Constructing Clienthood in Social Work and Human Services

of related interest

Inclusive Research with People with Learning Disabilities
Past, Present and Futures
Jan Walmsley and Kelley Johnson
ISBN 1 84310 061 4

User Involvement and Participation in Social Care
Research Informing Practice
Edited by Hazel Kemshall and Rosemary Littlechild
ISBN 1 85302 777 4

Learning to Practise Social Work
International Approaches
Edited by Steven M. Shardlow and Mark Doel
ISBN 1 85302 763 4

Welfare and Culture in Europe
Towards a New Paradigm in Social Policy
Edited by Prue Chamberlayne, Andrew Cooper,
Richard Freeman and Michael Rustin
ISBN 1 85302 700 6

The Working of Social Work
Edited by Juliet Cheetham and Mansoor A. F. Kazi
ISBN 1 85302 498 8

Research in Social Care and Social Welfare
Issues and Debates for Practice
Edited by Beth Humphries
ISBN 1 85302 900 9

Ethical Practice and the Abuse of Power
in Social Responsibility
Leave No Stone Unturned
Edited by Helen Payne and Bryan Littlechild
ISBN 1 85302 743 X

Narrative Approaches to Working with Adult Male
Survivors of Child Sexual Abuse
The Clients', the Counsellor's and the Researcher's Story
Kim Etherington
ISBN 1 85302 818 5

Constructing Clienthood
in Social Work and Human Services

Interaction, Identities and Practices

Edited by Christopher Hall, Kirsi Juhila,
Nigel Parton and Tarja Pösö

Jessica Kingsley Publishers
London and New York

First published in the United Kingdom in 2003
by Jessica Kingsley Publishers Ltd
116 Pentonville Road
London N1 9JB, England
and
29 West 35th Street, 10th fl.
New York, NY 10001-2299, USA

www.jkp.com

Copyright © Jessica Kingsley Publishers 2003

Library of Congress Cataloging in Publication Data
Constructing clienthood in social work and human services : interaction, identities, and practices/edited by Chris Hall ... [et al.]
    p. cm.
Includes bibliographical references and index.
ISBN 1-84310-073-8 (pbk. : alk.paper)
1. Social case work. 2. Social work administration. 3. Social interaction. I. Hall, Chris, 1948-
HV40.C6615 2003
361.3'2--dc21
                                                                2003041609
British Library Cataloguing in Publication Data
A CIP catalogue record for this book is available from the British Library

ISBN 1 84310 073 8

Printed and Bound in Great Britain by
Athenaeum Press, Gateshead, Tyne and Wear

Contents

Preface

The four of us met at the 1997 conference, hosted and organized by the Department of Social Policy and Social Work in Tampere on the theme of social constructionism and social work. In fact there are a number of contributors to the book who were present with us also. This was perhaps the first time that we realized that the area of social constructionism was one of considerable interest to a variety of different practitioners and researchers in the social work field, and that it was well worth trying to develop international collaboration. The idea for the book started to develop seriously in 1999. We then contacted a number of people we knew were interested in the topic. We engaged in all kinds of face-to-face, e-mail and telephone conversations and started to put the book together seriously in 2000. As a part of the process we also built in two seminars which took place in the first half of 2001. One of these was held in Tampere, Finland, and the other in Huddersfield, UK. Approximately half the contributors were able to come to the Tampere seminar and the other half to Huddersfield. By this point we had all drafted our different papers and we spent many hours together discussing, developing and refining our thinking. The seminars proved very enjoyable, very instructive and very helpful both in terms of putting the book together and in terms of developing our thinking.

There are a number of people we would like to thank. First, our contributors, all of whom have been a delight to work with and have kept to the promptings and deadlines we have suggested throughout. Second, the translators, particularly in relation to some of the Nordic papers, who have provided an invaluable service. Third, and by no means last, Sue Hanson, the Research Assistant in the Centre for Applied Childhood Studies at the University of Huddersfield, who has acted to co-ordinate and bring the various papers together in preparation for the publication.

We see this publication as very much part of a process and expect there will be other projects that will be developing both alongside it and as a result of it.

Transcription Symbols

The transcription symbols employed in some of the chapters of this book are derived from the system developed by Gail Jefferson (see Atkinson and Heritage 1984). The authors of the chapters follow these symbols flexibly. Depending on the topic and analytical focus of each chapter the detail of transcription varies and also the number of symbols used in data extracts. These symbols are used thoroughly or partly in Chapters 2 to 8.

Symbol	Explanation
[	A square bracket marks the start of overlapping speech
↑ ↓	Upward and downward pointing arrows indicate marked rising and falling shifts in intonation
Underlining	Signals emphasis
°soft°	Raised circles indicate obviously quieter speech
>fast< <slow>	'Lesser than' and 'greater than' signs indicate talk that is noticeably faster and slower
hhh	Out-breaths
.hhh	In-breaths
.hhh	Inspiration
yes::s	Colons show degrees of elongation of the prior sound

=	Equal signs indicate no gap between utterances
(1.5)	Numbers in round brackets measure pauses in seconds
(.)	An untimed pause (just hearable)
Yes,	Commas mark a continuing intonation
Yes.	Periods indicate a stopping fall in tone
Yes?	Question marks indicate a rising intonation
( )	Empty parentheses indicate the transcriber's inability to hear what was said
(word)	Parenthesized words are possible hearings
becau-	Hyphens mark a cut-off of the preceding sound
#	Creaky voice
((laugh))	An additional comment from the transcriber

Reference

Atkinson, J.M. and Heritage, J.C. (eds) (1984) *Structures of Social Action: Studies in Conversation Analysis.* Cambridge: Cambridge University Press.

1

Introduction

Beyond a Universal Client

Kirsi Juhila, Tarja Pösö, Christopher Hall and Nigel Parton

The client in social work

The client is at the core of social work. The debate on social work, whether focusing on the profession, ethics, politics and ideology or research, inevitably takes a stand on what is called the client-citizen. This client-citizen is considered if not the only, then at least an essential target of and motive for, social work. The same applies to other human service professions. Their basis lies in the actors who use and need them. The practices and methods of social work may be defined through the client even to the point of being described as client centred. When this is the case, the aim is to underline that the client, as the partner of the social worker, has a guiding role for the content of social work. Such client centredness has become a self-evident ideal for social work. Good social work starts out from the client and the client's needs, and bad social work is understood as the opposite of this, as a work approach which makes the client into an object.

The tendency to define social work as good or bad, drawing the attention to the position of social work in relation to the client, omits to problematize the question of who or what the client is in concrete social work terms. This has prompted criticism of the client concepts in social work. It has been stressed that an abstract client does not exist, but the process or event of becoming a client is determined in social, cultural and economic terms. For this reason, attention must primarily be paid to the mechanisms and processes which create clienthoods. The client, just as the subject in general, is socially constituted (Leonard 1997, pp.32–60). It has been emphasized that clienthoods are intertwined with such factors as gender, race, ethnic identity, social class and age. It has also been noted that the condition of being a client is only one factor determining an individual's life. In addition to clienthood, there exist many positions or actions which are meaningful for the individual and have often more significance than clienthood. In the client discussion which approaches the issue through the meanings of the actors and actions, more and more attention is paid to a scrutiny based on narratives and the client's life history. Clienthood is to be understood and interpreted in relation to the client's previous life, and at the same time it is emphasized that the individual her- or himself positions the role of client in her or his life history (e.g. Parton and O'Byrne 2000). In this context it is significant that the so-called client and the worker together discuss the meanings of clienthood. Clienthood is not accepted as given, but as situational and narrative states and interpretations, and being so, they may be subject to change. Thus, the client is multiple, not something that can be reduced to a single abstract category.

The same multiplicity of the client is visible in the institutional and administrative environment of social work. The identity of modern social work has been strongly linked to welfare state systems, which is why the emphases and changes in these systems are also reflected in the clienthood of social work (Chambon and Irving 1999). In child protection, the client is not understood in the same way as in social work which focuses, say, on poverty. The clients of child protection are the child and its parents in a mutual interaction and care relationship. In issues related to livelihood, the person interpreted as client is often an adult whose life management is examined by social work, particularly from the point of view of daily coping (e.g. Forsberg 1998). Institutional routines also differentiate clients, beginning from decisions on who is entered as client in the information systems of each organization and what basic data is entered about them.

In social work research the client has been very much a focus of differing conceptual standpoints. This can clearly be seen in textbooks written as introductions to various theories underlying social work. One example of this is David Howe's *An Introduction to Social Work Theory* (1996) which summarizes the way in which different theoretical strands of debate have defined, explained and positioned the client. For instance, psychoanalytical theory conceptualizes the client and simultaneously also social work through the client's internal, partly subconscious, world. This interpretation is clearly different from, say, behaviourist approaches or radical social work, in which the client is understood through external behaviour or socio-economic structures and the focus of change work lies in the client's behaviour or the immediate socio-economic life situation. More important than the client concepts of individual schools of thought in this context is the fact that they all contain and create interpretations of clienthood and may diverge significantly. Thus, social work theories also produce multiplicity.

An important element in the debate on the client of social work comes from critical research, which emphasizes the control and management aspect of social work and thus discredits its 'innocence' (Chambon and Irving 1999). To take an example, Amy Rossiter (2001) writes how, as a social work teacher, she grapples with the problem of trying to find a client-centred locus of innocence which can be taught as the correct direction for social work. Finding a direction is made more difficult by the understanding that social work always also involves managing and categorizing people in order to control a range of deviations and to make people compatible with the outlooks of institutions based on normalizing people. Thus, cate-gorization is often negative and based on the definition of shortcomings and problems. This places the social workers hierarchically above the client and allows them to manage the shortcomings and problems of the clients.

However, Rossiter (2001) does not remain imprisoned in a black-and-white, either-or approach. She is of the opinion that there also exists a middle ground in social work. The solution is to make social workers conscious of their participation in governmentality and of the problems related to their own identity. In this way it is possible to identify not only one's own controlling power but also other types of client–worker en-counters and moments of categorization. Thus, our interest is turned to the everyday practices of social work in which client categories are produced, maintained, modified and broken. These practices also form the focus of this book. Through a study of various practices we attempt to provide multiple answers to the question of who and what the client of social work is, that is, we seek to go beyond a universal client.

The individual becomes a client of social work when he or she enters or is forced to enter into a relationship with a social worker and an organization carrying out social work. Clienthood may be based on a face-to-face relationship but it may also be situated more vaguely, such as in shared ways of understanding the client in local organization cultures (Jokinen *et al.*

1999). These bodies, organizations and social workers, are present in this book, although in the background. Our gaze is now directed expressly to the client. There exists a lively debate and research concerning the institutional place of social work and the social worker, concerning the differences between societies and cultures, concerning educational and support systems etc., but there is clearly less research which attempts to position the client conceptually and empirically. Bringing the client on to the agenda of empirical research in social work is the essential task of this book.

Terminological pressures

Parallel with the ongoing debate on the multiplicity of clienthood in social work there has been a focus on the use of language. The concept of client has attracted negative connotations and has been regarded as stigmatized by social work approaches which deny the client's autonomy. Especially in Britain, alternative concepts have been searched for which would bring greater equality to the activity and autonomy of the citizen as client than does the word client. However, language is always bound with a culture, and in Finland, for example, the word generally used for client does not carry particularly negative connotations. In fact, in certain contexts it is considered progressive, so that within recent memory it has been debated whether social work related to health care has clients or patients. However, certain sectors in Finland, too, particularly those related to direct benefits, have introduced other concepts besides that of the client (such as applicant, beneficiary, etc.). In particular, the concepts of service user and consumer have been suggested as alternatives to client. The choice between these is significant, as they refer to different relationships and also reflect different ethical commitments. 'Service user' is well suited to describing clienthood in the welfare state, based on social rights. A 'service user' is a fully empowered citizen who, thanks to this position, may expect and demand services of a certain kind and level. 'Consumer', on the other hand, refers more to a person active in the 'social services market', who chooses the service with the best price/quality ratio (see Niiranen 2002; Banks 1995). Changing the concept also changes the meaning, which is why these changes may confuse issues. For instance, 'service user' – even though it emphasizes activity and autonomy – primarily refers to the universal social services accessible to all citizens, and is less well suited to the kind of 'marginal social work' which is strongly needs based and/or which contains the possibility and obligation of compulsory measures. To some extent, this is an issue related to the general change in human services terminology: we also speak of judicial services and police services in such contexts as violence between couples (Nyqvist 2001). These are defined as 'service' from the point of view of one of the parties, but as 'control' from that of the other.

The pressures towards new vocabulary in social work do not arise out of nothing. They are linked to broader societal changes and the academic debates analysing these. This broader context has been described in some texts as a move to the late or reflexive modern society (Beck *et al.* 1994; Giddens 1991). Late modernity is characterized as an era of individualization, during which the self has become a reflexive project. There are no clear pathways or rules to follow throughout the course of one's life, but people continuously encounter different choices and decisions. Harry Ferguson (2001; see also Karisto 1997) writes that the task of social work in the late modern society is to act as a resource for the individual self projects and life planning, to empower people by promoting their opportunities of self-actualization. We are dealing here with a citizen-based life politics, with which the social work tradition, based on guiding the client towards a certain set way of life, is poorly compatible. The viewpoint emphasizes a clienthood based on activity and autonomy, and a vocabulary which is compatible with this.

The pressure towards changing the vocabulary of social work can be placed into another societal context and the research commenting on this as well. What we are dealing with here is a neo-liberal spirit of the times based on both economic arguments and individualism. On the one hand, markets, entrepreneurship, profit, competition and efficiency are emphasized, on the other the responsibility of individuals themselves and that of collectives other than the welfare state (Julkunen 2001, pp.163–164). Welfare state benefits and the way of life of those who do not meet the criteria for people active in the markets are evaluated in an increasingly rigid and controlling manner. At the same time, social work is pushed into the margin as a controlling profession run by the state, in which the client is defined as a dependent and passive object. Opinions have been voiced in Britain that as a result, the public image of social work has been so badly tarnished that new names must be sought for many activities which could otherwise happily be called social work; among the alternatives are 'projects' and 'project workers' (Jordan and Jordan 2000). In Finland, Britain and elsewhere one can discern attempts to replace social work by the labels and practices of case management, for instance, which serves as a means of transferring tasks to other than social work actors. Simultaneously this helps to interpret the educational qualifications of practitioners less rigidly. This may lead to a situation where the activity termed social work is narrowed down and stigmatized as a profession which carries out control and co-ordination tasks, defined in detail by law, which will also produce a very limited understanding of the client.

Constructionist approaches to clienthood

All in all it is hardly wrong to say that the notion of the client is in a state of change. There are many ways in which social work reformulates the conceptual and operational approaches to the social worker's 'partner'. The present book brings its own angle to this discussion. We will highlight the ways of understanding the client of social work and human services from the viewpoint of one research tradition, that of social constructionism. Doing this, we are rejecting an abstract and universal concept of the client and instead asking from an interactive angle how the client is constructed in the various encounters within social work. Constructionism stresses a negotiable clienthood instead of an universal one. The client is not a client all the time. This is why we must speak of clienthoods, separated from the individual.

A commitment to the idea of negotiable clienthood means that the focus of the book is on action. We are interested in what takes place in the practices of social work and in the broader sense of human service work when clienthoods are negotiated, that is, how social workers' partners are produced. We understand practices in a broad sense. The reality of social work and the way in which it is continuously being constructed is present wherever it is spoken or written into being: when encountering clients, when speaking or writing of them. In the chapters of this book these practices become data which are used to interpret the processes of social reality in which multiple clienthoods are constructed.

The research tradition of social constructionism stresses precisely action as a significant research topic (Burr 1995; Gergen 1994; Holstein and Miller 1993a; Potter 1996). The phenomena to be studied do not self-evidently exist in a given manner 'out there', simply waiting for the researcher to come along and report on them. Instead of being inert, the research topic continues to evolve. Thus, each set of data – whether interview, conversation or text – is in continuous movement. It is the researcher's task to analyse this movement and present it as like a film: what stages are taken by the characters in the film, what roles they do assume, what relationships the roles have with each other, how the story unfolds (see Goffman 1959). The completed film, the research report, can only contain some of the material collected. The researcher always makes interpretative choices, but still the purpose is to present the processes which are essential for the question being studied and which produce social reality.

Social constructionism, especially in the ethnomethodologically tuned traditions presented in this book, deals with the study of interaction: movement is created by the mutual action of people. Social reality is something that people construct together. When meeting each other on whatever stage people talk with each other, agree, argue and disagree. In other words, they negotiate social reality and construct interpretations of it. A monologue, i.e. a speech or text by one person only, is also interactive, an interpretation of social reality always produced for a reason and always spoken or written for someone. The study of interaction from the angle of constructing social reality brings into focus the use of language. Thus social constructionism is placed in the framework of the so-called linguistic turn of social and humanist research. The turn had the result that language, speech and text, was no longer understood only as a tool for describing reality, but as action which produces reality in and by itself. Bringing linguistic practices into the focus does not, however, mean that the other elements of human encounters – physical locations, gestures, expressions etc. – are no longer important. Constructionist research is interested in the overall context of interaction.

Social work includes many different stages for interaction where the actors meet. The work is carried out by a range of organizations specializing in different problems – neglect and abuse of children, substance addictions, mental health problems, regional deprivation, poverty, homelessness, etc. Clienthood has its links with the organization and also with the service system in the sense of what organizations and experthoods there are on offer and available. The special fields of these organizations determine the roles which clients and social workers may assume on each stage in relation to each other. In other words, in the organizational sense, the contexts open up different actor positions and thus also call up different clienthoods (see Gubrium and Holstein 2001; Hall 1997; Holstein and Miller 1993b; Juhila and Pösö 2000). This does not, however, signify that the client positions in organizations would be completely defined and simply waiting for someone to fill them. The actors evoke the roles in their interaction, and many variations are possible. Variations are produced by many factors, such as narratives which are recounted by people themselves or attached to client histories through various client documents and which thus become part of the interaction, or previous encounters between the actors and meanings constructed through age, gender and race. Thus, clienthoods are always ulti-mately produced in local negotiation. This is why it is necessary to study in detail the practices in which this negotiation takes place and to present inter-pretations on how the partners together construct the realities and clienthoods of social work.

Social work research based on social constructionism may be regarded as a methodical direction which contributes to the debate on the locus of knowledge related to social work expertise. Nigel Parton (2000) has defined social work as a professional practice in which uncertainty, complexity and doubt are continuously present. The reverse of this is what creates the strength of social work: the capability of a dialogical and interpretative approach. A similar approach to work has been defended in other human service professions as well, especially in therapy (McLeod 1997; McNamee and Gergen 1992; Miller 1997). Social work expertise, dealing with many kinds of people, situations and personal problems, cannot be reduced to the application of external theories, empirically tested work methods or legislation. Instead, expertise is about local negotiations, which use different narratives to organize and articulate 'messy' issues together with clients and other professionals. In this sense, we are dealing with a locally constructed knowledge, in social work literature called by various names, including 'practice' or 'tacit knowledge'. Some even speak of practice theory (e.g. Fook 2002; Pease and Fook 1999). In our opinion, this local knowledge, its construction and use can be made visible by the tools of constructionist research, by asking, among other things, how knowledge of clienthood is constructed in social work practices.

Constructionist approaches have inspired an application of the methods of qualitative, empirical research in and to social work. It has been claimed that this has formed a kind of basic research into social work, especially from the angle of essential client work practices. At the same time, this direction has also aroused strong criticism. The criticism has been targeted very much to the relativism and avoidance of universal claims typical of con-structionism.

Ian Shaw and Nick Gould (2001, p.6) claim that the dominance of methodology is one of the topics of criticism levelled against qualitative social work research. There has been concern over the fact that advocacy tasks regarded as part of social work are bypassed by methodological discussions. Thus, research could not take part in the debate on societal policy or promote the interest of individuals and collectives which serve as the objects of research and social work. However, the situation can also be defined in an other way: qualitative research with close links to the practices reveals many processes, drawbacks and positions related to daily practices which would escape notice in a different research orientation. This makes it possible for the qualitative and constructionist researchers to take part in discussion about societal change. It matters how client categories are constructed in social work interaction: categories have real consequences for people's lives.

Constructionist research into helping work is anchored not only in social work. This angle has been adopted for the broader study of institutional practices, including among others the study of therapy and counselling work and the activity of courts of law and homes for the aged (Holstein 1993; Gubrium 1990; McNamee and Gergen 1992; Mäkitalo 2002). The data sets and methodology typical of constructionist research enable a dialogue between studies dealing with different disciplines and professional domains. As an example, this book assumes that the construction of clienthood can and should be studied in different human service organizations. Some of the texts in this book are dominated by questions specific to social work. However, the interactive variation in the construction of clienthood is a central theme in all chapters, irrespective of whether the organization discussed represents social work or, perhaps, therapy or counselling.

Content and the background of the book

Clienthood is studied in the following 13 articles by 19 contributors. All the articles share an interest in clienthood constructions in different human service contexts. Ethnomethodological tones on social constructionism are strong as well as an emphasis on the detailed analysis of empirical data. There are, however, exceptions as well, as the book aims to present a variety of analytic and empirical approaches to studying clienthood constructions.

The book is divided into three parts, each of them looking at clienthood constructions with a different emphasis. Part I, 'Constructing Client Identities and Morals', focuses on how client identities are created and re-created in interview situations and other forms of institutional practices of human service work. Identities are not seen as fixed entities but as the interactants' orientations to relevant roles in human service settings. The detailed examination of these orientations makes the 'seen but unnoticed' moral order visible.

Part II, 'Categorizing and Negotiating Clienthoods', explores institutional dialogue in worker–client and in professional–professional talk. The emphasis is on the ways the participants jointly categorize clienthoods and produce case descriptions. Clienthoods are not approached as taken-for-granted roles but as positions which are constantly being negotiated, justified and argued.

The chapters in Part III, 'Client Work in Professional Contexts' consider the ways in which professional or organizational frameworks, ideologies and conceptualizations are constructed in social work practices as well as the implications of such constructions. On a more general level, the issue of the practical implications of the social constructionist approach is discussed in the final chapter of the book.

The book has four editors who share an interest in the constructionist approach in social work research. The individual paths and reasons which brought us into this book project are, however, different ones. Let us end this introductory chapter with the brief autobiographical histories of each of us. The histories seek to answer the question, how did I end up editing this book?

Christopher Hall

Srikant Sarangi and I went to Tampere in 1997. I was carrying out fieldwork in a social work agency, researching policy implementation but surrounded by everyday professional talk. I'd met Srikant some years earlier, a linguist interested in professional talk. We both liked each other's territory – I envied the rare opportunity to analyse talk, he appreciated my access to professionals and clients. However, our activities took place outside social work. I was warmly welcomed at linguistics meetings and we wrote for linguistics publications. My doctoral thesis in a sociology department explored the clash of professional and theoretical voices. But in social work my work was considered 'arch', 'will not be taken seriously by funders', or even 'will do terrible damage' (Pierson 1998). My then employer did not support such work and I paid for the trip to Finland myself. I was astonished to find kindred spirits at the 'Constructing Social Work Practices' conference – researchers, teachers and practitioners who saw in social constructionism and discourse analysis the potential for rethinking social work practice, theory and research. I had set my sights rather low, carping at the sidelines at the growing orthodoxy of scientism in social work, but ultimately they were peripheral. Working with Tarja, Kirsi, Nigel and the other contributors has challenged me to move to centre stage. In particular we have tried to celebrate the complexity and diversity of how social workers and clients interact with one another and make available 'seen but unnoticed' practices (Garfinkel 1967). It is here where the stuff of social work is done and statuses of clienthood created. Most social work research chooses to ignore such arenas, seeing social work through medical models and abstracted notions like assessment, intervention and outcomes. Social constructionism returns us to social work, not only to be more 'social' but also to recognize the 'work' required by all parties to produce it.

Kirsi Juhila

Homelessness has been one of the areas of my research interests for about fifteen years. I conducted, in collaboration with Arja Jokinen, my master's, licentiate's and doctoral dissertations on this particular topic. We soon came to realize that the lack of housing or financial resources was not sufficient to explain the homelessness. In addition to these explanations it seemed to have a great deal to do with the categorization of homeless people. This notion brought us to discourse analytical and social constructionist studies. On the basis of our empirical material, which contained the talk of local politicians, housing officers and social workers and conversations between social workers and clients, we argued that homeless people were often defined as incapable of living independently. We ended up making the very critical conclusion that this definition had tremendous consequences for some homeless persons who were 'sentenced' to live in shelters without hope of ever getting anything better. In recent years my focus of study has been on the practices of social work, especially in the organizations which can be categorized as last-resort helping places in the Finnish welfare state. I have been examining the business that is going on in institutional interaction where both parties, 'social workers and clients', are involved and the ways in which people construct their 'client careers' in narrative interviews. I have asked how are social problems and clienthoods constructed in different social work settings and with what consequences? I have several colleagues in my department, Tarja Pösö among one of the closest, who share similar interests and with whom I have created research projects, analysed data and written texts. We noticed very early on that social work research based on social constructionist and discourse analytical premises is not widely practised internationally. This notion led us to the idea of organizing a symposium around this topic in Tampere in 1997. Nigel Parton and Chris Hall in particular were scholars who we wanted to attend this event. Luckily they decided to accept our invitation. This book is one important outcome of the fruitful collaboration that started then.

Nigel Parton

My story as to why I came to become involved in this book goes back many years. In the early to mid-1970s I was working as a social worker for a local authority in northern England. The period coincided with the first contemporary public inquiry into a child abuse death in Britain, the Maria Colwell Inquiry (Secretary of State 1974). It was to prove a major event in the modern history and changes in England for social workers in that a whole variety of new procedures and training were introduced to encourage us to identify and respond to a problem which had previously received little attention. However, I had an uneasiness about what was happening to both clients and social workers as a result. In particular the problem did not seem nearly as clear cut as was often suggested in much of the training material and guidelines which were being promulgated at the time. Increasingly I wanted to develop a more critical analysis about what was happening and why. I found the social constructionist approach to social problems very instructive in helping to clarify my thoughts and subsequently used that as the organizing framework for writing *The Politics of Child Abuse* (Parton 1985). I have used this perspective ever since to try to analyse how the nature of the social problem and policy responses to it have changed over time. However, it was only in the 1990s that I realized its potential for both analysing social work practice at a more micro level (Parton, Thorpe and Wattam 1997) and also its potential for contributing to social work practice theory itself (Parton and O'Byrne 2000). An important part of this journey was an invitation to attend the Constructing Social Work Practices conference in Tampere, Finland in August 1997. This was the first time I had met Tarja and Kirsi and was delighted to spend time with Chris Hall as well (this was some twelve months before Chris came to work at Huddersfield). It was also the first time I had spent time with a group of people with very different backgrounds but all of whom were keen to discuss and share experiences in relation to social constructionism and social work research, policy and practice, and also theory. It proved a key meeting for me and I have kept in contact with many of the people at the conference since. But the conference also provided something of a catalyst for the four of us to try to start working together, to keep the dialogue and the work going and to see what joint research and projects might develop. Throughout we have tried to extend the networks within our own countries and across northern Europe, North and South America and Australia. This book is a key exemplar of this. Prior to the conference in 1997 I had felt – apart from a very few exceptions – to be one of the few people in social work who was interested in social constructionist perspectives; I no longer feel this.

Tarja Pösö

My relationship with social constructionism is not very straightforward. Yet despite my periodic agonies of doubt I still always return to the constructionist standpoints whenever looking at the issues of social problems and social work. I have had the privilege to work in a research community where there have been several people sharing the same interests. That is how we came to organize a small international seminar on social constructionism and social work in 1997 and publish a book *Constructing Social Work Practices* (Jokinen, Juhila and Pösö 1999) based on the papers which had been presented. That is also how we started a research project in 1997 in Tampere and Jyväskylä, Finland, where our specific aim was to look at social work practices from the point of view of social constructionism. A variety of practices was studied and we learnt a lot, but as the focus was on professional practices, mainly on the interactive practices between social workers and clients, I was still confused about the position of the client in this research agenda. The approach to construct and analyse data and the concepts used seem to be linked more to the institutions of social work than to the people needing and using social work. Therefore, on a personal level, the focus of *Constructing Clienthood in Social Work and Human Service* is important to me as it adds to and expands the issues previously studied. The book is a sign that the analytic tools and interests in social constructionist studies on social work and other human service work are very similar across several countries and research teams. Thus, while working with this book, the ease with which the editors and contributors have been able to communicate about social work and social constructionism has been striking. Of even greater importance to me has been the fact that the project to make this book has not only been about academic interests but also about social work practice itself. Indeed, the main core of the book, clienthoods, takes me back to my early years as a social work student. Nothing seemed to be more important than the position of the client. I hope the book manages to contribute something to the controversy of being, becoming and surviving as a client in social work.

PART I

Constructing Client Identities and Morals

2

Legitimating the Rejecting of Your Child in a Social Work Meeting

Christopher Hall, Arja Jokinen and Eero Suoninen

> There's no denying the truth in any way that you're giving your children
> away in exchange. You should realise that and think about that yourself.
> And that's something you will never be forgiven for.

This challenge by a grandparent to her daughter-in-law is from a highly
charged meeting in a social work office where the children's custody is being
discussed. What is at stake is the identity of a mother who is prepared to give
up her children. Mothers are expected to love and care for their children
unconditionally and failure to do so is 'a grave charge' (Dallos and Sapsford
1995, p.163; Dingwall *et al.* 1983, p.73; Vuori 2001, p.358). Writers from
various perspectives, however, have questioned the 'naturalness' of family
roles. As Muncie and Wetherell (1995) put it:

> The notion of the family depends on and works through ideas about cer-
> tain identity positions – mothers, fathers, adolescents, grandparents and
> so on. Now, of course, motherhood is not just an idea, it involves an obvi-
> ous physical state, but in every culture 'interesting physical conditions' of
> pregnancy, mothering and infancy are shot through with ideas and
> expectations about behaviour, attitudes and practical conduct. (p.70)

Feminist writers in particular have criticized the notion of family roles as
fixed or natural (Smart 1992), seeing expectations of mothers and fathers as
a product of gender relations. Discursive approaches to the family share the
constructivist approach in much feminist thinking (Rapp 1979, p.181) without necessarily exploring macro explanations. Gubrium and Holstein (1990)

argue that the family should be seen as process rather than an entity, concerned with how identities are actively constructed in everyday situations.

As with other papers in this book, identities are treated as multiple, fluid and negotiated (Antaki and Widdicombe 1998). As Gill, Potter and Webb (1991) put it:

> One of the characteristics of the rhetorical approach, with its emphasis on a detailed analysis of discourse is that it addresses the deployment of notions such as 'the family' in terms of the way their sense [is] developed on specific occasions of use...The point is not that 'family' does not come with a wide ranging set of potential connotations and sense; but precisely that it does and these are overwhelmingly positive. (p.21)

While accepting an approach to 'family' which investigates how identity categories are used, it is the implications of managing the violation of ordinary positive connotations that we will consider. Leaning on social science traditions which see explanations as accounts which justify or exonerate speakers from moral or social sanctions (Antaki 1994, p.43; Garfinkel 1967; Losake and Cahil 1984; Scott and Lyman 1968; Suoninen 1997) we try to identify the morally laden episodes of negotiations in social work encounters.

Our data consist of two meetings in social work offices at which the anomalous identity of mothers who are giving up their children is negotiated. Given that such an identity is morally questionable, how do participants reach agreement that giving up your children is justifiable? While there are many differences between the meetings in terms of nationality, legislation, circumstances, etc., we are interested in the way that in order to handle sensitive topics mothers and social workers deploy similar processes of identity construction. Our interest is less in an explanation in terms of comparing the different contexts and more in the investigation of similar interactional exchanges, in which 'context is inherently locally produced and transformed at any moment' (Drew and Heritage 1992, p.19).

Anna's case (the custody meeting)

The first meeting is considering the custody of two children (Pekka, a boy of 11, and Sari, a girl of 6). The parents are divorced but have joint custody. The children have lived with their mother, Anna, for five years, but she has remarried and wants now to 'give' the children to their father. Anna is suggesting that she leaves the flat and the father moves in to live with the children.

Those present are the social worker (SW), the mother (M), father (F) and the paternal grandmother (G).

The focus of our analysis is the negotiation of identities between Anna and the social worker. What sort of person and what sort of mother gives up her children? How can she be considering the children's needs?

Extract 2.1: *Mother as a rational decision maker*

(SW = social worker, M = mother)

1	SW:	But wellhhh what if we begin by you starting Anna, .hh and telling us,
2		(1) .hh what y<u>ou</u> would wish and suggest [and what y<u>ou</u> have been thinking
3	M:	[Yes.
4	SW:	that that the children's, (.) hhh the children's matter is decided and how long
5		the children have lived with you and wh<u>y</u> this change is n<u>o</u>w at this moment in
6		this situation necessar[y.
7	M:	[Yess, (.) the change is necessary because, (1.5) because
8		well I have thought it best and I have come to the conclusion that it will then be
9		better for the children to be with their father and then rather live in the flat
10		where they are now so in my opinion this is, (.) the best sol<u>u</u>tion.
11	SW:	Wha[t grounds do you have for this solution.
12	M:	[Now.
13	M:	What grounds I hav[e.
14	SW:	[Mm:.
15		(1.5)
16	SW:	F[or how long to begin with have you lived with the children.
17	M:	[(How) well, (.)
18	SW:	The children have be[en with you,
19	M:	[Five years.

((SW continues by collecting background information.))

The social worker offers the floor to Anna, but resists her first contribution (line 3) by specifying the nature of her answer. She emphasizes that the issue at hand is the 'children's matter' and that background information and explanation is required (lines 4–6). Note the insistent tone of the enquiry: 'change now, at this moment, in this situation', in the form of a 'three-part list', a particularly persuasive form of talk (Atkinson 1984, p.151). In reply Anna contends that the change is necessary because it is better for the children. Her own situation is not mentioned. She emphasizes that she has thought a great deal about it and 'come to the conclusion...' (line 8). In formulating this position, Anna constructs herself as a rational decision maker who considers what is best for her children.

Anna's use of 'I' opens the possible accusation that this is her decision alone, with no allies recruited (Latour 1987). This potential weakness enables the social worker to seek further justification (line 11), implying Anna's answer is inadequate. Anna appears confused; she repeats the question (line 13), and after the social worker's 'continuer' ('Mm:' line 14) signalling that an answer is required, there is a long pause (line 15). There is now a shift from an open invitation to tell her story to a question–answer format (Hall 1997, p.46). The formulation (line 16) 'to begin with...' announces that a series of questions of this nature is likely to follow, implying that Anna is not yet authorized to make unsupported decisions about what should happen to her children.

After asking for further background information, the social worker starts again insisting on further justifications for the mother's proposal.

Extract 2.2: Not coping mother

(SW = social worker, M = mother)

1 SW: ... .hhh well why do you think thathh it is better for the children that they go

2   and live with their father.

3   (3)

4 M: Well see, (.) we have sort of, (.) problems, (.) in the family,

5   (1.5)

6 SW: With whom.

7   (1.5)

8 M: Ah well see, (1) .mt (1.5) the problem is kind ofhhhh me and, (.) my current

9   husband.

10   (4)

11   SW: .hhhh krh rhh ((coughs)) your husband ge-(.) gets along, (.) with the children

12   from your prev-, (.) previous marriage, (.) or, (.) or how do you mean.

13   M: No he gets along with them all right. (.) But I c[an't cope.

14   SW: [Well ho- how does the

15   problem come a[bout.

16   M: [I can't cope with this, (.) circus.

17   (1.5)

18   SW: So who do you not get a[long with.

19   M: [Well, (.) children and, (1.5) this, (.) combination,

20   (1) husband and, (.) children,

21   (1.5)

22   SW: Husband and children.

23   M: Mm.

24   SW: .hhh Then what kind of hhh, (.) problems, (.) do you have, (.) in your home

25   situation, (.) family situation.

26   (1.5)

27   M: Well mainly sort of mental health problems.

28   (2)

29   M: I have mental health problems and, (.) then well, .mthh, (.) my husband has

30   this alcohol problem (.) and I think that's two good reasons for, (4) for well,

31   (.) me being here now(.)

32   SW: Mm.

33   M: Mm.

34   SW: .mthh So you feel that you cannot take care of the chil[dren.

35   M: [Yes.(.)

36   SW: .Yes. (1.5) .hh That you haven't got the strength to see to their basic-, (.)

37 M: N[o.

38 SW: [Basic needs and things (.) .yes.

Anna outlines problems in the family (line 4), marking this as a 'delicate' issue (Suoninen 1999) by pauses and hesitations (lines 3, 4, 8–9). The social worker's enquiries now have a 'soft' manner, notably lines 11–12. She hesitates, repeats words and offers a candidate answer for her earlier question: the problem is between the children and the new husband. Anna resists the formulation that her husband does not get on with her children and shifts the blame to herself. She cannot cope 'with this circus' and the 'combination of husband and children', hinting at problems with everyday family interactions.

Seeing the mother's formulations as rather vague, the social worker presses for further clarification of the family situation (line 24). Hesitantly, Anna identifies that she has mental health problems and her husband's alcohol problems. As she notes, these are powerful categories and should be enough to legitimate her position 'for me being here now' (line 31). This is a strong reflexive move and implies that the social worker should now stop her questioning. The social worker is now able to link these problems to an inability to look after the children, so much so that Anna cannot see to their 'basic needs'. Anna has reluctantly constructed herself the identity of a 'not coping mother' by invoking strong categories of social disfunctioning in such a way the social worker can see potential harm to the children. By now there are few pauses in the interaction and a consensus is emerging.

Next the social worker questions the father for several minutes about his availability and asks his opinion about the mother's sincerity: 'Will you believe it if Anna says that she is unable...'. The father answers: 'It's difficult to say...'. With this lack of corroboration, the social worker returns to test if Anna is really a 'not coping mother'. There are then a series of exchanges in which the social worker remains unconvinced that the problem is serious since Anna has continued to work – there is not enough 'abnormality' to justify the mother's decision. The social worker also asks if Anna's husband might get treatment.

Extract 2.3: *Mother as an abused woman*

(SW = social worker, M = mother)

1 SW: Have you talked it over with him that you're worried about his use of alcohol

2   and,(.)

3 M: °Yes° ((weeping))

4 SW: Something ought to be done.

5   (4)

6 SW: Is he violent or, (1) .hhh (.) what is your concern.

7   (.)

8 M: He [is.

9 SW: [What is your concern regarding the children over his use of alcohol.

10   (1.5)

11 M: He is violent.

12   (.)

13 SW: Against you or the children.

14 M: Against me.

15   (1.5)

16 SW: Not against the children.

17 M: No.

18   (.)

19 SW: Yes.

20   (7)

21 SW: Have the children seen situations where he's attacked you.

22   (2)

23 M: No:t that I can think of.

24   (6)

25 SW: °.Ye-es.°

26   (2)

27 SW: Now there's no way, .hhh one could accept that, (1) .hhh (.) that there is such

28   violence in the family, (.) .hh family, (.) and if the children see that, (.) that

29   their mother is treated like that then, (.) then of course they are afraid like for

30   you and worried about you and, .hhh and well hh (.) are of course afraid of th-,

31   (.) this new father possibly, (.) stepfather.

The social worker moves the focus away from the mother's abilities to the new husband's problems. Now the mother's tone changes dramatically. At the beginning of extract 1 her voice was determined, then somehow irritated or embarrassed, but now she starts weeping (line 3) and her voice becomes tremulous. The social worker begins to upgrade the seriousness of the situation (line 4), and after a long pause, she asks if Anna's new husband is violent (line 6). Anna confirms this, and her identity becomes reconstructed as an abused woman, a victim herself. The social worker clearly articulates her opinion on family violence (lines 27–31): 'there's no way one could accept that there is such violence in the family…'. The abnormality of the new family is now accepted as adequate enough for legitimating the transfer of custody. Having accepted the mother's position and confirmed her damaged identity, the social worker discusses the practical arrangements of the transfer of custody and about the children's rights to meet their mother after they have started to live with their father.

It turns out that Anna is reluctant to make firm commitments concerning future contact with her children. Instead she proposes that it is enough that the children have her telephone number and they can call her if they want to. The social worker does not accept such vague arrangements and she gives a very strict piece of advice to the mother by appealing to the children's interests.

Extract 2.4: Always a mother

(SW = social worker, M = mother)

1 SW: Even if you didn't, (.) want it, (.) even if you yourself didn't want it ((laughs)) even

2   then I think it would be in the children's interest, .hhh (.) that well, (.) the contact is

3   kept up even if you must force yourself a bit.

((A moment later the social worker answers the grandmother's question
about why is it necessary that Anna should meet her children.))

4 SW: The children feel bad if they don't see their mother. After all for ten years they

5   have lived with this person, .hhh she is their mother. Anna is and always will be

6   their mother. And they think about their mother they love her she is important to

7   them, So they actually want to see, (.) from time to time their mother to see how

8   she is.

The social worker strongly emphasizes the specific meanings of motherhood: Anna will always be their mother, has emotional ties with her children
and be responsible for seeing them at least from time to time. The message is
clear: a mother cannot be released from her obligations towards her children
even if she is giving them away and even if she herself wants to give up the
rights and commitments of a mother. Motherhood is a category you cannot
quit. Note how Anna is talked about in the third person; the audience is the
father, paternal grandmother and possibly wider superaddressees (Bakhtin
1986, p.126).

In summary, we have seen that through a series of highly charged exchanges,
Anna and the social worker can agree that it is appropriate for her to relin-
quish custody of the children. However, this was only achieved through
intense questioning of Anna's identity as an adequate mother and person.
Her opening position that it was her decision as to what is best has been
ignored in the requirement to produce a damaged identity of an abused
woman living with a violent and alcoholic husband. In these circumstances
it is not only legitimate to give up her children but also probably in the children's best interests.

Mrs Jones's case (the care placement meeting)

While our second meeting differs markedly, similar identities of motherhood are constructed and negotiated. This meeting concerns Jane Jones,
aged 15, who was recently admitted to public care. Unlike Anna, Jane's family have been involved with social services for several years. She has had
periods of respite care but now Jane and her parents want her to remain in
care.

Present are the social worker (SW), mother (M), father (F), social worker responsible for fostering (FPSW), residential social worker (RSW) and team manager (TM). Jane is not present, having absconded from the children's home. This meeting is mainly concerned with finding Jane and arranging accommodation rather than exploring the mother's perspective. However, in several exchanges the mother is challenged to justify why Jane cannot return home.

The team manager is new to the case so the meeting opens with the social worker outlining recent developments, after which the team manager seeks clarification.

Extract 2.5: Mother as rational decision maker

(TM = team manager, M = mother)

1 TM: Can I just sort of (.) gather my breath on this one cos I see that she was placed

2   at ((children's home)) on the fourth of January (.)((cough)) this was a case that

3   (.) came across from ((previous social worker)) I believe, (.)

4 M: [°That's right°.

5 TM: [.hhmm

6 M: She's had several placements in (.)

7 TM: She's had several placements in [((children's home))

8 M: [((children's home)) yeah that's my

9 TM: Over the last year or [so,

10 M: [yeah, (.).hh that's they're my safety net,

11 TM: ((cough))

12 M: they've ehm (.) we've decided that's the best thing, (.) .hh when things got too

13   heated.

14 TM: hmm

15 M: there if I had somewhere to send her, (.) rather than sort of beating her into a

16   pulp on the floor then phone somebody up ((laugh)) and say excuse me I've

17   done this that and the other so when things got too heated we sent her to (.)

18   ((children's home)) and ((previous social worker)) arranged (.) like weekends

19   away through the holidays: (.) and this sort of thing for me (.) and aa: (.) but

20   this time we decided it had to be at bit more (-) permanent because things just

21   don't work out between us

Like Anna, Mrs Jones makes claims to be the authorized 'teller of the tale' (Smith 1990, p.25). The 'facts' of the case have been outlined, so Mrs Jones claims authority by explaining the reasons behind the facts – why Jane is currently in care and cannot return home. She takes the floor without a specific invitation and her speech is quiet (line 4), suggesting a non-verbal signal to speak.

Mrs Jones puts the current placement in context. There had been several placements, part of a service negotiated with the previous social worker. It is a 'safety net', somewhere for Jane to be sent when 'things got too heated'. Note that it is 'my safety net'; the mother needs the service, depicting herself as the social work client. The service is also made to appear a measured response contrasting the 'safety net' of the children's home with the mother beating the child (Smith 1993). An extreme case formulation is deployed (Pomerantz 1986). It is not merely that the mother and daughter would have problems without this service but also that the mother might seriously assault her, 'beating her into a pulp'. However, the laughter (line 16) serves to show listeners that this formulation is not to be taken seriously. (For a discussion of laughter in this case, see Hall, Jokinen and Suoninen 2000.)

Jokes require some affiliation (Haakana 1999) and its absence here raises an interactional problem for Mrs Jones. She quickly changes her tone and reports that they now want Jane to stay in care. This new situation is introduced delicately, describing not having Jane home as 'it had to be a bit more (-) permanent' (line 20). Note the pause before 'permanent', which is emphasized. Anna also understates her decision in terms of the 'children living with their father' rather than her leaving the children (Extract 2.1). The justification is also low key, with no blame attributed: 'things just don't work out between us'. As with Anna, Mrs Jones constructs her decision as rational. A respite service has been established to handle difficult relations in the family but now a permanent placement is required. Also like Anna matters are introduced delicately.

In the next few exchanges the team manager explores the work that has been carried out in this case and the mother depicts herself as a co-operative client. However, she introduces some uncertainty as to whether it is her or

Jane who is making the decision. While not initially taken up by the team manager this uncertainty resurfaces as the team manager summarizes the case.

Extract 2.5: Mother offers to have her child back
(TM = team manager, M = mother)

1   TM: °Hm° (.) so, (.) the current situation or the one that was, (.) when the last planning

2   meeting happened on which was on the eh,

3   (1)

4   SW: 25 of Janu°ary°.

5   TM: 25 of January, (.) .hh was that e:hm, (2) she'd definitely not go back home to you.

6   M: .hh as that's what I've said if she really wants to, (.) then e:hm I'm willing to give

7   it another tr:y, (.) not making any promises, (.) but I'm willing to give it

8   anot- another try, (.) .hh but Jane wasn't interested.

9   TM: So you said she could come back and Jane said didn't want to

10   M: °That's right°.

11   (3)

12   M: But saying that I didn't really want her back, ((laugh joined by Dad)) .hhe:hm, (.)

13   but [I didn't want her to have that

14   TM: [Yym

15   M: option of not being able [to come back if that makes any sense [to you

16   TM: [right (quiet) right (quiet)

17   (2)

18   TM: .hh Right that's just cleared a bit up for me °thank you°, (.) e:hm, (1) and at the

19   moment Jane is: (.) missing.

The team manager reformulates the position as unambiguous, 'she'd definitely not go back home' with a stress on 'definitely' (line 5). The pause before this statement has the effect of emphasizing that this summary is of some importance. In a similar way the social worker in Anna's case sums up the mother's position, 'haven't got the strength to see to their basic needs'

(Extract 2.2 line 36). Whereas Anna accepted the clarification, Mrs Jones makes it more complicated. She was prepared to have Jane back home with provisos. It is dependent on Jane wanting it and she does not expect it to succeed, 'making no promises' (line 7). However, Jane did not take up the offer. The team manager repeats the position: Jane is doing the rejecting.

Mrs Jones changes the position again. Not only did she have reservations but hoped Jane would not take up the offer (line 12). Note how this further complication is presented. First, the rejecting mother status is not accepted and a second identity is proffered, a mother who will try again. She is not a rejecting mother. However, this would open up the possibility that if Jane could be persuaded to change her mind then she could return home and all the placement problems would be solved. The pause before this further complication separates the 'surface identity' from 'real identity' (line 11). The irony of the position is emphasized by laughter from both parents, and the difficulty of justifying this complex position is recognized: 'if that makes any sense to you' (line 15).

Throughout this series of exchanges the team manager has done little to challenge the legitimacy of the mother's rejecting status except to ensure that therapy has been tried. This can be contrasted with Anna's case where a series of attributes were explored to establish the legitimacy of her rejection. The team manager completes this phase of the meeting as if things were now clear and shifts to discuss placement matters.

Extract 2.6: Mother giving double messages

(TM = team manager, M = mother, F = father)

1   TM: So we've got a situation where, (.) e:rm (.) she's supposed to be at (children's

2   home) (.) and has absconded, (.) e:rm (children's home) is saying the placement

3   ended anyway, (.) e:rm mum, (.) was saying that she, (.) could look at having her

4   back but Jane does not want that, (.) so at one level you you're still, (.) a bit open

5   about, (.) trying to do some work with her. (.) hh

6   M: E:rm, (.) I wanted her to know that I'd be willing to give it another try, [(.)

7   TM: [Ymm.

8   M: I wanted her to know I was willing to give it another try, (.) [but I don't

9   TM: [(Is that)

10 M: want to give [it another try.

11 TM: [(Is that true) of you Mr Jones

12 F: Oh yeah.

13 TM: Ymm.

14 M: So e:hm, (.)

15 TM: But you don't want.

16 M: I don't want to h<u>a</u>ve to try give it another try, (.) because it won't w<u>o</u>rk it'll fall

17   through again, (.) but I just wanted Jane, (.) n<u>o</u>t to think I've actually g<u>i</u>ven up

18   totally.

19   (2)

20 M: that don't make sense to you does it [((laugh)) it d<u>o</u>es to me. ((laughing))

21 TM: [No

22 M: hh e:hm how can I explain it b<u>e</u>tter e:rm, (2) being out of the h<u>o</u>me and knowing

23   there's an option I can go back, (.) e:rm doesn't seem anywhere near as bad as

24   mum saying you're out and n<u>o</u>t, (.) coming back, (.) yeah (.)

25   [<u>to</u> to Jane, (.) .hh a:nd e:rm, (1.5)

26 TM: [So to (.) hmm

27 M: but also I don't actually want her to t<u>a</u>ke me up on that option ((laugh)) and(h) say

28   (.) .hh ok come back and let's give it another try because it is, (.) so obviously

29   much easier without her there it's incredible, [(.) .hh and e:rm it's going to break

30 TM: [So, hh

31 M: down again if she come's back I'm sure it will.

32 TM: So it sounds as though you will find it really difficult to say, (.) I I can't have you

33   back.

34   (2)

35 M: I wouldn't say I can't have you back if she came and said, (.) please mum I want to

36   give it another try I'd say OK we'll give it another try, (.) but <u>I</u>'m I'm telling <u>you</u> I

37   don't want, (.) her back, (.) yeah.

38   TM: That sounds like a double message to me.

39   F: It [is, (.) it is.

40   M: [Probably yes it is, (.) .hh e̠:rm, (.)

She raises again the possibility of Jane returning home, although the enquiry is qualified, 'at one level' (line 4). She appeals to the early identity of the 'mother as a cooperative client' willing to 'do some work' (line 5). These are preferred identities, ignoring the mother's 'offering but not wanting' position.

Mrs Jones initially responds to this invitation by appearing to agree with these preferred identities (lines 6–8). However, the phrase 'I wanted her to know that I'd be willing to give it another try' addresses Jane, emphasized in the repeat 'I wanted her to know' (line 8). Using the past tense, it suggests the offer is no longer available. The 'offering but not wanting' formulation is justified by an appeal to realism, 'because it won't work' (lines 16–17). Again, Mrs Jones assumes the team manager will not accept this position (line 19), prompted by the lack of affiliation (line 20). She now takes a long turn to explain and legitimate this position (lines 21–36). It starts with a reflexive comment, 'how can I explain it better' and a pause. The position is initially formulated in the abstract, any young person away from home would feel better if the route home was not closed off. But she hopes Jane will not take up the option – it is easier without her and will break down again. There is a strong appeal for affiliation 'yeah' (line 24).

The team manager now criticizes the mother's position. She cannot be straight with Jane (line 32). Mrs Jones agrees and reformulates her position, 'I'm telling her but I'm telling you', shifting responsibility to social services. The team manager categorizes the mother's position as a 'double message'. Two versions of motherhood are now juxtaposed. For Mrs Jones, she is promoting Jane's welfare by letting her believe that home is always an option, that it is her decision to leave and social services can take some responsibility. For the team manager, however, the mother is being deceitful by not making it clear that she is rejecting Jane.

This juxtaposition is elaborated further by both sides in the next few minutes. Father develops the mother's position, that they would try again if asked, it would make Jane feel better, but would rather not as it will fail. The professionals criticize it – Jane can see through it, you are just avoiding making a decision, Jane does not want to come home. The final criticism is by the residential social worker: 'So the door isn't closed on her, (.) but it would be easier if it wasn't a permanently open door.' While the parents are not completely rejecting Jane, they should be honest about the true nature of her welcome at home. Note the graphic metaphor of the door to the family home. The rest of the meeting is taken up with placement and education matters and the mother's identity is no longer discussed.

As with Anna's meeting, the identity of a rejecting mother has undergone negotiation and reformulation. The initial formulation of a rational decision maker has been undermined. Mrs Jones as a social work client has not been explored. Instead, an identity has been formulated in terms of double messages, insincerity and not really understanding Jane. Also like Anna, future obligations are defined in terms of a limited but clear contact. In both cases, identities of motherhood are built on top of one another, with new damaged identities established which fit better with the social work context.

Conclusion

In comparing these two encounters, the atmosphere is different. In Anna's meeting emotions are raw with tears and recrimination. In Mrs Jones's meeting there is laughter and little explicit blaming. However, there are surprisingly important similarities in process, topic and negotiation, suggesting shared notions of motherhood and rejection. We might want to ask why it is necessary for social workers to reformulate mothers' identities in disparaging terms before agreement and a way forward is established. Three lines of enquiry are suggested: societal, (cultural concepts of motherhood and the confession), institutional (processes within welfare bureaucracies) and interactional (the dynamics of social worker–client encounters).

At the beginning we indicated some of the themes in the literature about the socially constructed nature of family identities and obligations. What is noted is the central importance of motherhood for protection and nurturing of children, but also the legitimacy of alternative family arrangements (Nätkin 1997; Vuori 2001). Recently feminist writers have explored wider notions of fulfilment in motherhood. These include recognizing that women have their own needs and priorities, that there is ambivalence in the mother–child relationship and, on occasion, women may feel compelled to leave their children (Featherstone 1999). Featherstone explores the case of Ruth Neave, who was jailed for cruelty to her children, one of whom died. She had continually asked for her child to be removed but was not heard. Featherstone (1999) discussed a range of factors around the circumstances of lone mothers, the relationships between social workers and their clients and the need to discuss the 'unacceptable side of mothering' (p.52).

From a different orientation, Foucault's (1976) concept of the confession might also offer some understanding of the way in which broader cultural concepts are located in mechanisms of power

> [the confession is] also a ritual that unfolds within a power relationship, for one does not confess without the presence of a partner who is not simply the interlocutor but the authority who requires the confession, prescribes and appreciates it and intervenes in order to judge, punish, forgive, console and reconcile. (p.61)

There is a large literature on institutional processes and in particular the way in which professionals interpret rules to manage particular cases (Kullberg and Cedersund 2001). Much of the negotiation of eligibility for welfare is in moral terms as social workers struggle to assess the legitimacy and credibility of clients' claims (Hyden 1996). As Holstein and Gubrium (2000) say:

> Formal organisations significantly concretize self construction. Their service mandates, such as specialized institutional missions or professional, therapeutic outlooks and orientations, provide publicly designated resources for producing selves. (p.165)

The negotiation of rejecting mothers could be seen in terms of social workers creating morally validated identity categories in order to fit them into institutional processes. Perhaps in subsequent discussions social workers will be expected to produce reports of Anna and Mrs Jones to justify their decisions.

Cultural and institutional processes come together in the interactional encounters that realize damaged identities. The meetings we have discussed bear some of the characteristics of what Garfinkel (1972) calls 'degradation ceremonies' that transform the public identity of an individual: the event must be out of the ordinary, the person being denounced must be shown to be morally blameworthy and unable to be redeemed, and the denouncer must be a supporter of ultimate community values. Garfinkel associates such degradation ceremonies with the law courts, but we can see similar characteristics in other institutional encounters as well, such as everyday meetings between social workers and clients. Further research will enable identification of the characteristics and circumstances of such processes and promote discussion of whether such categorization processes enhance the needs of children separated from their mothers.

3

Caring but Not Coping

Fashioning a Legitimate Parent Identity

Stef Slembrouck and Christopher Hall

Introduction

Parents whose children are in public care are likely to face serious challenges to their self-identity and moral character – how can they maintain that they are adequate parents when their children are being looked after by others? Are they to blame for their family's difficulties or are they victims? For professionals, too, how to approach parents is uncertain: are they the source of the trouble and the target of social work intervention or are they a detraction diverting attention away from promoting the child's needs? Current policy and practice in social work throughout Europe points in both directions, working in partnership to support families but also the welfare of the child is 'paramount' (see White, this volume).

In this chapter we will consider how parents explain the circumstances and offer explanations of their child being in public care and so manage a 'spoiled identity' (Goffman 1990a). At the same time we will insist that such explanations are established interactively and this has implications for practice. We will in particular explore how parents rely on a specific rhetorical device we have identified as 'caring but not coping'. By this we mean that parents strongly resist any suggestion that they do not care for their children, but for various reasons they cannot cope with looking after them.

Research interviews as eliciting accounts of moral adequacy

The data extracts examined here are taken from interviews with parents in several studies carried out in Belgium and Britain. These studies were

concerned with presenting the views of parents involved in child care systems and are reported elsewhere as displaying consumer perspectives (Hall and Featherstone 2002; Packman and Hall 1998) or as narrations of parenting (Slembrouck 2002). Interviews for research purposes are usually treated as a method for gathering answers to specific questions, these answers being treated
as 'evidence'. However, research interviews are also social events. The formulation of replies is far from straightforward, particularly when the issues under consideration are sensitive topics which might call into question a respondent's motives or moral integrity. Some sociologists have questioned the usefulness of research interviews for gathering facts; instead they approach them as an opportunity to consider respondents' (and researchers') overall methods of explaining events and people, what Silverman (1985) calls 'displays of perspective and moral forms' (p.171).[1] Collins (1998) sums up such a position.

> My interviews comprise accounts of events together with attempts to interpret them on the part of interviewer and interviewee, but the process is haphazard and tentative. Rather than mere facts (which have an existence independent of the means of their discovery), such exchanges precipitate narrative: narrative that is emergent and indexical. Events and experiences are constituted, partly at least, in their telling (and re-telling).
> (p.4)

Talk, especially formal talk, revolves around occasioned depictions of a situation, which attempt to portray the speaker as morally adequate. To understand such depictions, one has to attune the analysis to the dynamics of the telling.

In a similar vein, Goffman (1990a), in his essays on 'stigma', pays much attention to the two-headed role-play that comes with the management of information as people interactionally and situationally pass into and out of a stigmatized category. In his view, the 'normal' and the 'stigmatized' are not persons but rather perspectives 'generated in social situations during mixed contacts by virtue of the unrealised norms that are likely to play upon the encounter' (p.164).[2] The management of tension and information control (for instance, concealment, revelation, particularization, qualification, etc.) by the stigmatized person is to be understood as an interactional accomplishment in which 'the role of normal and the role of stigmatised are parts of the same complex…the very notion of *shameful* differences assumes a similarity in regard to crucial beliefs, those regarding identity' (pp.155–156).

In the speech data under consideration here, both interlocutors – parent(s) and researcher – are in the know about the discredited identity:[3] the parent is known to the interviewer to have (had) children in public care; the parent knows the interviewer will already have certain details of their case. The parent might expect a more sympathetic hearing as he or she is addressing a neutral outsider who professionally speaking at least comes to the encounter with an attempt to understand rather than judge and carries an institutionally legitimized ticket to enquire into great detail. Assumptions of this nature will undoubtedly affect the interviewee's position as to what/how much will be revealed/concealed and the degree to which particular categories of parents, children, care, etc. will be particularized and given a specific interpretation. Revelation is perhaps to be expected more than concealment. At the same time, however, the interviewer is also likely to be perceived – in some respects, at least – as a person with a set of 'normal' family attributes/experiences. On his or her part, there is no pressure to reveal anything at all about his or her own particular family attributes, although he or she probably will have to reveal certain attributes about his or her researcherhood; and, of course, there may well be moments when he or she feels ethically or otherwise compelled to go on record as expressing understanding, sympathy, etc. On the part of the interviewee, the pressure to account for one's actions and particular events/state-of-affairs *vis-à-vis* an interlocutor is tangible (why would a researcher be different and not pass a verdict on the interviewee's moral adequacy?). Despite explicit disclaimers ('this is a research interview', 'I am not connected to social services', 'our aim is to try to understand a parent's perspective', etc.), we analyse the interviews on the assumption that, for the interviewee, the encounter comes with a 'charge' inviting a 'rebuttal'.[4]

Caring but not coping

It is suggested that the formulation 'caring but not coping' is used by parents as a defence against possible unfavourable evaluations – presupposed or implied by certain specific questions or being up in the conversational air. 'Caring but not coping' is a rebuttal to the accusation that they are not adequate parents since their children are (or have been) in care.

Parents' love for their children tends to be seen as unquestioned. Mothers in particular are assumed to be ever attending to their children's needs. Feminist writers have noted the high expectations of motherhood and the extent of censure when these are not met (Graham 1982). Wetherell (1995) talks of 'the Angel in the House' to indicate the idealized view of mothering and links it directly to a specific sense given to the idea of 'coping':

> Good mothers are expected to be able to expand their own personal resources and to 'cope', that is meet the needs of the situation whatever the personal cost and to make their work invisible by absorbing stress. (pp.230–231)

Dingwall *et al.* (1983) also note how the accusation that parents do not love their children is so extreme that child protection workers will try to avoid making such allegations.

> If the love of parents for children is an event in nature, instinctive rather than motivated, then those who fail are, in some sense, not members of the same species as the rest of us... An allegation that they have failed to love their children is a matter of such enormity that it can seldom be contemplated in the absences of substantial corroborating evidence which thoroughly undercuts the parents' moral character. (p.73)

We take the notion of 'caring' to be associated with the nature of the relationship between parent and child, the love, the concern, the responsibility, whereas 'coping' is associated with notions of managing the family and the home. It is summed up in a comment by a social worker in a case conference contrasting loving and controlling capacities of a mother:

Extract 3.1

> Social worker: yes I my feeling is their's a good relationship in terms of I don't question at all Katherine's love for her children or their's for her I ehm I think they're very clearly very very attached and very fond of her ehm I suppose I can see though that that can be jeopardized by other things going back again to controlling them ehm but in terms of relationships the actual basic relationship I think that that love and affection is there.

Elsewhere (Hall, Sarangi and Slembrouck 1999b) we have developed this as a distinction between the mother and the parent role – a balance between loving your children and looking after them. Given such notions of caring and coping are available in discourses around child welfare agencies, it is not surprising that parents' stories of why their children are in care are likely to attend to the dimensions of caring and coping and will often include versions of a balance between them.

The formulation 'caring but not coping' is available as a rhetorical device in the form of an excuse. As Dingwall *et al.* (1983) say:

> Excuses recognise the deviant nature of the acts in question but withholds moral liability because of the impairment of the actor's capacity-responsibility... They are the moments at which agency is overwhelmed by forces beyond its control, either chance or mysterious inner urges. Excuses, then, are a particularly powerful account. If accepted they are likely comprehensively to exculpate the alleged deviant, since he or she was not capable of being responsible for the acts complained of. (p.86)

No matter how much the parents love their children, they are/were not able to look after them because of outside pressures beyond their control.

Kilroy

The most explicit version of the formulation from our data is available in an exchange from a confessional TV programme, *Kilroy*. The theme was 'foster care'. The formulation came at the beginning of the discussion as a mother was asked to justify her decision to 'put her daughter in care'. In the previous exchanges the mother uses the phrase 'I couldn't cope' three times. The talk show host does not appear to accept this as an adequate justification and presses her further. She admits that she has 'failed as a mother' and 'blames herself for everything'. Kilroy then provides the caring juxtaposition – 'perhaps you gave her all the love and affection that you could' – but continues to press culpability: 'a mother above all has to be there always for their child'. Such an interactional move indexes the real pressures that come with the naturalized premise that parents – especially mothers – are biologically predisposed to be best suited to look after their children. After a six-second delay (on live television), the mother provides a formulation in which 'not coping' is juxtaposed with 'caring'.

Extract 3.2

(M = mother, K = Kilroy)

1   M: erm (2) er I feel Emma going into foster care (-) erm I feel that

2   I made the right decision I'm glad I've put my daughter in care

3   K: why

4   M: because it's guided her I couldn't do that (-) I couldn't cope I

5   couldn't guide my daughter at the time I feel being in foster

6   care has guided her to where she is now and we now have a (-)

7   marvellous bond

The decision to place her daughter in care was not merely a response to her 'not coping'. It was also a sign of caring. Emma has benefited from being in foster care and now they have a good relationship (lines 6–7). Note the change from the essentially defensive talk of the excuse of 'not coping' to the more positive talk that public care has 'guided her' (line 4), a justification that she had made the best decision.

Kathy Malcolm

Kathy has three children one of whom has started short stays in foster care. She has had long-term contact with social services: her first child was adopted and the other children spent periods in care. There are also child protection concerns. The majority of the interview is concerned with behaviour problems of her oldest daughter, Anne, how Kathy has coped and the kind of help she has received from the social services. The youngest child is at home.

Extract 3.3

(I = interviewer, M = mother)

1   I: so so ehm when did did problems first come up with with Anne

2   M: Anne (-)

3   when she was two just before she was two I had my dad staying with

4   me (-) and he had a stroke well they all moved in sort of like they had

5   one bedroom I had the other bedroom ehm there was my dad er his

6   girlfriend and the little boy and there was me and Anne in one room

7   and she seemed she to sort of start (-) yeah it was before she was two

8   she started and she was a right little madam you know

9   I: what sort of things

10   M: like in a tantrum or ((to the child)) alright go and put it in the kitchen

11   then she'd throw things on the floor and ehm (2) generally get out of

12   hand be out of hand you know couldn't hold her or do anything with

13   her so anyway they referred ((to the child)) don't do that come and sit

14   here

((Child plays with the tape recorder.))

15   ehm (2) ehm what do you call it (4) she used to just sort of play up

16   even now she does the same thing now it's even worse

((child interrupts again))

17   M: but you know social services don't get me wrong they have helped me

18   a lot (-) but

19   I: [but I can understand that

20   M: [I I it's ehm it's taken ages and ages to get help

21   with Anne now I've had a knife to my throat by Anne I've had a nose

22   bleed I've had black eyes ((laugh)) ehm she's pushed him over we've

23   had him up the (hospital) three or four times cos she's cut his head open she

24   picked him up one day and threw him across the floor now when I told

25   the social worker this all I got out of her was oh but it could be her age

Kathy locates the beginning of the problems with Anne at the time when her father and family were staying with her (lines 3–4). The implication is that they were living in very overcrowded conditions but this is illustrated by describing sleeping arrangements rather than reported directly (lines 5–6).

Prompted by the interviewer, she begins to describe Anne's disruptive behaviour. This is made available as two three-part lists, a particularly strong persuasive device (Atkinson 1984, p.151). The first list has the third part extended – 'in a tantrum', 'throws things on the floor' and, after a pause, 'generally out of hand', 'can't hold her', 'can't do anything with her' – and uses upgraded terms (lines 10–12). After the child's interruption, the mother provides a much more detailed three-part list of the daughter's attacks on the mother with each part starting with 'I've had...' (lines 21–22). Then a list is provided of assaults on the other children (lines 22–24). These lists of Anne's behaviour are vague at first, but after the interruption they become detailed and highly structured, providing a vivid depiction of Anne's behaviour. While at this stage there is no direct formulation of how this resulted in Kathy 'not coping', it is implied that attempts to get help are hampered by social services' inadequate response (line 25).

In the next few turns Kathy continues to illustrate Anne's behaviour problems, describing incidents during behaviour modification sessions and exclusion from a play scheme for assaulting other children. There are also ongoing complaints about social services' reluctance to help. An explicit formulation of 'not coping' is presented in the context of a comparison of different social workers. It is part of a complaint about social services and it is attributed to a social work voice.

Extract 3.4

(M = mother, I = interviewer)

1   M: social services turned round and said then they'd wash their hands cos

2   they didn't think I could cope with Anne they didn't think I'd be able

3   to do anything with Anne you know they thought well if I'd one child

4   put into care I'd have another one put into care sort of thing but ehm

5   they just said you know they didn't think I'd be able to cope but I just

6   proved them wrong didn't I

7   I: absolutely it's been a long time you have had problems that long

'Not coping' is a formulation which Kathy saw as aimed at her – she could not cope with Anne and was categorized as the sort that puts their children into care. Note how the 'not coping' formulation is first stated and then extended – 'not cope with Anne' to 'not do anything with Anne' (lines 2–3). As such the social services did not think she was worth supporting. However, Kathy considers that such a formulation has been proved wrong, as she has been able to cope with Anne's extreme behaviour. The tag-question 'didn't I' (line 6) counts as an invitation for the interviewer to support this formulation, which he does.

Just as the 'not coping' formulation is qualified and negotiated, so the 'caring' formulation is made available through hints and with the support of the interviewer.

Extract 3.5

(I = interviewer, M = mother)

```
1   I:    so how is she when she comes home, is she…

2   M:    ((laugh)) as soon as she walks through the front door and you say a

3         word to her and she'll NO ((to the child)) she'll come in and she'll

4         pick up her shoes and her coat and its pff on the floor so I says

5         Anne pick your coat up please grrrr so then she'll be fightin' kickin' and then

6         she'll start again and then it go on and on so I I mean she's quite big

7         so can that's her up there the middle one ((pointing to a photograph))

8   I:    oh right

9   M:    so you can imagine trying to control that

10  I:    yeah

11  M:    don't get me wrong I mean she's a lovely little girl when she wants to

12        be it's just these mood swings she has you know
```

The interviewer invites a comment on Anne's behaviour in the context of her stays in care. A description is provided of a typical entrance to the house, with displays of anger and the difficulties Kathy faces in managing her behaviour (lines 2–6). Again the situation is not merely reported but also the interviewer is invited to assess it: 'so you can imagine trying to control that' (line 9). The interviewer's agreement is followed by a positive comment on Anne, using a contrast device, 'don't get me wrong' (line 11). It might be suggested that such a 'caring' contrast appears here to tone down the previous description, which had ended with a highly derogatory formulation of Anne as an object 'that' (line 9).

Similarly, in the final exchange before the recorder is switched off, the most explicit 'caring' formulation is provided, following claims that single parents can give more time to their children.

Extract 3.6

(I = interviewer, M = mother)

1　I:　good oh well thanks very much for your time

2　M:　that's all right

3　I:　very interesting

4　M:　don't get me wrong I still like I still ((laugh))

5　I:　no you've put it very well that there's two sides to the whole thing

Note how the 'don't get me wrong' comment (line 4) is again used as a device to resist any misunderstanding that Kathy may not care for Anne. The formulation is far from explicit and it might be suggested that Kathy resists saying that she 'loves' her child. The word 'like' at line 4 tails off and it is followed by the repeated 'I still' and then the laugh. It does not sound a convincing exposition. However, when it is heard interactionally rather than as a self-standing comment which is to be taken literally, it can be seen as reinforcing an unspoken understanding which has developed between Kathy and the interviewer. The interviewer responds to the invitation with a direct supporting comment 'no' (line 5). He does not misunderstand the situation. 'Caring but not coping' is an interactionally established formulation in which parts may not be made explicit but are hinted at and duly supported.

Dutré-Verbiest

The second interview is with the couple Dutré-Verbiest. The interview was recorded just after their 18-year-old daughter, Sara, returned home from residential care following a troubled family episode involving (as listed by the interviewees): truancy, poor results at school, emotional blackmail and spending several nights away from home. Formulations of 'not coping' are made available at various points, but these are predominantly in terms of controlling an adolescent's breaching of 'rules' at school and at home. Even though these parents very much took the initiative by contacting the district youth care committee, leading to Sara's two-month stay in residential care, there was a preceding history of monitoring by the school team, family therapy, etc.

Extract 3.7

(F = father, M = mother, I = interviewer)

1	F:	yes the other thing that Sara didn't want (-) just a few weeks
2		earlier things had been difficult then we had suggested to her but that
3		wasn't through the committee to go to a crisis centre in [place name] but
4		that scared her off she was afraid of that because she couldn't see it
5		happen erm in the meantime between the proposal to go to [place name]
6		and the decision at the committee here in [place name] there were a
7		few weeks certainly a few weeks went by when things were coming to
8		a head and that she then started realizing herself yeah ok things can't
9		go on like this and ok we also clearly said things can't go on like this
10	M:	also at the school they said like she's not doing anything for you
11		something has to happen
12	F:	yes also at school drastic measures weren't far off one more instance
13		of truancy there was truancy all the time one more instance of truancy
14		and the school would have no other choice but to
15	M:	expel her
16	F:	expel her from school
17	I:	uhum

In the case of difficulties in coping with adolescents, children are increasingly likely to be held responsible for family crises.[5] Here an extreme case situation is being formulated – 'things can't go on like this' (line 9) and 'drastic measures weren't far off' (line 12). In it, an appeal is made to all parties to recognize that something had to be done, with considerable pressure from various agencies. A little later in the interview we learn from the father that the reception into care was timed carefully: after the Christmas holidays (so that the family could spend a holiday away from home together first) and in any case before Sara turned 18 – a decision which is presented as in the interest of all involved.

Extract 3.8

(F = father)

1 F: things went so fast (.) things went fast especially because we wanted

2   to make the best of the months before Sara turned eighteen (.) because if

3   we had let time tick away (.) this would have been bad for everyone.

4   then she should have been eighteen and said ((claps hands)) close the

5   door done I'm eighteen and I'm leaving.

This formulation suggests an amount of responsible, not to say rational decision making, which could easily be heard as a lack of emotional involvement.

A formulation of 'care', however, follows in a later sequence, when the father talks about their positive assessment of a preparatory visit to the residential home. At this point, the father makes a set of comparisons with other youngsters in public care.

Extract 3.9

(F = father, I = interviewer, M = mother)

1 F: I think that for her too it's been a bit of a shock (.) what she

2   experienced there (.) suffered there (.) youngsters who are brought

3   in handcuffed (.) a er couple months earlier (.) suicide (.) erm guys

4   who are heavily addicted (.) parents who never turn around to

5   look after their children (.) while we at least supported her were there

6 I: uhum

7 F: who were there pff ((distancing tone)) no more contact with the

8   parents so I think yes this has made her see things (.) made her see

9   one or two things ((ironic smile))

10 M: but we're still in therapy aren't we

The contrast with the list of other cases (crime, suicide, addiction and total abandonment, lines 3–5) redeems the parents in a number of respects. These are problems which lie outside the remit of this particular family. At the same time, these experiences had a positive effect on Sara: they made her see that her parents weren't doing so badly after all (lines 8–9). This can be read as a justification that the reception into care was the right decision. At the same time, the parents offer a powerful formulation of 'see how we cared, even if we did leave our daughter behind in a residential home', formulated contrastively with parents 'who *never* turn around to look after their children' (line 4). They are not parents who will just hand over their adolescent daughter to the professionals.

Just before the end of the interview, an even more explicit formulation of care follows.

Extract 3.10

(M = mother, F = father, I = interviewer)

1	M:	yes but also at the Boterhoek[6] erm these conversations you don't have
2		the feeling like [F: no] you're being blamed [F: oh no] you are
3	F:	they offer a framework don't they [M: yes]
4	I:	and you don't feel inclined to do this yourself
5	M:	well at that at that moment you do off course
6	I:	yes yes yes yes
7	F:	oh yeah yeah. especially at first during the first days that that she was
8		there
9	M:	after the first day yes then ((long pause)) and then she will know
10		exactly how to play at that too (.) Sara ((ironic smile))
11	F:	oh yes (.) she's clever she's shrewd (.) yes ok (.) well ok (.) now it is
12		the these six or these eight weeks made things a bit more relaxed here
13		during the week [M: a bit more relaxed] (.) in the weekends the home
14		gave her a very clear frame like Friday night at home Saturday night
15		going out and other things and so that then even after three four
16		weekends we were able to relax that and now she more or less goes

17   along with what we've agreed doesn't she (.) ok

18 M: I think it's also done her some good

19 F: only

20 M: for everyone in a way

21 F: only you keep worrying about her future that stays doesn't it

22 M: it does

23 I: uhum

24 M: like how is this going to end (.) that uncertainty stays

25 F: yes. well ok

26 M: even after

27 F: that's the same way even with an 84-year-old mum about her

28   youngest son

     ((shared laughter))

29 M: this will always be the case

30 I: indeed

Although the parents did not feel they were being blamed by the family therapy centre, the interviewer's question may well come with a charge ('and you don't feel inclined to do this yourself', line 4). In their co-constructed response, the mother first and then the father report feelings of guilt and doubt immediately after the separation from their daughter. What follows then is a depiction of how this, too, was exploited by their daughter (she will 'play at that too', line 10), which again casts the daughter at the problem. This negative characterization is counter-balanced by a list of positive effects attributed to the period in care, which did Sara and the parents some good (lines 12–20). However, to the extent that this counts as an expression of confidence for the future, it is balanced by the parents voicing concerns about the long term (lines 21 and 24). This kind of worrying indexes a commitment to one's children which can be generalized to all parents. Note also the mild irony in the father's final turn, as the lifelong worry is also somewhat exaggeratedly there in his own relationship with his 84-year-old mother (line 27). Care for one's children is indeed a 'strange thing', as interviewer and mother agree.

Conclusion

In this analysis of instances of parental talk about why their children are in care, we have shown one frequently used rhetorical formulation, 'caring but not coping'. While parents are having difficulties coping with their children's behaviour, they still care about them and hence their parenting credentials should not be challenged. The three cases we have considered involve children aged between 10 and 18 and, as we have suggested, the formulation may be used differently for young children or babies. We have also suggested that to work as an excuse such a formulation is produced in normal talk; what all speakers might understand. In particular, the talk show host and the interviewers have contributed to the construction of formulation by supporting ('indeed' in Extract 3.10), pressing ('why' in Extract 3.2) and even commending the explanation ('you've put it very well', Extract 3.6).

While this formulation has only been explored for parental talk concerning children in care, we would suggest that versions are likely to appear elsewhere. For example, conversation between parents at the school gates might include talk about how parents are coping with their children. Rosanne Barr in the TV comedy commented that 'if I can get to the end of the day without nailing my children to the wall I've done pretty well'. Similarly, the media frequently present features on how parents will cope over the long school holidays. However, in such talk we would suggest that the 'caring' part of the formulation is less likely to surface explicitly since these parents' caring credentials are not under scrutiny.

Caring and coping are explored from a very different perspective in the literature on disability and illness. Here caring is associated with the everyday tasks of tending to an incapacitated relative rather than necessarily the nature of that relationship. (e.g. Szmukler 1996). The carer's love and affection for their relative is not in question, and 'caring' is seen in the way in which they are able to continue tending to their relative's needs. Coping here is associated with how the carer is able to maintain increasing levels of self-sacrifice without damaging their own physical and mental health. Carers are not required to justify their care for their relative.

If caring and coping are indeed a part of everyday descriptions of bringing up children, then why do the parents of children in care appear to have to make extra justifications of their caring and coping credentials? Could it be that the parents' stories of why their children are in care are not really believed? Kilroy certainly did not appear convinced of the mother's story: 'a mother above all has to be there always for their child'. In Extract 3.1, the social worker, while accepting the mother's 'love and affection', still felt that the children were being damaged by her not coping; that is, 'not coping' can become 'not caring'. This scepticism of adequate caring can be contrasted with for example families caring for disabled children: 'Caring for a developmentally disabled child can be stressful for many parents' (Chan and Sigafoos 2001, p.253). Similarly, White (this volume, Chapter 5) suggests the sentiments in case files concerning parents with disabled children are more service delivery orientated and contain supportive comments about the parents' moral worth.

We would suggest then that parents' concerns about maintaining a balance between caring and coping talk is a justified response to a situation in which it is likely they are surrounded by scepticism concerning their parental capacities and moral worth. Social workers, neighbours, family and they themselves appear to associate their children spending time in public care with parental inadequacy. This is not the intention of legislation in Flanders and the UK. In the latter case, periods away from home in council establishments are referred to as 'accommodation' rather than 'care' which policy statements identify as a service to support the family without stigmatizing connotations (Department of Health 1991, p.11). Yet it seems that unless children can be provided with a label of developmental or behavioural disability, such interventions will continue to lay parents open to the accusation that they are not only not coping but also not caring for the child. Indeed, social work may be a key part of such stigmatizing processes.

Research in social work and social policy has developed Goffman's concept of stigma, discussed by Offer (1999, Chapter. 5). Such research sees stigma in terms of discrimination. For example, professionals through assessment, screening or means testing systems categorize clients in various disparaging ways in order to establish whether they qualify for services or benefits. Such an approach, however, sees stigma as a one way process – professionals imposing on clients a stigmatized identity. It also identifies stigma in terms of particular attributes rather than, as we have tried to do, located within an interactional order. While Offer (1999, p.96) points out Goffman's inconsistency in this matter, the overall direction of his work suggests the need to investigate the dynamics and management of stigma. As we have seen, parents resist the stigma associated with their children in care: they anticipate criticism and develop counter arguments. As noted by Atkinson and Drew (1979), the rebuttal comes before the charge.

If the development of a stigmatizing perspective is indeed so closely tied up with 'normal' conditions of interaction (as Goffman seems to be suggesting), then a speaker's interactional orientation towards 'feeling accused' and 'feeling one has to justify and explain' is inherent in the dynamics of interaction. Such a stigmatizing perspective will develop almost inevitably as soon as speakers are in the know about one of the two possessing a discredited property. Although, like many others, he stresses socio-cultural and historical contingency, Goffman's insights lead to a pessimistic conclusion about the chances of stigma being overcome by simple appeals to political struggles, to a change in mentality or an inscription in legislation. Offer (1999) correctly observes that in Goffman's work 'we are actors in a play, performing a script already written' (p.111), but we take this point to be more about social-interactional dynamics than the immutability of discreditable attributes.

Payne (1980) has suggested various ways in which social workers might challenge stigma. While support of the client with 'self management' (as we recommend) locates action in the interaction arena, persuading them to disregard potentially stigmatizing identities does not. The thrust of Goffman's analysis raises the question to what extent social work, rather than hearing parents' explanations as 'excuses to be ignored', can take on board that it is almost inevitable for parents to experience pressure to account and to redeem their moral worth. What calls for our attention is not so much that parents should not feel accused but rather that they will almost certainly feel accused. Developing an analytical/reflexive sensitivity to the varied display of rhetorical figures such as 'caring but not coping' can contribute to social work practice which anticipates the dynamics of client self identity.

Notes

1   See Silverman (1987), who considers how the mothers of diabetic teenagers, when talking to the doctor, carefully present themselves as concerned but not neurotic parents.

2   Goffman (1990a) stresses that one enters encounters with the anticipation of meeting a 'normal' person with a set of 'ordinary' attributes (this is the domain of 'virtual social identity' as opposed to 'actual social identity' which is the domain of attributes that a person can be 'proved' to possess). Stigma arises when interlocutors become aware that the person they meet possesses an attribute which makes him or her different and less desirable, with the result

of being reduced in the interlocutor's mind from a whole and usual person to a tainted and discounted one. Of course, discreditable attributes will vary in kind and degree and are socio-culturally and historically contingent. Therefore, by 'imputing identities to individuals, discreditable or not, the wide social setting and its inhabitants have in a way compromised themselves; they have set themselves up to be proven the fool' (p.161). At the same time, understanding how stigma bears on interaction, requires a language of relationships rather than of absolute attributes. The gaps between virtual and actual social identities leads to questions of information control, revelation and concealment and such questions are faced by all. Stigma 'involves not so much a set of concrete individuals who can be separated into two piles, the stigmatised and the normal, as a pervasive two-role social process in which every individual participates in both roles, at least in some connexions and in some phases of their life' (p.163).

3   In Goffman (1990a), the term 'stigma' conceals two categories: the stigmatized individual assumes his or her differentness is known about already or is evident on the spot (the plight of the discredited) or assumes it is neither known about by those present nor immediately perceivable (the plight of the discreditable).

4   See Atkinson and Drew (1979), who investigate how talk in court is defensive in nature, organized in charge and rebuttal sequences.

5   In contrast, consider what another client had to say about the context of small infants:

    CL: yeah. two came round. and they saw that I wasn't coping very well with Nathan. which. I tried to explain to people that I wasn't coping with Nathan it's a very difficult thing to explain to people that you're not coping with a baby very well

    IN: mm

    CL: it's hard work telling someone that you are not coping with your baby and. you can't admit to it

6   The 'Boterhoek' is the informal name for the family therapy centre (named after the street in which it is situated).

4

Negotiating Clienthood and the Moral Order of a Relationship in Couple Therapy

Katja Kurri and Jarl Wahlström

Introduction

In its theoretical self-understanding, couple therapy usually constructs as its object of treatment the inner worlds of the partners and their mutual interdependencies, the limitations in communication skills between the spouses or the malfunctional interactional patterns of the relationship (Crowe 1996). These formulations appear, from a constructionist point of view, restricted in not taking into account the institutionally framed constructive work of the spouses. A constructionist point of departure would hold that people do go into couple relationships driven by 'a passion for living together', but that this passion does not inform them on how to actually live together, i.e. to construct a joint form of life (Wittgenstein 1953). What then informs them? It seems that in (post)modern society there are fewer opportunities or necessities to rely on traditions, such as gender-divided labour, and fewer cultural rituals exist to perform such a task. 'Negotiations' have an increasingly central part in the process of establishing a social and moral order of a relationship.

Couple therapy can be seen as a special arena for these kinds of 'negotiations'. Here the spouses bring their private business to 'public ears'. In this situation it is not uncommon that the position of 'client' is offered by the spouses to each other, and the therapist is called upon to work on the problems of one of them on behalf of the other. In this chapter we will analyse a part of a conversational process of one couple therapy session. We will show that negotiating clienthood is at the core of the therapeutic process and forms a necessary frame for establishing the session as an arena for dealing with other issues in the couple's life.

In this chapter we will ask how the discursive practices of the participants in the couple therapy process establish an arena for problem formulations, membership categorizations and other means of clienthood constructions, and how this forms a frame for negotiating the social and moral order of the relationship overall. We will do this with special reference to the usages of emotion talk. By scripting emotional experiencing as orderly, it is possible to perform manifold discursive actions in the social and communicative tasks of identity construction, positioning, defending, and accusing, to name a few (Edwards 1995, 1996, 1999). In order to address these issues we will take a close look at extracts of text data from one session of couple therapy, analysing them with close attention to sequential turn-by-turn interaction (Schegloff and Sacks 1973).

The session

The analysed session took place in a university psychotherapy clinic in Finland. This is the fifth session out of seven. The clients referred themselves due to the distress and tension the family's eldest daughter had brought about for the rest of the family members. They did not seek help for this daughter, who had already moved away from home, but explicitly for the repercussions of her troublesome behaviour on their couple relationship. There are five participants in the session – the two spouses, two male trained family therapists and one female student in training. The clients are both academically trained professionals in their early fifties. The first six extracts to be subjected to a detailed analysis consist of the transcription of seven minutes from the one-and-a-half-hour long video recording of the session. The seventh extract begins 11 minutes after the sequence in Extract 4.6. Conversational flux is marked with the continuous numbering between extracts; where the extract does not immediately follow the previous one the numbering begins with number 1.

At the beginning of the session the spouses relate an incident that occurred the day before. Their eldest daughter had been in an accident, caused by her own carelessness due to an intoxicated state, and had almost died. After the account of this dramatic and very stressful event, 16 minutes into the course of the session, there is a 17-seconds pause in the conversation. Then the husband starts to talk on a more generic level, commenting on how the troubles with this daughter have affected him emotionally.

Extract 4.1: Emotional scripting as a starting-point for negotiating clienthood

(H = husband, W = wife)

1		(17)
2	H:	°But anyway. (.) you have to. (1) go through
3		considerable, (.) storms kind of, (.) in your own,
4		(.) emotions and, (.) then when both, (.) our
5		reactions clash together then it's always a bit
6		problematic°
7	W:	°Yeah we have completely different, (.) different
8		these (2) habits, (.) but yeah,°

The formulation of the husband (lines 2–6) constructs emotions, through the metaphor of a storm, as naturally and temporarily occurring phenomena (see Edwards 1999). An image of a natural event, which cannot be controlled, is created. It just has to be lived through and endured. An impression of inevitability is given. However, on the other hand, storms do not last forever, they eventually calm down. This metaphor creates an impression which locates the experiencing outside the realm of the speaker's agency. Emotions are not represented as actions or feelings chosen. They are constructed as phenomena one has to go through, without options. Hence, the responsibility of the speaker *vis-à-vis* his emotions is lessened.

In his turn the husband also locates emotional experience within a relational context. This is done through the use of the word 'reactions'. Emotions are constructed within a relational matrix – they are caused by something. However, also here we have the image of uncontrollability. A reaction is immediate and spontaneous. The script formulation 'our reactions clash together' (line 5) orientates the conversation to construct the problem at hand as a relational issue, involving a mutuality of behaviours. And here the 'problem' is interestingly, and somewhat contradictorily, produced as something constantly present, 'it's *always* problematic', but at the same time of minor concern, 'it's always *a bit* problematic'. This latter emphasis renders the 'problem' a quality of manageability.

In her turn the wife continues the constructive work. Her formulation introduces a shift in what the conversation should be orientated to. By saying 'we have these completely different', and after a two-second pause, 'habits' (lines 7–8), she introduces a new contextual frame. The pause in the wife's turn can be seen marking hesitation and delicacy, but perhaps also deliberation, in relation to the choice of the word 'habit' (in Finnish, *tavat*). The word, which translates into Latin as *mores*, puts the issue under discussion within a frame of morality and responsibility. Here, in contrast to the husband's version, the possibility of making choices and of acting differently is highlighted. A person can have good or bad habits and is also expected to be able to choose between them. When emotional experience is scripted in this way the speaker is rendering the subject of that experience a higher share of agency. The extreme formulation (see Pomerantz 1986; Edwards 2000) 'we have these *completely* different' included in the wife's turn contrasts to the husband's mitigated formulation and marks the 'problem' as an issue hard to solve. However, by ending her turn with the phrase 'but yeah' (line 8), she seems to open the possibility for further negotiation.

The therapist responds to these turns by posing a question (lines 9 and 10).

Extract 4.2: Focusing on the interaction

(T1 = therapist 1)

9   T1:   So has today, (.) and, (.) yesterday something like

10   this been going on between you,

The therapist's question retrospectively elicits (see Peräkylä 1995) further the topic introduced by the spouses, and thus marks it as an issue worth talking about (Bergmann 1998). The formulation of the question, though, is obscure enough not to subscribe to either of the emotional scripts of the previous turns. The use of the wording 'something like this' orientates the conversation to what has been offered, and in this way marks it as a legitimate 'problem' to be dealt with within the therapeutic context. The wording, however, leaves the definition of 'something like this' open for further negotiation. This calls for more information on how the conflicting script formulations are lived out in the concrete exchanges between them.

Extract 4.3: Constructing the husband as 'the client'

(W = wife, H = husband)

11 W: [>Last last night just that this thing again of

12 H: [Mmm-mmm,

13 W: Erkki's, (.)

14 W: kind of it seems to me Erkki's worries and distress

15   always appear as a kind of aggression<, (.) .hh and

16   coldness that that so it's kind of for me tough that

17   mm 'cause I I can't, (.) express .hhh myself kind of that

18   I could fight properly over which of us has though

19   yesterday I said it straight out but kind of no you

20   don't answer. (.) like you just go silent. (.) so it

21   is somehow [like

22 H: [.Hhh hhh

23 W: that but then one has learnt to.hhhh grhm, (1) umm be

24   sort of on one's own somehow kind of one realizes that

25   he won't speak any more and now he won't I I can't

26   stand that kind of aggression and .hhh that sort of

27   mmhh,

28 H: Yeah I think you should stand it a little.

The wife's response to the therapist's question (lines 9–10) does not take the form of a retrospective account of events (which could have been one way of taking up the thread) but produces a description of her husband's way of expressing emotions: 'Erkki's worries and distress always appear as a kind of aggression and coldness' (lines 14–16). Here the husband is constructed as the possessor of a characteristic, that of presenting emotions differently from what they actually are. This characteristic is constructed as permanent – 'yesterday this happened *again*' – and the emotions '*always*' appear like that. The wife's utterance, 'it's kind of for me tough' (line 16), makes it clear that this description is to be heard as a blame.

Through the use of the words 'again' and 'always' the formulation shifts the focus of attention from whether the description of the husband's characteristic is true or false as such. The extreme formulation concerns the frequency of appearance, and is as such viable to objections. The presence of the characteristic in itself is not opened to question; it appears as indisputable. This choice of word can be seen to serve the credibility of the description – the understanding of the permanency of the conflict is constructed as shared by the spouses. It also, however, seems to pave the way for a more drastic membership categorization of the husband, to be seen in Extract 4.5. By ascribing a generic feature to her husband the wife is also strengthening her blame and building a basis for a categorial problematization of the husband's actions and features. This rather long turn performs the complicated and delicate task of constructing blame while trying to manage the consequences this has for the speaker's moral status (see Kurri and Wahlström, 2001). This is done by softening the blame by nominalizing the husband's behaviour and sharing the blame (Edwards 1995, 2000). Further, the account is constructed as constitutive by the use of extreme formulations (Pomerantz 1986): blaming is justified because this is always the case – not only sometimes. The turn also orientated the therapeutic conversation towards the task of dealing with the difficulties of the husband to express his 'real' emotions. The husband, however, refuses to accept the wife's attempt to place him in the category of the client (line 23). His turn makes relevant only the last lines (lines 25–26) of the wife's turn. When responding to only the last utterance, 'I I can't stand that kind of aggression and that sort' by saying 'Yeah I think that you should stand it a little', the husband justifies the aggression by admitting it and denying the negative moral character related to it. Consequently he constructs the scripting (see Edwards 1994) of his emotional expressions as 'faulty' to be the problem; rather the problem is his wife's inability to stand aggression.

In a sequence following Extract 4.3 the wife tells of how, in some instances, the husband's 'whole being' becomes 'repulsive' to her. These instances refer to her description in lines 15 and 16 of his way of expressing emotions. A few turns later the therapist picks up this account in a question.

Extract 4.4: *Challenging the grounds for client categorization*
(T1 = therapist 1, W = wife, H = husband)

1   T1:   Then the the immediate reaction that arises in you when

2   Erkki:.(.) changes like you just described is is then what,

3   W: Disappointment

4   T1:   Disappointment

5   W: Disappointment aa-a sort of disappointment but it's maybe not

6   so #mmm# it's not so kind of mmmh. total like it used to

7   be no it isn't yes it lasts a moment

8   T1:   And and can you get hold on what's what's the main idea which

9   is behind your disappointment (3) if you tried to put it into

10   one sen[tence

11 W: [Awful it's something so disgusting that I can't say

12   it out loud

13 H: ((laughing)) Wha:t what

14 W: Kind of sort of like like when I'm disappointed then like

15   mm mh I don't know how to say it

16 H: I also have a problem with how it is possible to verbally

17   describe everything [what happens there

18 W: [Yeah I I kind of I have that like awful

19   that comes that kind of feeling that .hhh what am I doing

20   with that kind of person

21 T1:   Mmm,

The therapist's question (lines 1–2) changes once again the context of talk. In face of the dilemma of what the conversation should be orientated towards, arising after the husband's rejoinder in line 28 (Extract 4.3), this question offers a new path. The discursive structure of the question is twofold. The wording elicits a relational context. Something happens in reaction to something else. The wording 'what arises in you' through the use of a spatial metaphor, points towards the 'inner life' of the wife. The wife picks up this potential thread by naming a feeling, 'disappointment' (line 3), echoed by the therapist in line 4 and, interestingly enough, qualified and mitigated by the wife (lines 5–7).

The therapist follows the thread offered by the wife's answer and further elicits an account of the cognitive process 'the main idea' behind the disappointment (lines 8–10). This formulation strengthens the orientation towards the 'inner life' of the respondent, and, in so doing, towards the realm of the wife's agency and her responsibility. The 'disappointment' is elicited not only by the husband's behaviour but also, and perhaps decisively, by her thoughts. The three-second silence (line 9) during which the wife does not produce an answer, and the therapist's need to spur on by formulating the question further, can be read as marking the potential repercussions of this context shift into the moral order of the conversation. The wife picks this up immediately (overlapping line 11) by explicitly wording the condemnable consequences her thought, if made public, would have on her moral identity. Now, suddenly, the blame she was constructing in Extract 4.3, is on her!

Furthermore, the wording 'comes that kind of feeling' (line 19) obscures the agent. The original word 'idea' used in the therapist's question changes into 'feeling' and the phrase is worded in the passive voice (comes). These discursive markers can be seen to serve to 'save' the speaker from her predicament, stemming from focusing on her realm of agency. The feeling 'comes over' her, she does not 'originate' it. She announces that she is conscious of the unacceptability of her sentiment. Only embedded in an utterance softened by an excessive use of delicacy markers can the sentiment be made public.

Here again a turn back to the blame construction in Extract 4.3 is offered. The phrase 'that kind of person' (line 20) can be read as a second step on the way, paved already in Extract 4.2, towards a construction of the husband's identity as essentially being of a particular quality. This constructive work will be completed in Extract 4.5. It should be noted that the husband's three turns within Extract 4.4 are not strongly orientated towards the wife's blame construction. The first one (line 13) suggests perplexity and the second one (lines 16–17) offers an invitation to discuss a shared difficulty in verbalizing experiences. In short, the previous extract, when read from the viewpoint of managing clienthood, offers many interesting points of departure. First the therapist challenges the categorization in which the husband is offered as a client by focusing on the wife's thoughts and actions. This leads to confusion after which the wife returns to the construction in which it is the qualities of the husband that should be the object of treatment.

Extract 4.5: Focusing on the wife's cognitive processes
(T1 = therapist 1, W = wife)

1	T1:	If this is your, (.) your first idea that. (1) how can
2		he be like that. (.) and, (.) or something like that
3		and what am I doing, (.) [with that kind of person
4	W:	[Yeah,
5	T1:	who, (.) .hhh reacts in these
6		situations so differently than you [think one
7	W:	[Mmm,
8	T1:	should react so, (.) now in this situation kind of when
9		you can think about it. (.) sort of reflectively and
10		think over everything that is actually
11		happening there in this calm situation,
12		[(.) then what in this situation do
13	W:	[Yeah,
14	T1:	you think is the thing that get's Erkki. (.) to act
15		such a way.
16	W:	Well I think that he's so, (.) mmh I think that he's
17		so emotionally handicapped this Erkki that he kind of
18		doesn't that he is so shocked that he doesn't have any
19		means, (.) kind of #mmm# then I start sort of
20		feeling sorry for him, (.) and sort of feeling that I
21		should then be able, (.) #aaa# bec- I I then there's
22		again a kind of, (1) .hhh mmhh äh that that mmhh. on
23		the other hand I realize that I should then mmhh. be

24   able to show to get close or somehow kind of, (.)

25   comfort him or something like that. (1) but, (.) I am

26   then, (.) somehow there comes to me something like,

27   (.) .hhh pride or something like that why should

28   I always. (3) #th:at# when I mmmhh kind of myself

29   expect something like that, (.) in some situations

30   sometimes then, (2) mmmhh, (1) that one could trust

31   that, one could break down however tired weak and then

32   the other would say that, (2) is's

33   okay we are together, (1) that's what I kind of, so

The therapist responds to the wife's expression of her sentiment by continuing to construct the focus of the conversation in her realm of agency. This is done through the formulation of an extended question (lines 1–3, 5–6, 8–12, 14–15) with a rather complicated temporal and indexical structure. The question starts (lines 1–3) by repeating and partly rephrasing the wife's earlier account (Extract 4.4, lines 19–20), using the same kind of undetermined terms 'like that...that kind of person' when ascribing to the husband a certain quality. There is an important rephrasing, though, in the opening of the turn. The therapist replaces the wife's vague expression 'feeling' with the word 'idea', thus returning to the phrasing of the question in Extract 4.4 (line 8) and so eliciting an account of a more active and responsible 'inner process'. In his question, the therapist interestingly uses a first-person structure 'what I am doing with that kind of person' (line 3) when quoting the wife's earlier turn but then shifts footing (Goffman 1979) back to a second-person structure 'than *you* think one should react' (lines 6 and 8). The use of the first-person structure functions to mark an adoption of the recipient's perspective and is validated by the wife's overlapping mini-response 'yeah' (line 4). The turn back to the second-person structure again seems to mark a distancing from that perspective. This may serve two functions. First, it questions the potential identity construction of the husband as 'that kind of person' by framing this categorization within the bounds of the wife's judgement ('than you think'). Second, it may signal to the husband that the therapist is talking from a position of a 'non-interested' party.

The therapist's question also functions to construct two different contexts. The first one (lines 1–3, 5–6) contains the situation in which the sentiment arises, and the second one (lines 8–12) the 'here and now' of the actual therapeutic conversation. This is presented as a situation in which it is possible to think and reflect upon the issue calmly. Again, two possible functions of this constructive work can be seen. It provides an opportunity for the wife to adopt a position of agency with respect to her initial sentiment. 'Now', when she is not driven by the agitated situation, she can construct her opinion in peace, and from this point of reflection seek a new understanding of those kind of situations. Second, the separation of the two different situational contexts can be seen as an invitation to the wife to construct and display an empathic understanding of her husband's reaction.

These opportunities, however, are not grasped by the wife. Instead she brings her own constructive work concerning the husband's characteristics, started in Extract 4.3, to a closure. The husband is assigned membership in the category of emotionally disabled persons (line 17). Interestingly the wording of this categorization, 'I think that he's so emotionally handicapped this Erkki', is quite straightforward and declarative. The speaker signals full responsibility for the statement. What could be the consequences of such a bold act in terms of her position within the moral order of the conversation?

On the one hand, when making such a statement, the speaker, by constructing herself as someone able to evaluate the emotional capability of somebody else, is positioning herself as an emotionally able person. To say that someone is disabled requires that the person making this evaluation is able within the field being described, in this case emotions. Such a person can be seen as representing normality (Garfinkel 1967) and would in that capacity have strong grounds for claiming authority when the grounds for the social and moral order of a relationship are delineated.

On the other hand, ascribing someone disabled in his presence could be seen as invalidating the emotional ability and moral status of the speaker. The wife's turn, starting with the 'disability-statement' (line 17), becomes quite elaborated and includes a number of similar discursive devices as in Extract 4.3. Also here they function to sustain her moral status within the conversation. She formulates her statement in an active way thus signalling responsibility for it. She produces an empathetic and socially approved understanding of the rationale behind his disability: 'he is so shocked that he doesn't have any means'. She constructs herself as empathizing with her husband as being an important constituent of her phenomenological reality: 'I start sort of feeling sorry for him'. She shares the blame by giving an account of her failure to do what should be done: 'I realize that I should then be able to show to get close'. The impediment is something outside the realm of her agency – the feeling of 'pride' which 'comes' to her. She also provides a morally viable explanation for this failure – the lack of mutuality in showing comfort and support: 'why should I always'. The extreme formulation, 'why should I *always*', is contrasted with the wife's wish that 'in *some situations* and *sometimes*' she could trust that the husband would do the comforting. This contrast structure (Smith 1990; Potter 1996) constructs the wife's wish as a modest and realistic one.

From the point of view of the construction of blame as one of the central threads of the conversation, what happens in Extract 4.5 poses an interesting question. If the core of the 'problem' to which the therapeutic conversation should obviously be orientated is the husband's constitutional disability to handle and express emotions, is there any more room for blame or therapy? There is, of course, also a more hopeful interpretation. The therapist has in Extracts 4.4 and 4.5 challenged the wife's client categorization and has orientated towards her inner thoughts. The wife's open, straightforward and declarative remarks regarding her inner logic may be seen as one way of trying to be a client in couple therapy – 'to tell honestly what I think about the other'. In Extract 4.6 this constructive work continues.

Extract 4.6: Opening space for mutual blame construction
(W = wife, T1 = therapist 1, H = husband)

1	W:	So I expect kind of [that that when for once such kind
2		of that
3	T1:	[You expect it, (.) you expect it,
4	W:	[(1) yeah that hey we are together and share this thing
5	T1:	[Yeah sorry I misunderstood.
6	W:	that it will pass [that
7	H:	[Well of course th- it should be like
8		that.

9   W: In a way it's like this I kind of realize it's like this

10   usually between us because they are solved quite, (1)

11   #ä# the closeness is however strong between us #umm#but

12   both of us have a kind of inability that we can't go

13   [halfway

14   H: [Mm.

The wife further elaborates on her vision of the preferred state of affairs picturing togetherness and sharing as values to be aspired to: 'hey we are together and share this thing that it will pass' (lines 4 and 6). The husband immediately rejoins with a confirmative comment. His wordings, 'of course' and 'it should be like that' (lines 7–8) construct the wife's vision as self-evident, and hence subscribe to that vision but also assert his ability to grasp the requirements for the moral order of a 'good' relationship. Now the wife again rejoins in the affirmative, acknowledging that there actually exists togetherness, and even a strong one, 'closeness is however strong between us' (line 11) in their relationship. In light of this, she finishes her turn by once more redefining 'the problem'. What should be orientated towards is their mutual inability to 'go halfway'. This is a quite significant turn in the path of her blame construction. This sharing of the blame is different from the previous extracts for it does not function to save face. The problem is not formulated as an essential feature or characteristic of a person but as a mutual difficulty to initiate a process.

Shortly after this, in a reflective conversation (Andersen 1990), the therapists wondered whether what the wife saw as an incapacity of the husband could also be seen as something useful – as a means of maintaining a capacity for action. Further, they reflected that, in spite of the potential usefulness, it is possible to understand that the husband's behaviour might not be something that the wife wishes for. After this the spouses engaged in a discussion – at times quite heated – on their differences in expressing emotions, and of the gains and losses related to these. Extract 4.7 shows a sequence of this discussion.

Extract 4.7: *Constructing the relationship as 'the client'*

(T2 = therapist 2, H = husband, W = wife)

1	T2:	#Mm# Wh- what do you think about that Tuija, (.) Tuija
2		charges so much emotion to that situation then. (.) or
3		that.
4	H:	Well for me it's kind of pretty pointless. (.) .hh,
5		(.) that with less we would be better off kind of °I
6		think like that.°
7	T2:	Why does she charge. (.) do you have any idea about
8		that,
9	H:	Well it's her habit and °characteristic.°
10	W:	I'll say ((with a smile)) this [that
11	H:	[that she's she's just
12		such a fanatic, (.).hh [tha:t hhh
13	W:	[then that I have, (.) emo-
14		emotional arsenal I, (.) therefore, (.) because of so
15		much I feel that Erkki hasn't got Erkki doesn't risk
16		anything at all. (.) .hh that therefore I perhaps
17		using that, (.) .hh umm mhh. I attempt, (.) something,
18		(.) c- could it be that I attempt using it something
19		because you freeze up. (.) so it is kind of irritating
20		when when one feels that, (.) .hh what ever [happens
21	H:	[Yeah,
22	W:	or whatever threat or distress or worry there is then
23		Erkki freezes up [like >those few emotions he has kind
22	H:	[Well it's, (.) yeah.
23	W:	of they don't come
24	H:	[well because you (.) in a way you

25 W: [out at all, (.) and<

26 H: kind of in ad[vance kind of prevent them my chance

27 W: [well it's somehow mmm,

28 H: [in that situation you block my chance

29 W: [I don't don't know it,

30 H: to e- express in that situation

31   [I feel like you, (.) lock up that route

32 W: [I block well why do you let me block it, (.) kind of

33   just it [that why then

34 H: [well there we are.

35 W: no no.

36 T1:   Mm that's probably what we are trying to talk about

37   here.

38 ((general laughter))

In the extract above we can observe something both similar and different from in the previous extracts. The main difference is the mutuality of the blaming. The conversation above is quite heated which can be noticed from the several overlapping instances of talk. The talk is also louder and the wife's turns more rapid than usual. The husband's first answer to the therapist's question (lines 4–6) constructs displays of emotions as both 'a habit' and 'a characteristic' of his wife. This draws an interesting continuity to the conversational thread; the conversation began with the different emotional scripts which ascribed different amounts of agency and responsibility over emotions. Further, after the wife's attempt to interrupt, the husband produces a description of the wife and uses a membership categorization; she is a 'fanatic' (lines 11–12). This rhetorical choice constructs a defence against the wife's categorization of him as 'emotionally handicapped' and manages the blame by suggesting that the wife's description should be heard from the viewpoint of her being a(n) (emotional) fanatic.

The wife continues (line 13) to explain her emotional arsenal in relation to the lack in the husband's arsenal and display of emotions. The interesting feature in this turn, from the point of view of constructing clienthood, is the changes in the addressed recipient. First, the wife is talking to the therapists and producing a description of her husband. Then she directly addresses the husband as 'you'. After this, she changes back to the description addressed to the therapists. Another interesting feature in this turn is the way of describing her own conduct in a reflective way – by suggesting interpretations of the possible reasons for her action 'perhaps' (line 16) and 'could it be' (line 18). The husband tries to take over the turn (line 22) and succeeds (line 24). He directly addresses his wife (line 24) and accepts her blame but offers an explanation of his behaviour and also blames her '...you kind of in advance kind of prevent them my chances...'.

The wife's defence and counter-blame is directed towards the husband and is in the form of a question (line 32). The husband, however, does not react to it as a question but states 'there we are'. This is read quite differently by the wife and by the therapist. The wife's turn, 'no no', seems to suggest that she hears the husband as refusing to 'catch the ball' thrown by her, and that she objects to seeing the conversation as settled. The therapist's turn (lines 36–37), again qualifies the husband's turn as marking the previous conversation as something that is the core of what is happening between the two of them. It is followed by shared laughter which works to end the escalating conflict.

In Extract 4.7 the accounts are addressed not only to the therapists but also directly to the other spouse. There is a lot of mutual blame and conflict. It is as if the conflicts of the relationship were now actually on the stage. Responding to each other's blames and accounts enables the spouses to turn away from descriptions of individual 'characteristics and habits' and address mutual interactions and the constructive work they are doing together in their relationship.

Discussion and conclusions

In this chapter we have analysed one couple therapy conversation and focused especially on the negotiation of clienthood and the moral order (Harré 1983) of the relationship. In the analysis of the couple therapy conversation we observed the construction of clienthood by tracking down some of the practices the conversationalists used to qualify what the therapeutic conversation should be orientated towards. The practices of the clients consisted of introducing new topics, blaming each other and thus offering each other the client position, and finally a devotion to mutual dispute and blaming. These practices themselves were constructed by using several sophisticated discursive tools. The clients also used several discursive ways to resist or change client categorization: excusing, justification, counter-blame and rephrasing. The negotiation over who is the client was linked to issues about the possibilities to influence experiences, acts and events, and to the obligation to take responsibility for them. We also analysed the ways in which blame, excuses, justifications, and counter-blame (Austin 1961; Buttny 1990; Edwards 1995) were constructed and handled as constituents of the continuous and tensioned process of establishing the moral order of the conversation. 'Emotions' had a central function in the flow of the conversation (see Stearns 1995; Edwards 1999). Emotion talk seems to have been not only a negotiation about emotions as such but also a privileged position of laying out the rules of the relationship and thus being able to influence the moral outline of the joint form of life. Further, we pointed out some of the means used to promote and protect moral status within the conversation.

Feminist theorists have criticized systemic family therapy practices for neglecting individual agency and voice, and for reducing a person to one component in the system (Vatcher and Bogo 2001). Further, the critique has argued that traditional family therapy has a tendency to consider therapy successful when conflict within the relationship is diminished. Feminist theorists have been concerned that this silence might be a sign of women's well-learned cultural trend to 'keep quiet' and keep on taking care of their male partners (Gilligan 1982; Vatcher and Bogo 2001). When analysing a couple therapy conversation with a focus on clienthood, we come to conclude that managing clienthood forms a central avenue for understanding therapists' actions in the course of a therapy session. If the turn-by-turn analysis of the conversation had not been performed, there exists a possibility of interpreting the therapists' discursive actions as having a male bias (given also that both therapists were male). However, we argue that the contextual shifts made by the therapist(s) were aimed at producing talk in which the problem constructions of both partners could be heard and thus negotiated. In our extracts one might also get a misguided impression that only the wife's blaming was challenged and that only her cognitive processes were focused on; this was not the case. We argue that the therapists' activity to focus on cognitive processes functioned to prevent the positioning of one spouse as the client. It also functioned to maintain the alliance between the spouses since, when brought into the realm of the speaker's agency and responsibility, the blame construction eventually developed into a shared one.

If the therapists had disregarded the meta-level of negotiating clienthood and instead joined in the conversation with their own understandings of emotions, there would have existed a danger of obscuring and preventing the voice of the spouses. The discursive moves of the therapist not only countered the one-sided ascription of clienthood but also focused to specify and retell the problem. They also actively introduced an alternative construction of the relationship itself as 'the client'. It could, in fact, be claimed that when the 'relationship-as-client' ascription is finally achieved, most of the therapeutic work would actually be over. Thus, the negotiation over clienthood can be seen to be one of the central issues to be solved in the therapy. This calls for an orientation of therapist talk towards the meta-level, not the contents, of controversial issues and disputes. By adopting a new language game of mutual involvement the spouses can enter a new form of life where troubled talk may take the form of negotiations with less likelihood of drifting to a dead end.

PART II

Categorizing and Negotiating Clienthoods

5

Creating a 'Bad' Client

Disalignment of Institutional Identities in Social Work Interaction

Kirsi Juhila

It can be claimed that there are two basic categories available for participants in social work settings, that is, the categories of a social worker and a client. This means that the participants constitute themselves in certain asymmetrical roles. The position of the social worker contains, for instance, mapping the client's troubles and delivering remedies and advice, whereas the client's role is to seek professional help, to provide information about his or her personal concerns and to receive help and advice. Thus, there are some culturally shared features and activities associated with these categories which are related to institutional rules that the participants are expected to respect when they encounter each other in social work settings. This phenomenon of reciprocal orientation that Erving Goffman (1990b) calls 'working consensus' (p.21) does not mean, however, that people would automatically follow the rules and take the roles like marionettes. On the contrary, the participants apply the rules and use their situated knowledge by actively orientating themselves towards the assumed categories (Silverman 1998, p.35). The categories are flexible tools which the participants employ in such a manner that makes sense and is relevant in a specific institutional context (Mäkitalo 2002, pp.49–51).

In most of the cases there are few problems with communication; the interactants play the roles of a social worker and a client. But there are also deviant cases, where the maintaining of a 'working consensus' is not apparent. By a deviant case I mean an uncertainty about the main purpose of an encounter. This kind of uncertainty emerges when the participants' expectations about each other's institutional roles do not coincide, i.e. there is no alignment of institutional identities. This chapter explores one such encounter.[1] In this case study a client produces such an identity for himself which two social workers come to treat as an inappropriate and disruptive one. This is why this chapter is entitled 'Creating a "Bad" Client'. I argue that by analysing exceptional cases like this it is possible to make visible the 'taken-for-granted' rules designed for the clients in social work talk.

The location of my case example is the crisis centre Mobile, which operates in a medium-sized Finnish town. In a brochure directed to the general public, Mobile describes itself as a place 'open to all' and goes on to say that 'When you are in need of support, visit or call us' and that it is 'open 24 hours a day, seven days a week'. The brochure allows the visitor the power and right to define how he or she makes use of the crisis centre. The word 'client' is not used in the text. This official policy of the crisis centre which stresses the absence of strict criteria of clienthood – all people in need of support are welcome – works as an interesting context for my study. How is it possible to be a 'bad' client in an open place like this?

Ethnomethodological spirit as the point of departure

In this study I attempt to follow the so-called ethnomethodological spirit based on the work of Harold Garfinkel (1967) and Harvey Sacks (1992). Charles Antaki and Sue Widdicombe (1998, p.2) describe this spirit.

> The ethnomethodological spirit is to take it that the identity category, the characteristics it affords, and what consequences follow, are all knowable to the analyst only through the understandings displayed by the interactants themselves. Membership of a category is ascribed (and rejected), avowed (and disavowed), displayed (and ignored) in local places and at certain times, and it does these things as part of the interactional work that constitutes people's lives.

Identity categories are thus co-constructed by the participants through concrete activities in real time (He 1995). My interest is focused on finding out which memberships of which categories the interactants construct for themselves, which they ascribe to and avow, and how they respond to ascriptions and avowals by others. In my analysis I try to bear in mind that we are dealing with institutional dialogue, the character of which has been aptly summed up by Paul Drew and Marja-Liisa Sorjonen (1997, p.94; see also Drew and Heritage 1992):

> The institutionality of dialogue is constituted by participants through their orientation to relevant institutional roles and identities, and the particular responsibilities and duties associated with those roles; and through their management of institutionally relevant tasks and activities. The study of institutional dialogue thus focuses on the ways in which conduct is shaped or constrained by the participants' orientations to social institutions, either as their representatives or in various senses their 'clients'. Analysing institutional dialogue involves investigating how their orientations to and engagement in their institutional roles and identities is manifest in the details of participants' language, and their use of language to pursue institutional goals.

Based on these characteristics of institutional dialogue, I will study my data from the following angles. To what kind of institutional identity categories and tasks do the interactants orientate themselves? What responsibilities and duties do these identities and tasks ascribe to the other party? How do the interactants propose a different alignment of identities? The most important question is the last one, since what interests me here is to study such instances in social worker–client conversations where there appears to be *a conversational disagreement regarding the institutional identities and tasks.*

In a particular way co-constructed institutional selves, 'workers and clients', are inevitably needed when accomplishing institutional business (Gubrium and Holstein 2001). Don H. Zimmerman (1998) writes that the alignment of identities is a fundamental interactional issue and achievement. He has studied how the failure of alignment produces trouble in emergency calls, for instance if the call-taker speaks 'seriously' and the caller aligns him- or herself as a 'prank' caller (non-serious identity). This disalignment becomes visible when the client rejects the membership of a client category ascribed for him or her by the worker and/or when the client's contribution is defined as disruptive in the given context. The argumentation of category membership starts when the participants' expectations about each other's institutional identities do not fit together (see Widdicombe and Wooffitt 1995; Widdicombe 1998).

Adapting Zimmerman, I will examine trouble instances in the case example by focusing on the ways in which the client is created by the social workers as 'a not properly orientated client', i.e. a 'bad' client, on the basis of his contributions in the course of conversation. I will also look at how the client responds to these accusations and produces expectations towards the institutional duties of the social workers.

When the client does not behave like a 'good' client should

Of the interactants in the conversation fragment selected, I only know that they are two female social workers at Mobile and one male person. This scant knowledge is a benefit rather than drawback, as my purpose is to study the categories which the interactants themselves make relevant (see Edwards 1998). The man, henceforth Matti (M), describes himself at the beginning of the meeting as being 'at breaking point' and gives lively descriptions of how this is manifested. One of the workers categorizes the state of being 'at breaking point' as 'self-destructiveness' at an early stage in the conversation. The categorization continues later as follows.

Extract 5.1: Resisting passively an offered client identity
(SW2 = social worker 2, SW1 = social worker 1, M = Matti)

1   SW2: though I'm not the one diagnosing and it's not my task the doctor

2   makes the diagnosis but somehow, (.) I would, (.) sort of lean

3   towards the opinion that, (.) that you, (.) could have, (.) something,

4   (.) resembling depression, (3) you have, (.) behind, (.)and, (.) that

5   you know is quite easily treated.

6   (1.5)

7   SW1: and as regards mental illness so often the names of these places, (.)

8   very easily, (.) are linked with mental illness but I would actually say

9   that the majority of those who come to these places that they are, (.) for

10   a while for instance, (.) struggling with some other depression or

11   something else I mean on no account [should

12 M: [mm

13 SW1: they [be classified as mentally ill

14 SW2:   [( )

15 SW1: burnout depression the like so when you do get

16   help at the stage you need it, (.) you'll be able to return to the normal, (.)

17   routine [and and, (1.5) have strength, (.) cope, (.) in your life situation,

18 M: [mm. (2) mm.

19   (1)

In the first turn social worker 2 (SW2) designs her formulation in a way which displays an orientation to the category of a professional helper. By making a distinction to the category of a doctor and a doctor's duties (the doctor makes the diagnosis) she positions her own identity category and at the same time the tasks of the social institution she represents. These tasks do not include medical diagnosis. Instead, they do include the mapping of the problem and the discussion of measures needed to solve the problem, for these activities are invoked by the worker in her speech. The turn also constructs a certain kind of institutional identity for Matti. He is the one with a treatable problem. The social worker is thus treating Matti as a client, as the professional helper's counterpart. In addition to the client category and in association with it, the worker offers Matti a membership in the category of the depressed. Matti passes the turn offered to him, which suggests a passive resistance towards the client role offered to him.

The other worker (SW1) actually interprets the silence as potential resistance, for after the pause she further specifies the offer by beginning to speak of 'places' and 'those who come to these places'. The users of places are divided by her into the categories of the mentally ill and of those temporarily depressed or burned-out. Even though the worker does not specifically direct her talk to Matti by using 'you', but speaks on a general level, the function of this turn would still appear to be to persuade Matti to speak as a client who confesses his temporary need of help and accepts the indirect proposal for a treatment place. The invitation is thus designed in a way that seeks to save Matti's face: entering treatment does not mean that one becomes a member of the category of the mentally ill. The face-saving talk simultaneously contains an assumption of the stigmatizing nature of the category of the mentally ill. Matti gives a minimum response to the invitation and does not align in a marked manner with the client identity which was made relevant by the prior turns. Eventually Matti presents the following turn.

Extract 5.2: *Commenting on workers' suggestion and assuming an expert position*

(Continuing immediately after Extract 5.1)
(M = Matti, SW1 = social worker 1)

1   (1)

2 M: but to come back to, (.) Pakkavaara ((a psychiatric hospital)) I actually I,

3   (.) it can be totally excluded, (.) they have nothing to offer,

4   (1.5)

5 SW1: well, (.) we have by now, (.) mentioned quite a, (.) number, (.) of these, (.)

6   places well quite a number there aren't, (.) all that many but what we have

7   then you have knowledge of them and then you sort of torpedo everything,

8   (1.5)

9 M: [I'm no- I'm not torpedoing anything but.

10 SW1: [we'll be running out,

11 SW1: well you say you won't go to Pakkavaara you say that you're not going to

12   the mental health office or to the crisis reception, (1) well I at least have

13   nothing more left to offer you at this stage, (.) And yet in my opinion you

14   are sending the message that you want help and support in your current

15   situation that you wouldn't have to have this strong feeling of self

16   destructiveness and depression. (1) tiredness.

17   (.) unwillingness with everything,

18   (12.5)

Matti disagrees with the social workers' assessment of his client position, which is clear not only by the turn-preceding pause (see Pomerantz 1984, p.70), but also by the 'but' opening the turn. The disagreement can be interpreted in two ways. Either he rejects the membership of the category of the depressed, or he rejects the proposed help, the status of client 'in these places'. Of these, the latter interpretation is the more probable, for he refers to a psychiatric hospital by name and uses an extreme formulation (Pomerantz 1986) to define it as a place useless for him ('they have nothing to offer'). In criticizing the hospital he simultaneously assumes an expert's position, bypassing the workers: he knows better than the workers do that the treatment proposed will not be of any use to him. Despite the rejection Matti is orientated to the client identity after all, in the sense that he comments on the workers' turns as proposals of help offered to him.

How do the workers respond to Matti's disagreement about the proposed treatment place? Worker 1 takes a turn in which she does not ally herself with the criticism presented by Matti against the hospital; on the contrary, she challenges it by presenting an arguable turn in which the point of the criticism is directed against his behaviour. In fact, this is an assessment of how Matti positions himself in the client's category. The assessment is carried out in relation to the worker's identity and the institutional tasks related to it. The workers have acted according to their role: they have presented various options for help. In contrast, Matti does not fulfil the duties required by the client's role, or only fulfils them partially. On the one hand he does send the message of needing help, which the worker also assesses he needs, but on the other hand the options for help offered are not to his liking. As a result, the worker assesses that Matti assumes the client's role only half-way. Thus the worker appears to exhort him to adopt more actively the client identity and the duties and responsibilities related to it. At the same time the 'normal' helping conversation turns into an argumentative negotiation on the institutional roles of the participants.

A little later the roles of the assessor and the assessed are exchanged as Matti begins to describe his previous visit to the crisis centre which he reports as having led to his being banned from visiting it again. The worker attempts to fish for the reason for the banning with an indirect question.

Extract 5.3: Orientating to a critical consumer identity
(SW1 = social worker 1, M = Matti)

1   SW1: when they issued that ban well, (.) there must have been something

2   in the conversation, (.) something which then, (.) which sort of gave

3   grounds for the ban,

4   (1)

5   M: well what I said was this, (.) that I couldn't begin to accept this

6   activity I mean that you employ people for six months, (.) on an

7   employment subsidy or is it an obligation that, (.) then when they

8   begin to ma- make sense of their work then the employers are changed

9   so I, (.) I think that, (1.5) the same people should be there, (2)

10   permanently and not always a new set of people.

11 SW1: well as to that, (.) I want to, (.) say that we're here for ten months

12   at a time, (.) and we:, (.) are not, (.) on a subsidy, (.) w we are paid

13   by the city and the municipalities,

14 M: °mm°

15 SW1: and we all have social work or health care training and since this

16   is not a treatment unit in other words we give temporary help to people

17   then it has no significance whether people change because we are all

18   professionals and trained people anyway, (3.5) now if one was to think

19   that, (.) that you came often here while we are here well, (.) quite likely,

20   (.) practically every time, (.) there'd be different people,

21 M: °mm°

22 SW1: in spite of that this team is a solid one here [at this moment,

23 M: [°mm° °mm°

24   (3)

The fishing is successful and Matti describes the ban by remembering (see Middleton and Edwards 1990) his previous visit to the crisis centre. In the version constructed by him he describes, using his own quoted speech (Wooffitt 1992, pp.155–87; Potter 1996b, pp.160–61) as a device, how he then took up a criticizing position towards the operation of the crisis centre. Although he does not explicitly say that the criticism was the cause of the ban, this interpretation can be read into his speech. If the workers earlier criticized Matti's defective client identity, now he turns the criticism to the institution of helping. In so doing he takes a specific kind of client identity which could be characterized as the consumer identity. The rights and obligations of the consumer include the evaluation of and feedback on the service used. The consumer is an expert with the personal knowledge and experience necessary for the evaluation. Evaluation and feedback also challenge the representatives of the service to respond to the criticism. One of the workers (SW1) accepts this challenge, positioning herself in the identity of the institution's representative by beginning to correct the errors in Matti's feedback. The worker's 'we' talk further emphasizes the alliance towards the institution and the non-alliance towards the client. As regards the meaning content, an opposite manner of responding to this identity would have been to admit the justification of the criticism. The roles assumed by the participants (criticizer of the service/defender of the service) are compatible even though the conversational content contains a disagreement. In her turn the worker labels the consumer's criticism as unfounded. Matti does not present further arguments from the consumer identity (though he does not express an acceptance of the worker's defending arguments). Conversation on this topic comes to an end, as the other worker (SW2) uses a turn related to the conversational agenda of this specific encounter.

Extract 5.4: Referring to duties related to a helper category

(Continuing immediately after Extract 5.3)

(SW2 = social worker 2, SW1 = social worker 1, M = Matti)

1   SW2: Mm. (.) but, (.) I don't suppose the purpose was, (.) really to begin

2   a very heated talk about the operation of the crisis centre but, (.) to

3   try to find for you a, (2) a solution for this and I, (.) this this has

4   in a way, (.) gotten stuck [I mean there's been no progress

5   SW1:   [°mm°, in this conversation, (.) for the last,

6   (3) minutes in a direction, (.) towards finding something

7   [essential,

8   M: [well go ahead and make progress then.

9   (2.5)

10   SW1: I somehow feel that you've gotten a bit tired with this, (.) or or otherwise

11   in so- some way show a kind of, (2) by sighing this may be the

12   wr- wrong word perhaps but a kind of boredness with the situation is

13   what comes to my mind,

14   M: It's not this situation I'm bored with but every-, (.) just bored with

15   everything in general,

16   (4)

17 SW1: well now if one hasn't got, (.) a motivation,

18 M: Oh there's motivation enough,

19 SW1: a motivation then resources or will whatever words one wan- now wants

20   to use, (1) if one hasn't got them, (.) there are no grounds for the

21   conversation, (.) to go or the situation, (.) to progress so well, (1) do you

22   feel the need that, (.) that we go on from here and try to find a solution

23   for this situation or or is it more to the point to stop now,

24 M: No I think we should go on,

The worker (SW2) ends the topic of evaluating the operating principles of the institution by defining it as irrelevant for this encounter. The definition spells out the institutional purpose of the encounter: the purpose is not to discuss the operation of the crisis centre but to try to solve Matti's problem. Thus Matti is again 'reminded' of the institutional task and the kind of client identity which he is expected to take up. Together and in mutual alliance the workers name Matti's disorientation as accounting for the lack of progress in the task-appropriate action and the stagnation of the conversation. At the same time they again produce for themselves the identity of a professional helper: their task is to look for a solution to the client's problems. Matti passes the buck back to the worker by referring to the duties related to the helper category, which include continuing the conversation. In this turn Matti constructs himself as a client by transferring the responsibility for managing the situation to the professional, but at the same time he omits to respond to the comment related to his client identity. The requirement for furthering the conversation gives the turn and the challenge to worker 1, who also takes it up after a pause. Her turn continues the assessment of the identity category assumed by Matti. Matti is deficient as a client, he is bored and unmotivated. In the end Matti is given a choice. Either he positions himself in the client category expected and ascribed by the worker, or the conversation is terminated. Matti underlines his motivation and desire to go on, and thus appears to conform at least partially to the duties of client expected by the worker.

A 'bad' client makes an institution and its rules visible

In this text I have explored the process of creating a 'bad' client by concentrating on such instances of the case where there is uncertainty and disagreement about the roles and tasks of the participants. The selected case is an exceptional one in the sense that the actual business in the encounter is negotiation and argumentation about the relevant institutional roles and duties of the participants. Therefore, the business of helping never really begins. Erving Goffman (1990b) writes that the interplay between teams, in this case between the social workers and the client, 'can be analysed in terms of the cooperative effort of all participants to maintain a working consensus' (p.97). The members of the teams have, however, a power to disrupt the consensus. In the case studied Matti uses this power. He does not produce his institutional self in a way that would enable social workers to do their work (see Miller 1991; Spencer 2001).

The social workers attempt to spell out to the client the purpose of the encounter, they guide him to a relevant position and persuade him to accept their service (see Spencer and McKinney 1997). At the same time they happen to produce criteria for both 'good' and 'bad' clienthood. The construed characteristics of a 'good' client can be listed as follows: he takes on a client identity, i.e. accepts that he has a need for the help offered by the social workers; he has a good motivation to become helped by the professionals; he treats the social workers' suggestions as competent ones and does not question them with his own knowledge; he does not criticize the policy of the helping organization or the ways in which the social workers conduct their work. A reverse list would describe the features of a 'bad' client.

The creation of a 'bad' client makes the studied institution and its rules visible. In this particular setting it is slightly paradoxical to end up having these kinds of results since the crisis centre Mobile defines itself as a place which is 'open to all' and which thus has no officially declared criteria for client status. But even though the crisis centre is a place with a low threshold, there are some rules and criteria for clienthood to be found. It is not sufficient just to walk in and start a conversation with the professionals. Visitors are expected to have some reason for their popping in, some problems for which they are motivated to get help and advice from the social workers with special expertise. In that sense the roles of the interactants should be asymmetrical: one party is supposed to seek and accept help whereas the other party in entitled to give it.

In his study of doctor–patient interaction, Christian Heath (1992) writes that preserving asymmetry in such a way that the expertise of the doctor transcends the lay opinion is the prerequisite of a fluent institutional encounter (pp.260–264; see also Peräkylä 1995, pp.96–97). Without this asymmetry there is a threat that the reason for turning to the doctor will disappear. The asymmetry becomes unstable if the patient challenges the doctor's diagnosis and medical assessment. The instability of asymmetry and the disalignment of identities could in my opinion be seen as analogous: when the patient or the client (in social work) challenges the practitioner's expertise and produces himself as an expert in a matter under consideration, he is also disorientated to the identity of the helped.

At its extreme end, the instability of asymmetry or the disalignment of identities could be manifested as a complete lack of meaningful interaction. This can be seen in the above example where the reason for the encounter seems to have been lost. The participants negotiate over the exact task to be accomplished and the identity categories required by it. The social workers construct the matter in such a manner that the reason and the identity are lost for the client in particular: he does not understand what the allowable contribution in this setting is. Thus, the actual topic of conversation is disalignment, and the turns are characterized by an open conversational disagreement regarding the institutional identity and responsibilities of the client.

The conversational disagreement between the social workers and the client in the above example manifest in an interesting manner the unwritten moral rules of institutional dialogue. These unwritten rules give rise to two questions. The first question is whether there is anything negotiable in the manners of being a client, or does the positioning as a client always 'demand' an orientation to the discussion of the problem and to accepting help. In the above example such negotiable area would not seem to exist, for the worker poses a certain kind of client identity as a condition for the conversation. The other question is whether there exists an angle from which disagreeing and argumentative talk about the criteria for 'good' and 'bad' clienthood and about who owns the expertise can be regarded as a successful professional encounter. Shouldn't the answer to this second question be 'yes' if we intend to make real the widely shared and accepted principle of client-centredness in social work discourse? From this viewpoint we could celebrate the non-hierarchical, argumentative and disagreeing conversations between the social workers and the clients as chances that might open up new ways to understand clienthood and expertise in social work.

Note

1   The encounter is part of a data corpus that consists of naturally occurring conversations between social workers and clients in different social work organizations. The present chapter is part of two extensive research projects funded by the Academy of Finland: 'Institutions of Helping as Everyday Practices' and 'At the Edge of the Helping Systems'. All in all these projects have offered the necessary material and scientific resources that made it possible for me to become one of the co-editors of this book.

6

Parental Identity Under Construction

Discourse and Conversation Analysis of a Family Supervision Order

Carolus van Nijnatten and Gerard Hofstede

Introduction

Dutch family law knows two types of interventions in parental authority. Abrogation of parental rights is a radical shift in custody and generally a permanent measure. This chapter is about the second type of intervention: the family supervision order (FSO). An FSO does not deprive parents of their parental rights completely, it only restricts parental power. If the family court pronounces an FSO, the judge charges a family supervision agency with this (public) authority. The agency appoints one of its workers as a family supervisor (FS) whose task is to restore the bonds between parent(s) and child in order to return full authority to the parent(s). The FS and the parent(s) together take the essential decisions concerning the upbringing of the child. If both parties disagree, an FS may give the parent a written direction that has to be acted upon by the parent(s) or, they may be taken into family court as a last resort

The professional activities of an FS have a particularly discursive nature. In a sequence of visits to the family's home or at the agency, an FS at first makes the parents acquaintance and explains to them the (formal) aspects of the FSO and, at a later stage, tries to get agreement on the (analysis of) the problems and on (near) future activities aimed at improving the current family situation. This problem analysis and the goals for the future constitute the main ingredients for the care plan. FSs have a statutory requirement to present a written care plan within six weeks after the pronouncement of the family court. The first conversations between the FS and the parents will be directed for a great part on the construction of this care plan. The FS will gain information about the relevant elements for the care plan, present the parents with provisional formulations and negotiate the exact phrasing. These conversations are the object of our study.

The professional activities take place in a pre-defined institutional context in which the parents are pictured as unable to exercise their authority without the help of public authority. The FS will take up the court's description of parent and child, and plan a future course in which the client may retake parental responsibilities without the help of a guardian. Therefore, the FS discusses and negotiates with the parents to achieve a minimal agreement on the problem analysis and goals for change (see van Hout and Spinder 2001). Parents attach great value to being acknowledged as an interested party (de Savornin Lohman and Steketee 1996). FSs see a good personal relationship with the parents as a condition for successful intervention (van Nijnatten and van den Ackerveken 1998).

Most child welfare research is about attitudes of social workers (Gadsby Waters 1992; van Nijnatten 1995) and reflections on their strategies (Andersson 1992). Studies based on interaction analysis are of recent date (Hall and Slembrouck 2001; Hofstede *et al.* 2001; Hoogsteder *et al.* 1998; van Nijnatten *et al.* 2001). This type of research is relevant to the practice of child welfare because it may gain insight in the communication processes between professional workers and clients. Besides, it informs us about the operation of implicit concepts of parenthood in the 'management' of clients. Identity work is essential for parents, especially where their parenthood is under dispute. The institutional discourse of child welfare agencies inscribes parental identities (Sarangi and Slembrouck 1996). This has far-reaching consequences for the future of the family, because parents and children train themselves from the outside in (Goffman 1959) and identify with the descriptions of them in discursive constructions (Barker and Galasinski 2001).

Identity construction

Preceding the first conversation between the FS and the parents, the Child Protection Board and family court have already constructed the parents as temporarily unable to raise their children in a proper way. This situation has to be reversed, with the help of family supervision, so that the parents can function again as capable carers. In accordance with preliminary construction work, we expect the FS to construct a route towards parental identity, from temporary incapability towards recovery. On the other hand, we think that parents will emphasize their capability and trustworthiness. Parental identities are developed in the context of these two positions and negotiated in the dialogues.

Identities are constructed in everyday life encounters in which people present themselves to others and identify others by making sense of their presentations (see Goffman 1959). Identifications may appear on a pragmatic level, when people in interactions put meaning to the behaviour of others and themselves. They never lead to one 'true' identity that refers to a cognitive entity. Identity is not an essential core. People mobilize different identities according to how they are addressed or represented. We do not 'have multiple identities (which would imply a subject who possesses) we *are* a verbal weave constituted as multiple and contradictory identities which crosscut or dislocate each other' (Barker and Galasinski 2001, p.121). Identities are not self-evident but develop in social contexts. It is therefore essential to complete interaction analysis with the 'rhetorical functions of the cultural knowledge that is invoked by speakers in conversation' (Abell and Stokoe 2001).

This study is about the social construction of identity in encounters of FSs and parents. We look at how parents are signified. According to Antaki and Widdicombe (1998), people can be categorized by classifying them on the basis of some features and then attributing other characteristics of the category. Utterances are never coincidental, but are part of the identity formation.

Communication between an FS and clients takes place in an institutional context. In the interaction with parents, we expect an FS to try to construct parental identities that fit in the institutional frame. This is a process of (re)formulating (self-) descriptions of the clients in terms of parents of a child under family supervision. In our analysis of identity construction in family supervision we chose to use our knowledge of the institutional context; yet, the interpretation of other identity elements of the participants will have to be extracted from the actual interaction.

The institutional task of the FS is to produce 'proof' for parenthood at risk and to come to terms with the parents about it. The construction of identity is the description of current features of parenthood and a sketch of how it may be changed. We consider the moment the parents agree with the formulations in the care plan to be as the first formal establishment of the identity. Parental identity may appear at the level of content (participants present identities of themselves and others) and may sometimes refer to external categories. Besides, it appears at the level of discourse structure: participants give and take position, take turns, control topics, and so on. The FS will try to achieve a definition of the identity of the parent that fits with both the outcomes of the Child Protection Board's report and the institutional goals of the FSO, and which is acceptable for the parent. On the other hand, we expect the parent to try to present 'proof' that neutralizes the problematic nature of his or her identity. These discursive goals may, for instance, lead to a different positioning of the FS in the course of the conversations. By this, the FS confirms the image of temporary incapability. This will come out in the formulations about how parents raise their children, continuity of care, acceptance of professional intervention, reflective abilities, and so on.

Method

Participants

One case was selected from a larger study of 21 cases of videotaped interactions between FSs and parents. In the selected case the participants are: male FS; 20-year-old mother (M) who is pregnant from her new partner (Fr) and mother's two-and-a-half-year-old son (C). A reason to select this case was that we could videotape the first (T1) and subsequent conversations (T2, T3) up to and including the conversation in which the presentation of the care plan was the central issue (T4). This was also the only case in which the mother was the only parent with custody. Hence we could limit our analysis to what was said about, to and by the mother. The analysis was done on the four conversations and the care plan.

Data

Identity is constructed directly in interaction and indirectly by using external categories in conversation and by writing down in the care plan the progress in the conversations. In the interactions of this study we looked for verbalizations as a step in the construction of identities. We expect that identity work, especially if it concerns an identity with problematic features, will hardly be expressed straightforwardly. In our study, we looked for both (negotiations on) concrete evaluations of parenthood and face strategies that mitigate face-threatening utterances. We compared the identity work in the conversations with the wording in the care plan.

Data consist of video-recordings (T1 was recorded at the agency of the Child Protection Board, T2, T3 and T4 were recorded at the parent's home) and the written care plan. Videorecordings were transcribed according to strict transcription rules and conventions (see Transciption Symbols). All verbal utterances and a selection of non-verbal acts were transcribed. The excerpts in this chapter were drawn from the transcripts and translated into English. All names and places are fictitious. Our analysis is based on the principles of discourse analysis (Fairclough 1992).

First, we analysed the four transcripts of this case independently of each other, and then we reviewed each other's initial analyses. On the basis of these reviews and reconsiderations, we ended up with our definite analyses of the transcripts. We analysed the data on content and discourse structure. Analysis of developments in the description of central clusters of concern related to the (legal) grounds of the FSO. We compared the descriptions in the sequences of conversations and compared the total of these descriptions with the formulations in the care plan. After the initial analyses and the reviews we ended up with a great amount of characteristics of identity which were uttered and communicated in the subsequent conversations. Because in this case there were hardly any descriptions of the physical or psychological condition of the child (we will come back to this in the Discussion section), we limited clusters of identity that are related to qualities of parenthood to three: social skills, pedagogical skills and economic management.

We paid specific attention to conversational strategies of the FS and mother to (de)construct parental identities. We will describe the policies of participants to achieve a mutually agreed description of parental identity.

Results

Social skills

In the cluster of social skills, three characteristics of the mother are discussed: passivity, aggression and unpredictability.

PASSIVITY

At first, the mother presents herself as a passive parent: 'Nobody told me that I had to join that meeting'; 'They would learn me how to bring up my child'. The FS takes over this identity construct. The mother is portrayed as a passive woman who does not bother when other people take over her tasks so she will have more time and energy to spend for herself.

Extract 6.1

(FS = family supervisor, Fr = friend, M = mother, C = child)

1   FS: (to Fr) the question for M is because you sounded very

2   much surprised about the <u>question</u> when I called you or

3   M it is <u>very</u> clear there is nothing wrong about that (.)

4   <u>help</u> me (.) <u>in such a way</u> that C is not always here

5   because I that time <u>also</u> for myself also ( ) apart from the little baby in the belly

The FS says that friend may be surprised about the mother's passive attitude, but that it is no problem for the mother. The mother's passiveness is determined more convincingly by quoting her. Discussing the mother's nature with her friend makes it harder for her to object. The FS relates the mother's passiveness to the coercive character of the supervision order. From the mother's refusal of coercion, we learn that the FS's strategy to reach an agreement in this way is not fruitful or even effective. In the next encounters, the FS tries to develop another identity of the mother as a young woman with friends, having a partner and being a daughter of her parents. These qualifications are less threatening for the mother. The starting-point is no longer a passive mother but an active woman who has to find her way through life, needs time for herself and has a son to care for. From this identity construct the FS offers help to fight the problems, which he never stops to point at.

AGGRESSIVENESS

Much attention has been paid to the aggressive conduct of the mother, especially in relation to the staff of the day care centre where she regularly brought her son. In the first conversations, the FS repeatedly gives examples of the mother's lack of tactful behaviour and the rows she caused at the day care centre. The mother's identity as portrayed in the report of the Child Protection Board is confirmed straightforwardly.

Extract 6.2

(FS = family supervisor, Fr = friend)

1   FS: (no) ok did you ever have had a situation in your life

2   that you <u>so</u> terribly

3   = went =

4   Fr: = sj [to C] =

5   FS: out of your head so for instance got a row with him and

6   kicked him out of li/eh life out of the house (.) and after

7   that you <u>blow your top</u> that you think of 'the only' ( )

8   way to go out dancing stop nagging to my brains [pause]

9   and that on a certain moment you can not take care of

10   your child who will you let take care of your child?

Although the FS only asks the mother if she might imagine such a situation, it is quite clear that the mother may understand the FS has the idea that this may happen. The FS asks a closed question, and the mother is expected to agree or reject the FS's presupposition. The identity construction by the FS is not straightforward and this is consistent with our expectations. The mother's history is described as full of aggressive incidents with her parents. As a teenager, she was hardly manageable and put under family supervision. These examples are presented as 'proof' of the mother's aggressive nature. The mother attributes to her identity as an aggressive woman by saying that she used to have difficulties with female supervisors. In the third conversation, the FS relates the mother's aggressiveness to her psychotic nature.

Extract 6.3

(FS = family supervisor, M = mother, C = child)

1   FS: yes, but listen this is, this is very hard but it is not just C

2   (.) you are yourself also of course ( ) the last time we also

3   talked = about =

4   M: = yes but = now they can

5   say to me

6   FS: yet but that that story indeed is [pause] but the <u>only</u> I

7   want to <u>say</u> with this if I study the total file (.) you are

8   psychotic now and then

9   M: yes but that was before I got a child

10 FS: yes

11 M: changed a = lot =

12 FS: = yes =

Psychosis less than aggression may be considered as conduct to blame. Hence the shift from aggression to psychosis may be done in the expectation that the mother will be more willing to accept this label. The FS takes distance and objectifies his utterance ('If I consider the total file') and mitigates the seriousness of the mother's psychotic behaviour ('now and then'). The mother tries to redefine it by restricting it to the past. Yet, the FS says it is her nature because sometimes she still acts very aggressively. The mother agrees and this affords the FS the possibility to relate that personal feature to the family problems, which is that the child was not allowed in the day care centre any more. From this identity construction and common problem definition, the FS works up to a solution: help from a solid male helper. In the end, the FS and the mother are in mutual agreement on the way to solve the problems in the future.

UNPREDICTABILITY

Unpredictability is the third cluster. By giving examples, the FS depicts the mother as someone who does not stick to her words. The mother tries to change this picture of her by saying that after the birth of her child, all this has been changed. She feels pinned to her past and wants to pay attention to the future. She tells how she tried to participate at the day care centre but got no reaction. The FS continues his line of thought on another level. He reveals that social workers should have a very straight policy towards the mother, giving orders that leave no room for misunderstandings. As, in the third conversation, the mother cannot find some papers. The FS seizes this as an opportunity to say that in order to progress from her chaos she has to learn how to organize. The mother tries to show that she is capable of organizing her life by arranging things for her pregnancy and paying her debts.

The FS does not pay attention and neglects these efforts of the mother. The FS appears to be quite paradoxical in what attitude he expects from her.

Extract 6.4

(FS = family supervisor)

1 FS: if you would be a very nasty <u>bag</u> you have well go ahead

2   by all means for <u>me</u> you do not have to show off

3   because in the end it will not work it will really not

4   work (.) you are just who you are as you always have

5   been (then) you are changeable so you have periods that

6   you are very sweet and very kind and then periods that

7   you (.) eh sorry for the word but eh you are <u>really</u> a fiery bitch yes?

         (*pause*)

8 FS: is nothing wrong but say than I <u>know</u> and <u>understand</u> it

         (*pause*)

9 FS: what drives me round the bend is that one day I am

10   called by someone who is suave and the other day by

11   someone who bloody scolds me

The FS invites the mother to remain herself and not to show off. Then he says he detests people who behave in an unpredictable way. At the same time, the mother is asked to not pretend to and not be what she always is, capricious.

The FS presents the mother's unpredictability as a problem in the child's upbringing. The mother disagrees, but later agrees with the FS's offer (and solution of the problem) to accept help from someone who may bring stability in her life and that of her son. Like the Passivity and Aggressiveness clusters we find a mutual solution for the problem is achieved without a clear agreement on the definition of the problem.

Pedagogical skills

We found the same pattern of establishing absence of pedagogical skills in the first conversations and of ensuring control and future change in the last conversations. The FS starts referring to the mother's remarks in a conversation with the grandmother and a police officer that she can not take care of her child. The FS shows his doubts about the mother's skills in a rhetorical question: 'Can you expose a child that hardly can speak to a day care centre?' With this face-threatening question, the FS creates a distance between the mother and himself (negative politeness). In his view the mother is not fully capable of looking carefully at the needs of her child. The mother tries to restore an image of capability by saying that she does not want to hand over her child and by telling about her child's needs. Besides, the mother denies the problems as described in the report of the Child Protection Board. She quotes the grandmother who would have said that her situation has improved a lot. The FS insists that there are some serious problems according to the professionals quoted in the Board's report. The mother replies that these professionals were only present once a month. The FS explains that the FSO is meant to keep the child with his mother. This means that the mother has to convince the FS that she is a responsible carer. By that, she can also prevent her next child being placed under supervision.

In the fourth conversation, the FS says that the mother and child are attached well. The FS exposes the importance of this by explicitly saying that this item will return in the care plan. The FS says that the expectations are high and that mother therefore badly needs help.

Extract 6.5

(FS = family supervisor)

1 FS: I have the very strong feeling really I mean this in

2   honest that someone should be around who helps you

3   on a regular basis near with you is an adult

The FS stresses that if the mother does not accept help in raising her son this will be explained as her unwillingness to raise her child. The mother says that she wants a job and time for herself. The FS says that he appreciates the mother's openness and honesty, meaning that it is quite unconventional for a mother to confess that she needs more time for herself, and authorizes the mother's downgrade. In the third conversation, the FS returns to what the mother told in a previous conversation.

Extract 6.6

(FS = family supervisor)

1   FS: Last time, you <u>yourself</u> said that I can not give him

2   attention the whole day I have to look after myself I

3   need rest and time for myself

The FS confirms again mother's self-categorization.

The FS does not doubt the mother's qualities as a mother directly, but indirectly, by pointing at a report of the CPB, grandmother and a police officer. The mother tries to take the edge of these arguments by saying that these problems date from before she moved to her current lodging and by pointing at the good care for her son (bathing, clean clothes). No unequivocal identity of the mother as a pedagogical responsible parent has been established. Yet, in the final conversation, the FS shows that he is aware that the mother needs entertainment and personal growth. The mother will have to find out if her parents want to help her with the upbringing of her children or to limit her personal freedom.

Economic management

Much of the time in the conversations is spent on the mother's budget problems. Time and again, the mother and FS turn to this subject. In the mother's opinion, she is living on a shoestring. The FS relates the financial problems to the big spending of the mother, who buys expensive food and clothes for her child and cannot find a way to economize.

Extract 6.7

(FS = family supervisor)

1   FS: [...] (.) the child ought to know <u>where he lives</u> what his

2   <u>real</u> situation is Teletubbies are very nice but next year (.)

3   it will be the billydaddies

The use of the word 'billydaddies' sounds like 'Teletubbies' but refers to daddies checking their bills, and refers to the undesired identity of the mother as a big spender. He even mentions the strategies of other mothers who go on with making babies to get more money out of social security.

Extract 6.8

(FS = family supervisor)

1 FS: there are even people and this will not go for [name of

2 M] but there are people who if they know that if they

3 are pregnant that it finances is taken account of that so

4 they go on with making babies (.) not because they want

5 to have children but they do this because (.) because for

6 heaven's sake to have not more than 125,- guilders a

7 week that they know (.) so you they can not <u>different</u>.

Although the FS says that his remarks are not directed at the mother, the question is why he says this. The slip at the end of the quote (you they) is significant. In spite of the disclaimer at the beginning, we think it is evident that the FS actually meant the mother when he spoke about other mothers. The FS is not direct in his disapproval of the mother's economic management, but points at what other people might think when they see the mother having huge financial problems while buying her child expensive sodas. The FS thinks that the mother's financial problems, although they may not be her fault, cause her a lot of trouble, and that it is her parental obligation to solve them.

In the final conversation, the FS looks at the future. In order to pay her debts and create a sound budgeting, the mother should cut her coat according to her cloth. The mother might buy second-hand clothes at the agency of the Salvation Army. He says he used to buy things there and was ashamed too. But it is the only way out of the debts. The mother and her friend dismiss the relevance of this category (see Day 1998) when they laugh about the proposal. The FS says that he can imagine that the mother, as a young woman, wants to be dressed beautifully/nicely, but that she has to be aware of the result of her way of life. The mother, in reaction, compares herself with other women of her age who buy things for themselves. The FS tells the mother that she needs supervision, and tells of his work with families who made debts, that became higher because professional help was not intensive enough. But he knows a family that after two years of intensive help could still have their child at home. It is implied that the mother needs such an intensive supervision of her financial conduct. By this, we found that the mother is constructed as someone who cannot handle money and should accept intensive supervision of her financial conduct. The FS hopes that in the future the mother might arrange her financial business herself.

As in the other clusters, the FS, in the end, gives openings in his last formulations. In the first encounters, he underlines the problematic aspects of the mother's 'economic identity'. When they meet for the fourth time, the FS shows his understanding that the mother, as a young woman, also needs money to spend on herself and that she needs help to budget. Again, we find the FS using this strategy of lessening the threat for the mother, showing understanding and looking for possible solutions in the near future.

The care plan

The conditions for negotiating the content of the care plan are poor. In the third conversation, the FS does not mention the main issues he wants to take down in the plan. The mother did not receive a concept plan and was hardly prepared for the discussion. The FS even forgot to take the care plan in the fourth conversation and could only tell the mother the concept of the plan. Besides, the care plan is not a simple enumeration of the most important problem areas and strategies for improvement, but consists of 13 pages with answers on standard questions. It is divided into particulars, description of the problem and the care plan, which is a detailed enumeration of goals and plans for the short and long term.

The problem description of the care plan in this study is composed of the following parts:

- *Composition of family of origin.* C is the first child of M and her former friend. M is the middle of three children. She has a stepsister and a brother who suffers from schizophrenia. M is pregnant by her new partner.

- *Social and economic factors.* M says to stand for her son, but also that she misses her private time she used to have when her son was placed in day care. M created huge debts. M had to move because of supposed trouble, and was offered alternative housing at the very last moment. M's partner considers taking social and economic responsibility for M and C, but still separates his life from the M's.

- *(Threatened) development of juvenile.* In spite of his age (two-and-a-half) he hardly speaks. M is in great need of regularity and personal freedom. In view of her age and personal development, this is understandable, but it raises questions concerning the upbringing of her son.

- *Strong points that offer chances to support and possibly improve the pedagogical situation.* M is aware of the (cause of) the problems. M and her partner are willing to co-operate with the policy of professional helpers. M has a house of her own and a small benefit. M's partner promises loyalty and support. The son is fond of his mother and her partner.

- *Client's wishes for support.* M wants help in bringing up her son, structuring her day, arranging better housing and dealing with professional agencies.

- *FS's view of the heart of the problem.* M has been troubled by her own aggression for a long time and does not deal tactfully with the care agents. M has to learn to deal with volunteering care agents who want to help her to bring the relationship with her son on smooth waters and to receive the baby in a quiet situation. Since M and C spend days together, C knows how to manipulate M's weak sides and not let her correct him all the time. Sometimes she enters into a coalition with C and so undermines her parental authority. M is not able to raise her child 7 days a week and 24 hours a day. M often obstructs help, and cannot cope with the pressure of having not enough money for entertainment and nice clothes for C. When her children are a little older, M might look for a part-time job. It will decrease the economic pressure and create room for personal entertainment.

In the care plan description we found a continuation of this more mitigating strategy, the FS has taken in the last encounters with the mother. The FS creates the possibility for the mother to agree with the description of the problems and the future plans by describing a wide range of identity elements. The problematic elements of the mother's identity are presented in a palette that also contains promising elements. By describing negative and positive elements at the same time, the FS acknowledges that there is good hope for amelioration in the family circumstances. Besides, it is a less threatening strategy that enables the mother to accept her identity construct and promise her co-operation. The FS writes down that the mother, as a young woman, also needs money to spend on herself and that she needs help to budget. He takes away the threat for the mother, because it is generally recognized that it is quite hard for single mothers to live just for their child at the cost of their personal development. In the line of this identity construct, the FS makes his offer of support. The goal of this is twofold: to help the mother raise her child, giving her some extra time to spend for herself, and to force a breakthrough in the relations between the mother and her son in which the son claims more and more freedom and room.

Discussion

In this article we analysed one case. Generalization in the classic sense will be impossible. Yet, is not any child protection case exceptional? As Hall and Slembrouck (2001) say, any situation is too complex to be covered by a standard formulation or protocol. Yet we can still learn from the analysis of this case. The communication between the mother and the FS is almost exclusively directed at the mother's (in)capabilities. Except for the supposed language deficiency of the boy, there are no remarks about the condition of the child. The mother does say that she takes care of her son's hygiene and clothing very well, but this is meant as an evaluation of her maternal capacities and not as an indication of her son's state. The lack of attention paid to the actual condition of the child is striking. We consider this as a main cause of the vagueness of family supervision work and the absence of concrete goals in care plans (Slot *et al.* 2001). By concentrating more on the condition of the child, we think the FS might have had better chances to reach an agreement with the mother about necessary changes in the way she takes the upbringing of her son in hand.

The construction process of parental identity shows a regular pattern. In the first conversations, the FS establishes the problematic parental identity by giving examples that 'prove' pathology, shortcomings or absence of necessary skills. Much attention is paid to the chronic character of the pathology by emphasizing that problems have already existed for a long time. The FS relates the problematic parental identity only indirectly to the upbringing of the son. The mother tries to resist negative identification by giving counter-examples and by another use of history, underlining the temporary nature of the problems. She clearly indicates that she disagrees with the FS about the gravity of the problems but gives some negotiation space with regard to support in raising her child.

In the last encounters the FS pays more attention to the ways the problematic parental identity may be changed in the future. Besides repeated attention on the problems, the FS mentions some unproblematic sides of the mother's identity. This puts the problematic identity of the parent in a more positive perspective and opens ways to future amelioration. For instance, the FS tries to come to an agreement with the mother about the time she needs for her own life, and arranges family care to set off the poor parental care. At the same time he indicates his hopes that in the future the mother will get a job and that her family becomes financially independent.

In all clusters, the mother's identity is first constructed as troublesome and then set aside. Then, the FS constructs different identities of the mother – young woman, mother, daughter and partner – which may benefit from help to structure her (family) life. As the FS repeats the troublesome aspects of the mother's identity this way, he puts them in the perspective of more positive sides and the possibilities of future change. The result is that the problem is also shifted from the mother's conduct as the one responsible for bringing up her son to her personal affairs (not having enough time for herself). The FS achieves that the mother accepts help, but this help is directed at giving the mother more leeway in her personal development, which is not under discussion, rather than directed at solving the problematic aspects of her identity or improving the situation in which the child is raised.

In the care plan, the problematic aspects of the mother's identity that had been set aside are dug up. The FS did not reach agreement on these problematic aspects. This means that the conflict about these aspects is postponed and that the professional helper who has been called in has to confront the mother again with the need to change the problematic aspects of her identity. It may also result in a confusion about which problems have to be changed. It is very possible that mother, for instance, gets the impression that her passivity is not such a big problem after all and that she is helped to take care of herself. This probably does not lead to a reinstatement of the child's upbringing by his mother and replacement of her parental authority.

The identity constructions in this case are a perfect fit to the legal goals of the family supervision order, which indicates an actual threat to the development of the child and perspectives for change. Yet, the different constructions regarding the mother's authority and upbringing qualities are not cleared up. This may very well lead to future confrontations and delay in changing the conditions of the child

7

The Absent Client

Case Description and Decision Making in Interprofessional Meetings

Pirjo Nikander

Decision-oriented talk in interprofessional teams, consultations and meetings forms one focal interactional site where the practical work in human service organizations gets done. During the course of this chapter I will examine the dynamics of meeting talk by looking at professional client description and decision making within the Finnish social and health sector. The present chapter, in other words, focuses on professional–professional encounters from which the client, him or herself, is absent. The actual physical absence of the client in these encounters is filled in by textual documents and case files, by verbal descriptions, by first-hand or second-hand narratives and by joint, and sometimes conflicting, descriptions by professionals.

The particular interactional arena focused upon here consists of interprofessional meetings where decisions about elderly clients' long-term care – placements in nursing homes – are being made. The meetings comprise professionals from the social care and the health sectors: doctors, nurses, home help personnel and social workers. Using extracts from videotaped material, centre stage in this chapter is given to the joint practices whereby the absent client is discursively drafted and talked into being through descriptions and categorizations. The analytic focus will be on the routine flow of the meetings, the argumentation and criteria used when describing the absent client, and on how textual information and case files are used as a resource for decision making. The more general concern throughout is to show how detailed, interaction-based analysis can explicate the actual situated processes in interprofessional settings, and how different kinds of clienthood are negotiated in and through professional interaction. The objective is also to show how focusing on the local logic of institutional interprofessional decision making (Boden 1994) helps us engage in useful dialogue with existing professional practice and with the principles and ideologies that inform those practices.

The chapter draws upon prior work outlining the relationship between social constructionism and discursive analysis (e.g. Payne 1999; Potter 1996a; Nikander 1995) and more specifically upon studies examining micro-level practices of categorization in institutional settings and categorization in talk more broadly (e.g. Antaki and Widdicombe 1998; Baker 1997a, 1997b; Boden 1994, 1995; Gunnarsson, Linell and Nordberg 1997; Hak 1998; Heritage and Lindström 1998; Hester and Eglin 1997; Jokinen et al. 1999; Nikander 2000, 2002; White 1999). The chapter also provides a further illustration and analysis of institutional client categorization and decision making in action. Focusing on professional categorization practices, its aim, in other words, is to identify local cultural and interprofessional knowledge and logic in use (see Baker 1997b). I begin by briefly sketching meetings as an arena for client construction and meeting-talk as data. After this highly selective thumbnail sketch of previous research, I introduce the institutional setting in which the data were collected. The remaining sections of the chapter will then be devoted to detailed analyses of case-talk through which the absent client is described and categorized. I conclude with some further considerations about the step-by-step fashion in which decisions, the client, as well as the professionals' rights and obligations, evolve conjointly in interprofessional meetings talk.

Meetings as data

As both locally and temporally limited, meetings provide an economic and effective way of getting access to the reasoning of professionals and to the everyday practices in organizations. As interaction, meeting talk has immediate and often very concrete outcomes for patients/clients. Meetings consist of reporting, describing and decision making that are fashioned to establish direction and justification for institutional action in a time-bound and practical fashion. Concerned with decisions about absent clients' life situations, meetings in the social care and health sector are also about dealing out scarcity: scarce resources either in terms of financial support, of care or in terms of professional resources (Nikander 2002; Nikander forthcoming).

A growing set of literature now exists where meetings are analysed as the very social site where institutions produce and reproduce themselves. Part of this literature is somewhat technical in focus, as it limits its interest to questions of management styles or, for instance, features of successful communication in teamwork and meetings (e.g. Dockrell and Wilson 1995; Gorman 1998; see also Øvretveit 1993). However, meetings have also been approached as empirical windows into power structures, morality, routines, concepts and the everyday emergence of organizational practice (Baker 1997b; Boden 1994, 1995; Hall, Sarangi and Slembrouck 1997; see also Drew and Heritage 1992b; Taylor and van Every 2000). In her classic work on meetings interaction, Deidre Boden (1994) states:

> Caught in a meeting and connected through a series of interactions across time and space are the people, ideas, decisions and outcomes that make the organization. It is in the closed internal times and spaces of meetings, as well as in the many phone calls that link people, topics and tasks, that the actual structure of the organization is created and recreated. The interaction order contains its own autonomous logic and, reflexively, encapsulates the organizational domain. (p.106)

To date, a number of studies have shown how ongoing discourse in meetings can be analysed as the active site whereby organizations and institutions come into being in analysable ways. Analysis of such goings-on varies from the conversation analytic interest in turn-taking in conversation, in opening, closing or 'achieving a meeting' (Atkinson, Cuff and Lee 1978; Cuff and Sharrock 1985) to broader interest in the practices of categorization and description (e.g. Griffiths 2001; Hall, Sarangi and Slembrouck 1999a; Sarangi 1998) and to the analysis of stories and narratives (e.g. Hall 1997; Hall, Sarangi and Slembrouck 1997; Housley 2000; Schwartzman, 1989). The analytic emphasis in this chapter is not so much on the turn-by-turn organization of meetings but, rather, on the practical category-generative and category-reinforcing work in the interprofessional meetings in question. Before moving on to the detailed analysis of transcribed meeting talk, however, some further background on the data and the institutional setting is needed.

The data and the setting

The data presented here come from a larger corpus of videotaped material collected in meetings concerning elderly care within the social and health services of one Finnish town.[1] In these meetings, representatives of the social care and health sector from one particular district of the town come together to decide about elderly clients' long-term care, i.e. placements in nursing homes. Representatives of the home help team of the district, representatives of nursing homes, a doctor, hospital and nursing home social workers, and a secretary attend the meetings. The meetings were videotaped while the researcher was not present in the meetings. The tapes were then transcribed into text.

The Finnish name for the meetings in focus here translates into DAC, which stands for 'determine–assess–and commit'. The name also, to a degree, sums up the practical business taking place in the meetings. Combining the expertise and skills from different professions, the task for the meetings is, ideally, to guarantee sensitive and appropriate care. As with interprofessional co-operation and teamwork more generally (e.g. Øvretveit 1993), dialogue across professional boundaries is also in this setting seen as a practical tool for more holistic decision making. The professionals in the meeting represent different local teams and, again ideally, provide different and complementary perspectives into the life situation of the elderly client in question. Home care personnel and nurses are often familiar with the client's living arrangements and with the level of support and coping at home. The doctor represents medical expertise, while hospital or nursing home personnel can provide detail about shorter ongoing periods of institutionalization. The meetings are not the sole site for interprofessional co-operation, nor the only arena for decision making concerning elderly clients. Prior to the meetings, district home help teams and hospital social workers have already agreed upon a priority listing on the basis of their day-to-day contact with clients/patients. These lists set into order the elderly clients currently living in the district or those currently in hospital care according to how urgent the professionals judge their need for a long-term nursing home placement. Priority lists may then become visible in the level and style of advocacy during client presentations in the meetings.

The normal flow of interaction in the DAC meetings consists of a chain of case descriptions. Each case presentation is followed by collegial discussion that varies in length and usually by a turn that marks that a decision about a client case has been reached. After this, the next client case is introduced. The practical outcome in terms of elderly clients is either becoming rejected or accepted or having one's application for a nursing home placement moved to a future meeting. The business of the professionals is thus to provide criteria and arguments either for or against placing a particular client into a category of care recipiency.

As research on interprofessional co-operation has established, interprofessional encounters are often saturated with 'tribal' boundary marking (e.g. Beattie 1995), with displays of professional expertise and with different occupational knowledge claims. Such negotiation of professional boundaries also marks the data in question here. The sometimes conflicting interests of occupational groups – the pressure set by both clients and/or their families, by colleagues, by financial scarcity and by future workload resulting from specific decisions – are all evident in the data (Nikander forthcoming). Medical, practical, social, psychological, moral and economic arguments for and against accepting a particular client's case are used, taken up, developed and refuted in various ways in the course of joint negotiation (see Metteri 1999). Documents and files, first-hand eyewitness narratives, as well as second-hand knowledge and the voice of the client can all be put to use in various degrees and drawn upon to support a specific route for institutional action. The practical means through which professionals balance between conflicting and dilemmatic demands and restrictions concerning the decision-making process, as well as the detail by which the absent client is talked into being, become clearer as we now move into data analysis.

Routines and criteria in interprofessional client description

Client description, typification and categorization are the central business of people-processing talk in meetings within the human services. One possible question when starting to look into how clients are described in the DAC meetings is whether the age of the service seeker is reflected in the ways in which the client is constructed. Are there, in other words, special discursive features and detail in the ways in which the absent elderly client is put forward as the target of decision making? What, for instance, is produced as relevant about him or her (Edwards 1998)? Are there specifics in the descriptive practices by which clients are categorized that construct elderly persons' clienthood as different from that of people in other ages?

One tentative way of starting to answer such questions is to look at what categorizations and characterizations are chosen from the case files that form the basis of decision making in these meetings. The following short extract comes from the beginning of a case description given by a hospital social worker. She is describing a client who is currently in hospital care. All names of both clients and professionals, of places, and other detail that might enable identification have been altered in all the extracts. A list of transcription symbols used is at the front of this book.

Extract 7.1: A never-married female

(SW = hospital social worker, Fairfield = pseudonym for a hospital)

1   SW: OK the first one is Salme Jenny (0.8) on page three

2   (3.8) ((page leafing))

3   SW: a (0.8) never-married female who has come to

4   to us in Fairfield (1.2) in July and-a (0.8)

((the case description continues))

From this short extract, it is immediately evident that written documents and text files form a resource for the decision making in these meetings. The absent client is, in other words, present via documentation and via the detail that professionals choose to take up as relevant to the case description. Additional first-hand or other information on the client is then used to flesh out the description. In Extract 7.1, the hospital social worker starts by pointing to a specific page in the pile of case files that everyone has in front of them. As the first detail on the client after the name, she then starts by categorizing her via reference to marital status and gender 'a never-married female' (line 3).

Work on categorization has pointed out how speakers, through simple mobilization of categories, simultaneously evoke a multitude of predicates, activities and images that go together with them (e.g. Baker 1997b; Nikander 2000, 2002; Silverman 1998). What does the joint evocation of gender and marital status of the client achieve for the interaction here? We can note, first, that by this co-selection of categories, the social worker, in a very economic way, makes reference to the notion that the client in question probably does not have a family network, a spouse or children to fall back on when living at home. Given that the categorization is made at the beginning of the case description, it may also be treated as salient for how subsequent characterizations should be heard. This detail, as of course any used in the course of the client description, may thus be picked up, elaborated and used as part of the criteria and as justification for specific institutional action. The combined evocation of marital status and gender may also function as reference to greater vulnerability and isolation, and thereby, in a very compact way, position the client case in a moral frame of justified institutional worry and action. This kind of reference to a lack of wider networks of care *vis-à-vis* the official systems of care may, at least potentially, come to form the basis upon which a decision is taken.

Extract 7.2 provides an example of a case description where another category: the client's chronological age – is evoked as part of the decision-making criteria. This time the speakers are discussing a male client who is currently still living at home. One of the senior district nurses is presenting the client case.

Extract 7.2: A ninety-three-year-old

(SDN1 = senior district nurse 1, SDN2 = senior district nurse 2, HHH = head of home help, S = secretary)

1   SDN1: This one has help (0.8) home help nine times

2   times a week and-a (.) .hh <and-a> (2.4)

3   the daughter's quite involved in the network of

4   care fee- (.) now feels that she cannot

5   participate as much as earlier

6   confused day-rhythm sleeps a lot (.) tired .hhh mm

7   burners left on food left uneaten leaves home

8   gets lost cannot find his way home (.) age (1.4) the

9   rela:tive also hopes for a secure place of care and

10   for good quality of life for his final years

11   we from home care recommend institutionalization

12   (.) mm (0.4) home care [personnel (0.6) home-

13 HHH: [yes

14 SDN1: visitor so, .hhh

15   (0.8)

16 S: ninety-two years

17 SDN2: yeah

18 HHH: ye[ah

19 SDN2: ex[actly yeah

20 SDN1:   [so I guess that (.) that

21   (0.8)

22 SDN2: or ni[nety-three

23   ((three lines of unclear talk omitted))

24 SDN1: so the grounds are quite sufficient in this case

25   (0.6)

26 HHH: ye[s

27 SDN1:   [compared to many others (1.6) who

28   also have gro(h)und(h)s

29   (.)

30 HHH: right hih hih hih .hhh

31 SDN2: There's not a case without grounds

The senior district nurse is reading out a list of arguments and detailed descriptions presented in the case file. Some recurring items and detail about the client (line 6 ff.) such as level of home help currently provided, existing family ties and medical status are brought up early on as relevant background to the decision making. Included are detail about the client's inability to take care of basic needs such as eating, his tendency to wander off and, in passing, the client's age (line 8). Towards the end, the case description becomes increasingly polyphonic, as both the wishes of the daughter and the recommendation and wishes of specific members of the local home help team are read out from the case file. Note that the wishes of the daughter are brought in by naming the more general category 'relative' (line 9) and by repeating what appears to be the exact and somewhat morally loaded wording in the case files: 'hopes for a secure place of care' (line 9) and 'good quality of life for his final years' (line 10).

The case description seems to not only concern the individual client case in question but also to simultaneously evoke several broader and more general notions concerning ideals of care and moral responsibilities for the care of the elderly. The daughter is first depicted as belonging to the 'devoted' category type: she has – together with professionals – been quite involved in the care of her father, although she is now unable to carry on with this work (lines 3–5). Her wishes, as they are read out in the meeting, evoke not only the more general right for a secure and good old age but also the professionals' responsibility to help provide exactly that. So in a relatively short stretch of talk and on the basis of the case file, the professionals not only place the client into the '93-year-old, in-his-final-years' category, but also re-establish a division of labour that includes both the client's and his relative's rights and the professional care providers' obligations and responsibilities (for analysis on morality in interprofessional talk see also White 2002).

What makes the extract intriguing is that, in the end, it is the client's chronological age that is used as the bottom-line argument for the positive decision taken. It is this detail, the fact that the potential recipient of care is 93 years of age, that is picked up, repeated, and in the end, together with other arguments, used as the decisive criterion. It may well be that, given that all client cases discussed in the DAC meetings are elderly and that a number of similar, slightly or severely demented, equally well-established cases with good grounds for a positive decision exist, a detail somehow unique to the case in question needs to be emphasized to differentiate sufficiently between client cases. The professionals' difficulty with drawing distinct lines and of establishing solid and clean-cut grounds for or against client cases is also apparent in the laughter towards the end of the extract. In fact, the laughter seems to indicate that the professionals share an understanding about the difficult nature of their job and that, in the end, only subtle and not easily pinpointable differences exist between client cases.

Our, your and the client's best interest?

As seen in Extracts 7.1 and 7.2, marital status, living arrangements, frequency of home care and the medical condition of clients form a set of relevant and professionally shared currency for the criteria and argumentation used in meetings making decisions about nursing home placements. In Extract 7.2 we also saw how the fuzziness of the criteria may be referred to implicitly. The fact that a shared professional understanding exists over what counts as relevant or salient, and over what can legitimately be used as an argument for rejecting or accepting a particular client case, becomes even clearer in Extract 7.3. Here, a client who is currently in hospital care is described by a hospital social worker. The question this time is whether she should be given a place in the nursing home or whether home care is still an option. The extract also includes some explicit reference to conflicting institutional interests between professional groups.

Extract 7.3: Describing a client case

(SW = hospital social worker, CN = charge nurse (nursing home), S = secretary)

1 SW: Yes, well then the next one there is I think: hhh

2   Kuusjärvi Hilkka who's I think: from May

3   seventeenth onwards (1.2) come to the ↑hospital

4   decline in general condition has been (.) the reason

5   for hospitalization and (.) she's been (1.0) this

6   of course has nothing to do (0.6) w- hh I(h)me(h)an not

7   mitigating circumstances at all but she has already

8   been offered several times to the meeting so I mean

9   the situation has been completely (.) clear to us, =but

10   then she (0.4) just a sec (.) yes she's demented and-a:

11   .mt mm needs some assistance but: so >anyway

12   a person< who tends to leave (1.0)

13   the ward. =and th- therefore is now in ward

14   3B Dementia ward with closed doors. but I mean

15   the meeting did at some point support the idea

16   that she might still cope at home. and

17   that from our perspective is quite an impossible (1.0)

18   idea I mean (0.8) exactly because of this

19   tendency to escape. she will leave then.

20   (2.0)

21 SW: so a calm demented patient in need of some

22   assistance,

23   (4.0)

24 SW: can't cope at home.

25   (2.5)

26   to put it shortly

27   (4.0)

28 SW: lacks initiative.hhh (2.0) middle stage dementia at ↓this

29   moment↓ d- the dementia has developed however I mean

30   now (0.4) compared to (0.8) last spring.

31   (3.0)

32 CN: is this perhaps then a case for the nursing home's (.)

33   ward for the demen[ted.

34 S: [mm: mm sounds like °i[t°.

35 SW: [yes.

The case description delivered by the hospital social worker is typical in that the speaker keeps the floor with an extended turn during which specific detail and characteristics of the absent client's life situation, prior history and health are listed. Two points of analytic interest are worth mentioning. First, note that the social worker makes direct reference to the criteria that can be used to back up a suggestion for action. That is, in addition to the client's medical history and diagnosis, the level of assistance needed, length of hospitalization, etc. she also includes and keeps coming back to the detail that the client's case has been discussed in an earlier meeting (lines 5–8 and 15–19). Doing this, she simultaneously marks this detail as something that goes against the set of criteria legitimately used by professionals in these meetings: lines 5–8: 'she's been (1.0) this of course has nothing to do (0.6) w- hh I(h)me(h)an not mitigating circumstances at all but'. Several features in the way in which this detail is added as an aside point out that something of a breach in argumentation and rationalization is taking place and that the speaker herself makes an attempt towards self-censure. Laughter and talk with a smiley voice combined with the general knowledge token 'of course' (line 6), together show that the speaker is aware of using argumentation that goes against some mutually shared code for argumentation.

Two further observations on Extract 7.3 can be made here. Note how reference to an earlier handling of the client case coincides with reference to conflicting institutional interests. Using the institutional we ('us', on line 9, and 'our perspective' on line 17), the hospital social worker immediately brings forward potential differences in wishes and interests of the home help team on the one hand and of the hospital on the other. The extract thus provides an instance of the practical business of medical, this time geriatric, assessment via which the flow of patients and the availability of hospital beds is dealt with and secured (see Latimer 1997). In her case presentation, the social worker provides sets of detail and membership criteria in a step-by-step fashion. These persuasive and performative arguments together construct the client as a suitable, and in the end as an inevitable, candidate for a nursing home placement. The second and related analytic point to be raised concerns the ways in which decisions become made in these meetings. Let us again have a second look at how this was achieved in Extract 7.3.

Extract 7.3.1: (with lines 31–35 repeated)

(CN = charge nurse (nursing home), S = secretary, SW = hospital social worker)

31   (3.0)

32 CN: is this perhaps then a case for the nursing home's (.)

33   ward for the demen[ted.

34 S: [mm: mm sounds like °i[t°.

35 SW: [yes.

It has been pointed out elsewhere that in ongoing meetings talk, decisions are largely invisible (Boden 1994, p.22), and that decisions often become assembled as part of, and located in, the layers of descriptions themselves. In Extract 7.3 the case description already brings forward two potentially opposing views, places them in a dialogue with each other and provides a potential decision. Finally, after several attempts at closing the case description, a delayed uptake and a closing to the case are offered. In Extract 7.3.1, the decision stage is entered via a suggestive, overtly democratic question which is then responded to by two members of the meeting. In contrast to Extract 7.2 then, the final decision is made here in a veiled fashion and the uptake treats the outcome as evident and somehow logically following from the case description itself (line 34: 'mm: mm sounds like it').

Challenging routine criteria

In the data extracts so far, we have seen some features of how client description and the wrapping up of a case are done. We also saw how specific routine criteria become evoked and listed as part of the decision-making procedure. In the remaining space I would like to discuss one further extract in which one recurrently used criterion for or against a decision, the number of home visits a week, is challenged by the professionals. We join the interaction at a point where the senior district nurse has been describing a female client at some considerable length. The case seems problematic, as the client does not currently receive much home help but is none the less severely demented and, in fact, in need of constant care. So in terms of the recurrently used indicator of home help frequency, she does not quite meet the criteria, whereas according to medical criteria she might. Immediately prior to the extract below, the senior district nurse has described how the restless, unpredictable and confused female client wanders alone outside, does not know her way back home, resists all medical procedures, and seems severely disoriented, anxious and delusional. Following this lengthy description the senior district nurse then continues with the following.

Extract 7.4: *The forgetful and the demented*

(SDN = senior district nurse, HHH = head of home help, S = secretary)

1   SDN: so there is >of course< all this (0.6) so if it

2   was only [possible

3   S: [yeah

4   (0.3)

5   HHH: when you think that

6   (0.4)

7   SDN: but this level of home care is still real (.)

8   quite low of course I mean bu- damn it with the

9   forgetful and the demented home care visits

10   don't necessarily

11   (0.4)

12 HHH: the[:y (.) don't help the fact that

13 SDN: [bring the sense of security °that°

14   ((discussion on demented client cases continues))

In Extract 7.4, the discrepancy between set and solid decision-making criteria and the specificity of singular client cases is brought into discussion. The senior district nurse does this by making reference to the lack of latitude provided by the set of criteria 'so if it was only possible' (lines 1–2) and by mentioning a wider category of client cases. Drawing upon the list of specifics about the actions, predicates and characterizations mentioned about the client in the course of her longer description, the senior district nurse, in other words, proceeds to place her into the category 'the forgetful and the demented' (line 7). The discursive shift from the particular to a more general category of client cases is done here to explicate why an exception to customary practice may be in order. This kind of movement from the particular to the general and vice versa is a more recurrent feature of client categorization in the meetings talk (see Billig 1985). Here the move from the single client case to the more general category, 'the demented', is done to underline that although home help provides and supports such basic needs as bathing, meals, etc. it does not provide the sense of security and the level of monitoring that people suffering from dementia need 24 hours a day. Therefore, in these cases, the level of home help is not a good indicator of the client's needs.

Supported by her colleagues, the senior district nurse, in Extract 7.4, moves the client aside as a particular case that requires an exception to be made. The discussion then continues on the special needs of this general client category. From the above, it is clear then that the decision-making process consists not of straightforward or automatic categorization according to some pre-existing and fixed set of rules but rather of actively defining criteria, of splitting client categories into finer divisions with their own specific characters, needs and relevant procedure.

The principles and practices of interprofessional work

I have been concerned here with some of the features that characterize the joint professional practices whereby absent clients become discursively described, drafted and categorized in interprofessional meeting talk and interaction. More specifically, the analyses provided in this chapter aimed at examining and explicating some routine features of decision making and client categorization within elderly care in the social care and health sector. One central aim of the chapter has been to show how the analysis of local institutional interaction may help us engage in dialogue with the principles that inform and guide professional practice. On the basis of the analyses in this chapter, three potential areas of dialogue can now be identified. These points for dialogue sum up the discussion in this chapter, while also pointing to future areas of research and areas where research of joint clienthood construction in meetings can prove informative to existing practice. I will discuss each potential point for dialogue in turn.

Dialogue between professional principles/ideologies and actual situated practice
Interprofessional co-operation, decision making and teamwork in all their various forms are often characterized as central means of encouraging and supporting better practice within social and health care organizations. Co-operation across professional boundaries is depicted in policy documents, mission statements, the schooling of future professionals and in the professional literature, as a means of combining different kinds of expertise, as a quality assurance for making balanced, well-informed and grounded institutional decisions. It is, in other words, seen as a safeguard for sound organizational rationality.

Herein lies a paradox, however, as the workings of the tool simultaneously remain largely under-researched. There is a lack of detailed information on how and whether the outcomes of such co-operation are actually reflected back in the form of more holistic, multi-voiced and rational decisions. What I hope to have begun to show here is how the somewhat abstract and theoretical notion of interprofessionalism may be approached and studied in action. Studying the professional give and take in specific interprofessional institutional arenas helps us grasp the dynamics and the criteria on which decisions are made. Analysing the specifics of how different and conflicting local logics surface in the course of interaction may thus open new analytic paths that lead towards better understanding of interprofessional work. In the long run, analyses like these may also contribute to the professionals' own theoretical models and to their understanding concerning their work.

Mapping the everyday-level emergence of organizational practice

One of the prerequisites of any dialogue is sufficient knowledge. What I hope to have shown is that detailed interaction-based analysis provides access to the routines, concepts, tensions, and power and moral structures operating within institutions. Looking at specific interactional decision-making episodes in meetings provides a snapshot of the current but developing and changing logic of action. The analysis of situated categorization in this chapter, for instance, showed how such activities inevitably merge in informative ways with negotiation about the rights, obligations and responsibilities of both the client and his or her relatives, on the one hand, and of the official system of professional and institutional care on the other. Analysing situated talk thus provides a window into how specific, potentially sensitive issues are raised and solved on a moment-to-moment, day-to-day basis.

Studying clienthood in action

From the above, it is already clear that tracing how professionals make sense of their work, of their clients' problems and of their life situations, gives us immediate access into institutional rationality in the making. As such, detailed analysis of institutional practices also provides one possible basis upon which future policies, guidelines and practices can be moulded to suit the heterogeneity and changing nature of client needs.

Moving back to the specific interactional setting analysed here, the relatively few examples discussed already give us some handle on the ongoing tensions included in client categorization between moral, economic and practical argumentation, and between the rights and responsibilities between different actors. In the extracts we saw, for instance, professionals challenging the existing criteria that guides the placing of clients into categories of care recipiency and non-recipiency. There was clearly a discrepancy between available latitude for categorization and decision making that would make justice to the heterogeneity of their clienthood.

These kinds of ruptures in the flow in professional client work and case categorization can often prove informative. The social and health care service system faces a continuous flux of demands and challenges towards change and continuous development. Tracing ruptures and discrepancies helps to build a picture of the current tensions within a particular area of decision making, and helps to map the practical means through which professionals, as part of their everyday work, balance between conflicting and dilemmatic demands and restrictions concerning their work and the decision-making process. One of the key questions confronting elderly care in an ageing society, for instance, is whether the care system allows for the increasing heterogeneity of clienthood to surface and become visible. One way of allowing this to happen is via mapping and seeking to understand how decisions and clienthood are negotiated and constructed in practice, either in micro-level face-to-face professional–client interaction or in encounters where an absent client's case is in question.

Note

1   The data was collected (between 2001 and 2002) as part of the Academy of Finland funded research project (SA170002) titled: *Constructing Age, Health, and Competence: Argumentation and Rhetoric in Institutional and Personal Discourse.* The data consists of a 42-hour videotaped corpus of meetings interaction and of documents, interviews and participant observation. The videotaped data consist of two types of meetings: meetings deciding about elderly or handicapped clients' home care benefits, and meetings making decisions about nursing home placements. Only the latter type is focused on here.

8

The Dilemma of Victim Positioning in Group Therapy for Male Perpetrators of Domestic Violence

Terhi Partanen and Jarl Wahlström

How do male clients who have used violence against their female partners, and therapists, negotiate and construct clienthood in the context of group therapy conversations? In this chapter, we will look at some of the dilemmas arising from differences in how male participants, on the one hand, and therapists, on the other, construct clienthood and participation in treatment groups for male perpetrators. We will put one particular instance, the seeking of a victim position on the part of the clients, under close scrutiny.

We will also look at the question of 'good clienthood': what are the characteristics of a 'good client' in these treatment groups for male perpetrators of domestic violence? What kinds of qualities is the client asked to fit into within this institutional frame, and how is the institutional task constructed through the 'negotiations' of preferred and non-preferred client characteristics? How do the professionals in this setting fulfil their institutional tasks as therapists?

Programmes for male perpetrators of domestic violence began in the late 1970s in North America. In Finland, the treatment of such men did not start until the beginning of the 1990s. Group therapy is shown to be an effective mode of treatment for male perpetrators of domestic violence (Dobash *et al.* 2000), and has become a common form of treatment in use. There are, though, several competing views on whether perpetrators' programmes should be of a counselling, educational, or therapeutic nature (Adams 1988;

Gondolf 1997, 2001). There is, in fact, a great ambivalence concerning men's programmes (Eliasson and Lundy 1999). Some researchers have pointed out that if women are only encouraged to leave their batterers, and the behaviour of the batterer himself is not addressed, this can result in 'cycling through' of women victims' (Harway and Hansen 1993, p.10). Other critics have also expressed concerns over the terminology used when talking about violence against women, and the consequences this has for understanding the phenomenon (Hearn 1998).

Standard treatment approaches based on the idea of re-educating abusers with regards to male ideologies of power and control, which rely on a high level of direct confrontation, have been criticized (Daniels and Murphy 1997; Hydén and McCarthy 1994; Murphy and Baxter 1997). Several studies have shown that men have a tendency to drop out of treatment (Gerlock 2001; Taft and Murphy 2001) and move responsibility away from themselves (Stamp and Sabourin 1995). Batterers are seen to take very 'elaborate measures to construct nonviolent self-images, and minimize others' negative view of themselves' (Goodrum *et al.* 2001, p.238). It is often documented that female victims tend to talk about the violent act and incident itself, while male abusers tend to focus on the responses which led to their use of violence (Hydén 1994; Nyqvist 2001). Projection and blaming others are common features and often documented (Ptacek 1988). From this point of view it is essential, when working with male perpetrators, to break these projective systems and simultaneously support the participants' commitment to the programme and its objectives.

When managing this complicated task one important element of the treatment process is the exposure and elimination of verbal strategies which serve to minimize the violence (Wolf-Smith and LaRossa 1992). But how can this be done without disqualifying the speaker as a recognized member of the group and a client in his own right? As such he would be committed to working towards commonly shared and personally adopted goals of change, and thus also entitled to the support and expressions of sympathy from the therapists. It seems quite obvious that the conversations of the group therapy sessions will present many instances of the confusing dilemmas of psychological and moral discourses when talking about violence, and when constructing the participants as clients of these programmes.

Treating male perpetrators of domestic violence is a typical instance of what Juhila and Pösö (2000) have named 'specialised trouble work'. The orientation is towards a clearly specified problem. Maintaining the legitimacy of intervention is a constant element of this kind of specialized trouble work, and is closely connected to the construction of clienthood. If clients do not have problems matching the institutional task of the treatment programme, then the therapists as representatives of the institution could not justify their activities (Silverman 1997). Through constructing and maintaining a fitting 'troubles talk' the therapists manage to defend and fulfil their professional responsibilities. An essential feature in 'specialised trouble work' is that the clients should be aware of the functions and tasks of the institution and at the same time that they should be committed to these (Juhila and Pösö 2000).

The overall goal of the treatment, i.e. the central institutional task, is to encourage the male participants to change their attitudes towards the use of violence, to take responsibility for their own violent deeds and to end their violent behaviour. These are clear starting-points that will evidently influence how the concept of a 'good client' is defined and constructed from an institutional point of view. They will form a framework for how the therapists and clients are present and interact in these encounters. The question arises of what are the possibilities of constructing such a notion of clienthood in concrete therapy talk, and how can this be done, or at least attempted, in the discursive everyday practices of the group meetings.

Data and analysis

In Jyväskylä, a multi-professional co-operation programme in preventing and treating domestic violence started in 1995.[1] It consists of separate programmes for victims of violence, that is, women and children, and for male perpetrators. The treatment of male perpetrators begins with an immediate intervention and individual sessions with one of the male workers. The possibility of entering group treatment is presented during these individual meetings. Attending a group is voluntary, but most of the men who participate are under a certain kind of social pressure, for example the wife, girlfriend or employer has encouraged or persuaded him to participate. Only a few of the men have reported entering the group sessions completely independently.

An individual treatment phase lasts from one to six months, and is aimed at concretizing violent acts, taking responsibility for these situations and finding ways to avoid abusive behaviour (Laitila and Sveins 2001). Entering group treatment is possible only after completing the individual sessions and an assessment interview. The group programme consists of 15 sessions of one-and-half hours' duration once a week. The group sessions are conducted by two therapists; up to the year 2000 both were male, from then on there was one male and one female therapist. The groups have included from three to seven male clients. From 1995 up to the year 2000, ten groups have been completed, one each semester.

The data of our research consists of videotaped and transcribed recordings of the first three sessions of ten groups for abusive men. The first author watched the whole body of 30 sessions of videotaped data, and all the sessions were transcribed. As a result of the first phase of analysis, after multiple readings of the transcribed text, different themes of tensions arising in the conversations between the male participants and the therapists were identified.

In the second phase of analysis, text extracts connected to one of these tension-producing themes, i.e. those involving the construction of a victim position on the part of the male participants, were subjected to a detailed reading. This was carried out with close attention to sequential turn-by-turn interaction (Schegloff and Sacks 1973). We were especially interested in examining sequences including client–therapist interactions. We chose these interactions and the theme of victim positioning because they seemed to constitute a commonly appearing and visible area of conflict or, at least, tense conversations between the clients and the therapists in our data. We regard them as central and revealing areas of conversation in which the negotiation of clienthood in these groups takes place. They seem to perform as a prism, rendering visible some of the basic constitutive discursive practices of institutional talk of the treatment groups for male perpetrators.

Here we will share the results of our analysis by showing three conversational sequences. The text extracts presented and analysed are from two different groups and from three distinct conversations. The first, and the third to sixth extracts are from the second session of one and the same group. The first one is from the first half and the others from the second half of that session. The second text extract is from the third session of another group and from the end of that session.

Dealing with the dilemma of victim positioning
Ignoring and confronting the victim position

There seems to be certain established practices in the course of the first group sessions in this men's programme. In the first session the group therapy and research contracts are signed, and the conversation starts with presenting the idea of the group and practical issues. By putting routine questions the therapists repeatedly bring up certain themes and often take the lead in the conversation. The male clients mainly participate by answering the therapists' questions in turn.

One of the therapists' routine questions, 'Why have you come to this group?', seems to mark the beginning of the actual therapeutic conversation. The formulation of this question leaves open different options for the clients to define their situation. After that the group usually proceeds by self-presentations of the therapists and the clients. One theme that is taken up for discussion is how significant persons in the clients' life-context are in relation to their participation. In Extract 8.1, one of the clients responds to a routine question concerning this.

Extract 8.1: Client aiming at victim position – therapist ignoring
(T2 = therapist 2, M2 = client 2)

1   T2:   (3) what by the way did you say when she ((client's wife))

2   asked you about this group (1) or what was it (that she asked)

3   M2:   (3) (what was it) I told her how many people we have in the

4   group and (3) something about the rules which had been

5   T2:   (1) mmm

6   M2:   talked about but (nothing more) about the ( ) (2) content (1)

7   it slipped quite quickly (1) the conversation to these (.) interests

8   of hers (2) which like always we had again to start wondering

9   about around midnight (1) when I was just going off to bed (2)

10   (so) it's part of her way of tiring me out (1) you have to always

11   (.) go on about them in the middle of the night

12   (6)

13   T2:   has anybody else (.) been asked anything (1) about the group

14   (.) did anybody ask

The client's answer, given after a three-second pause, is quite insubstantial (lines 3–4). The therapist gives a minimal response, encouraging the client to continue his account. He continues answering the therapist's question (line 6), and goes on to describe his and his wife's conversation. However, suddenly he starts describing his wife's demanding behaviour towards him (lines 6–11), constructing himself in this conversation as a suffering party. The client uses terms like 'again' and 'always' (lines 8,10) when describing the incident, expressing an idea that this is a recurring pattern in their relationship. The use of such an extreme formulation (Pomeranz 1986) can be seen to mark anticipation that the other participants may not be sympathetic towards his account. It also works as a formulation of consistency information (Auburn *et al.* 1995) where it functions to construct his wife as having been responsible for similar behaviour in the past. The client depicts his wife's way of behaving as her strategy to tire him out (line 10). The therapist passes his turn (six-second pause in line 12) with silence, and after that he directs his question to other members of the group (lines 13–14). Thus, the therapist totally ignores the client's invitation to participate in this construction of his position as a victim of his wife's repeatedly annoying behaviour.

The second text extract shows a different course of conversation. It is from the third session of another group and from near the end of the session. Prior to the conversation presented in the extract, the client has said that he has 'laid hands on his wife' because of her 'cruel' attitude towards him. He has depicted the situation as one where he has been violent himself but in a quite vague way and mainly as responding to her 'cruelty'. He has also stated explicitly that he has not started the argument and that in this situation his wife has not been intimidated. The therapist has given only a minimal response to this. In Extract 8.2 the conversation continues.

Extract 8.2: Client aiming at victim position – therapist confronting
(M4 = client 4, T1 = therapist 1)

1   M4: it just been like that .hhh the wife has .hhh (.) been in a terrible

2   state about something

3   T1:   mmm

4   M4: (1) and (.) I've been anxious about the situation in such a way

5   that .hhh it has (.) it has felt like (1)[( )]

6   T1:   [have you felt li-] have you

7   felt like this kind of physical contact has solved then (.) relieved

8   your anxiety or

9   M4:   .hhh (.) i:t doesn't relieve it (.) th- not in that way (.) as such

10   T1:   (1) so in the end it doesn't work the way you've tried [( )

11   M4:   [yeah

12   well I don't know (um) I think it's maybe sort of .hhh hhh

13   ((sighs)) (2) some ki[nd of primitive

14   T1:   [( )

15   M4:   reaction

The client continues describing his wife's emotional state (lines 1–2). Here again, as in Extract 8.1, the client positions himself indirectly as a victim of his wife's behaviour and attitude. And again, the therapist only gives a minimal response (line 3), perhaps intending to mark the client's explanation as an inadequate and not preferred one. The client, however, continues to strengthen his construction by referring to his own emotional state – 'I've been anxious' (line 4) – and, at the same time, implicitly offers his emotional state as a reason for his violent behaviour. Here he attributes his use of violence to a psychological state differing from the normal and adheres to a discourse of disorder which gives strong explanatory power to his account (Auburn, *et al.* 1995).

The therapist responds by asking if the physical contact has relieved the client's anxiety (lines 6–8). Here the therapist seems to share to some extent a discourse of disorder but, on the other hand, does not show empathy towards the client's emotional state and his psychological explanation. The formulation of this question (lines 6–8), and especially the use of the word 'then', confront the client's explanation and cut off its edge. This confronting function of the therapist's question is confirmed by the client's response in line 9. The use of the phrase 'it doesn't relieve it...not in that way' seems to indicate that the client is not totally satisfied with the therapist's way of putting the question and can be seen as a way of resisting it, although at the same time he cannot defy it. And in line 10 the therapist strengthens his conclusions and hence his confrontation.

In lines 11–13, when responding to the therapist, the client hesitates again, using disqualifiers like 'I don't know' (Suoninen 1999) and partly confirms the therapist's construction while still partly rejecting it. He reformulates his construction of an emotional state (anxious) to a primitive reaction (lines 12–13). By naturalizing his deeds as determined by primitive forces, he puts himself at the mercy of something outside his own control. This can be seen as an attempt to maintain his victim position in the face of the therapist's confrontation. When doing this he qualifies his description by embedding it into his own experience (Peräkylä 1995), offering it as his own point of view ('I think', line 12).

(Co-)constructing and deconstructing the victim position

The following text extracts show a more complicated course of conversation. They are from the middle of the second session of the same group as in Extract 8.1. It is a continuous sequence of exchanges of interactions between one male client and one of the two therapists. Before this sequence, the therapist has raised the issue about trust in the group and in the clients' present relationships. The therapist has asked what other people (for example, their wives), who know that the men are in this group, think about their participation and how free the men feel to reveal their personal matters in the group. The therapist's first question in Extract 8.3 is referring to this discussion.

Extract 8.3: Client constructing a victim position
(T2 = therapist 2, M6 = client 6)

1   T2:   how free do you feel here to talk about (1) your wife's (1)

2   participation or about your wife (2) your situation

3   M6:   well yes I (2) I am like from m- my own point of view ((laughs))

4   .hhh (how) these (.) these when (.) she's (.) she is such a very

5   (2) very strong (.) woman (2) .hhh and then when i- it (2) when

6   the fight comes (1) .hhh (1) it is the (.) the nearest thing that she

7   gets her hand on will let fly immediately (that's right)

8   T2:   mmm

9   M6:   that from there (.) she will like explode then and (1) .hhh I will

10   try to sneak away from there then (.) .hhh ((laughs, others

11   laugh too)) away from ((laughing)) the flying objects .hhh

12   that I think that's s- some kind of violence too

13 T2:   mmm

14   M6:   (1) from her side (1) even if they are not (.) even if they are

15   not exactly thro- thrown towards me

16   (5)

The therapist's question in line 1 is one of the routine questions asked in the first sessions. The therapist uses the phrase 'your wife's participation' but repairs this after a two-second pause to 'your situation' (line 2). The therapist perhaps assumes that his first formulation might offer the client the option of interpreting the question as indicating some responsibility on the part of the wife for the violence in the relationship.

After having briefly and quite vaguely answered the therapist's question (line 3), the client starts to talk about his wife's behaviour. He laughs when answering the question, changes the subject and starts to describe his wife 'she is such a very very strong woman' (lines 4–5). The client appears to offer to the therapist an account of his wife as having some 'behavioural problem' and of himself as a person in trouble in the relationship. Interestingly the client responds to the therapist's question in this way. The question in itself does not in any way invite a construction of a victim position of any kind. In spite of this the client's turn seems to pave the way for such a construction. It also seems to work as some kind of preface to that later construction.

In this extract again the therapist responds very minimally: 'mmm' (lines 8, 13). These minimal responses can be seen as unmarked acknowledgements and as primarily having a continuative function in the conversation (Silverman 1997), clearly at least not confirming the accounts. Perhaps because of the lack of responsiveness, the client seems to hesitate to continue his constructive work of his wife as an aggressive person (lines 9–12).

The client's choice of terms – describing his wife as 'a very strong woman' (line 5), 'explode' (line 9) and 'flying objects' (line 11) – makes his account very detailed. A detailed description of situations is often used when the speaker wants to ensure the accuracy and truth of events (Edwards and Potter 1993). The client portrays himself as a person in trouble when using the phrase 'I will try to sneak away from there then' (lines 9–10). The client constructs his wife as a violent person first by depicting her characteristics and later by confirming this explicitly, saying 'that's some kind of violence too' (line 12). Here again, there is no intimation towards positioning the male client as a victim in the therapist's question and still the client starts constructing this positioning almost immediately. The extract ends with the therapist's silence of five seconds. Basically, here is the same kind of conversational flow as Extract 8.1: the therapist avoids any direct confrontation.

After a five-second pause when the therapist does not take his turn (at the end of Extract 8.3), the client actually responds himself to his own account ('no no they are not', 17, next extract), and continues his turn by changing the subject.

Extract 8.4: Strengthening of the victim position by changing the subject
(T2 = therapist 2, M6 = client 6)

17   no no they are not and m- my childhood has been such that that (.)

18   (already) (.) since I was very young (2) I've seen only violence

19 T2:   yhym=

20 M6:   =and my (.) parents like .hhh they g- got (.) even thrown out of

21   their own flat because they fought (so much)

22 T2:   yhym (2) you have seen when

23 M6:   I've been watching i[t (.) it]

24 T2:   [(your father) has h]it your mother

The client starts to talk about his childhood and constructs a picture of it as a traumatic, violent one (lines 17–18). The client uses extreme formulations such as 'already since I was very young' and 'only violence' (line 18) when describing his experiences. The therapist's minimal response, 'yhym', seems to have a somewhat more compliant tone than the previous ones. This appears to establish a turning point of the conversation. One can presume that it is very hard, if not impossible, not to react to this kind of traumatic childhood story in a compassionate way, at least as a therapist. It can, in fact, be seen that the therapist becomes active in participating in the co-construction of the client's traumatic childhood story (lines 22, 24). This is also indicated by the overlapping speech in lines 23–24. He specifies the constructive work of the client by stating 'you have seen when your father has hit your mother' (line 24), and introduces a presumption of gendered violence. This formulation also specifies what has happened in time and space, thus making a difference between the client's past and present experiences. In this way the therapist succeeds in validating the client's victim position in childhood and yet, at the same time, avoids giving support to the client's construction of a victim position in his present relationship. This is achieved without the kind of direct confrontation that was seen in Extract 8.2. The conversation continues.

Extract 8.5: Constructing an identity of a traumatized person
(M6 = client 6, T2 = therapist 2)

25 M6: yes and mother (.) mother is such that that she didn't give in

26   at all that (.) .hhh (.) for example she took an axe and mm

27   went to smash mm my stepfather's (.) windscreen (.) to pieces

28   (.) .hhh (it) hhh ((laughing)) that (sh-) .hhh she gave it him back

29   and I've watched it my whole life (1) then ( ) (3) but but it has

30   had its effects but (.) I have this thing that (2) between the age

31   of seven and twelve there's a dark area

32 T2:   (1) yhym

The client acknowledges the therapist's specification with a short affirmative 'yes', but immediately carries on describing his childhood and especially his mother. He constitutes the same kind of 'strong woman' theme about his mother (lines 25–29) as he did about his wife in Extract 8.3. The client's stepfather is depicted as an object of his mother's aggressive behaviour. This can be seen as contrasting the therapist's presumption of gendered violence and offers a picture of two equal parties participating in and co-constructing the violent lifestyle.

Using the phrase 'I've watched it my whole life' (line 29), with its extreme formulation, the client presents the violence he has been exposed to in his childhood as having had an extensive effect on his whole life. The client continues to constitute his victim position by stating these effects explicitly (lines 29–31). The effects have been so traumatic that he does not even remember many years of his childhood. Again, the client uses his childhood experiences to reinforce his construction of himself as a victim in his present relationship. The use of childhood experiences as support for the present victim position is a powerful way of cutting the edge off potential criticism. By referring to his own life course, he strengthens his position as an expert in his own life (Sacks 1992). From such a position he is also entitled to define his feelings as a victim. Besides constructing himself as the victim of childhood experiences, the client also constructs a more general theme of 'a man as a victim of a woman'. The client continues to comment on his childhood 'amnesia' and offers three possible accounts for its origin.

Extract 8.6: Deconstruction of the victim position
(M6 = client 6, T2 = therapist 2)

33 M6: (1) I don't really remember any- really anything (.) in that area

34   (1) so I like (2) somebody (.) has wiped it away (.) apparently

35   it's like that for a child the bad things get wiped away

36 T2: (1) so it's been so bad that one is not (.) one is not anymore able to

37 M6: yeah [hhh

38 T2:   [does not manage to remember

39 M6: mmm

40 T2: does not want to remember

41 M6: (1) or (.) (I just) would like to [but I don't remember (.) mmm]

42 T2:   [(yes yes but one is not able to])

43 M6: (2) ((swallows)) so I've seen it (.) a lot of it in my childhood

44 T2: mmm (3) (you p- probably) know how (.) a child feels when

45   he sees (.) his parents hitting each other

46 M6: yeah (.) ( ) (.)th- that's the thing that bothers me now that

47   I have my own children (and)

48 T2: mmm

49 M6: (1) having to see what (.) I've seen

In the first account the client himself has erased the traumatic memories (lines 33–34), in the second one this is done by somebody or something else ('somebody'), and finally, in the third one this is explained as a result of a common 'mechanism' ('for a child the bad things get wiped away'). The use of this general category of children and the 'mechanisms of trauma psychology' makes the client's statement more convincing: 'This is what happens to everybody, not just me, it is like a law of nature'. The word 'apparently' creates an impression of the client as a person observing himself from an out-side position (Goffman 1979) and, in this context, offers the speaker's utterance more credibility when said from such a reflective point of view.

The therapist rejoins this construction in lines 36–42. Interestingly he uses a sequence of different verbs when referring to the difficulty of remem-bering. First he says that 'one is not anymore able to' (line 36), and second 'does not manage to remember' (line 38). These two versions seem to con-firm the client's construction of a traumatized identity. But finally, the therapist uses the expression 'does not want to remember' (line 40). Here it seems that the therapist is offering the client the possibility of taking on more responsibility and playing a more active part in the process of repress-ing memories.

The client concludes his constructive work on the identity of a trauma-tized person and at the same time offers himself as a 'good client' who is willing to remember but does not have the capacity for it ('I just would like to but I don't', line 41). The therapist gives a minimal response (line 44) and, after a three-second pause, he seems to offer an alternative conclusion. He states 'you probably know how a child feels' (lines 44–45). This formulation manages two tasks. Talking on a general level ('how a child feels') the thera-pist avoids belittling the client's childhood experiences and even offers support. His formulation 'you probably know' can be seen as a slightly con-fronting attempt to offer the client a new perspective. The therapist opens up a possibility for the client to assume the position of a responsible parent and, indeed, the client responds with an affirmative 'yeah' (line 46). This can be seen as a marked acknowledgement (Silverman 1997) indicating the possi-ble acceptance of this offer.

The client seems to read the therapist's statement partly as a reproach, responding to it by stating 'that's the thing that bothers me now' (line 46). The wording 'that's the thing' implies a gesture of consent and the phrasing 'bothers me now' a sentiment of remorse. The tone of the therapist's minimal response in line 48, when heard on audiotape, seems to confirm this reading.

The therapist's statement changes the focus of the conversation from the unsteady area of the client's victimizing childhood experiences to the arena of present interactions. The client replies to this move by referring to his own children and their present status of witnesses of violence in the family (lines 46–49). Although the client, when stating (children) 'having to see what I've seen' (line 49), is not directly referring to his own use of violence, he however seems to open up some space for the possibility of negotiating his responsibility for it.

Discussion and conclusions

One of the main findings that emerged from the first reading of our data was a strong inclination among the male participants to position themselves as victims. Negotiations around victim positioning were chosen for detailed analysis because of its significance in constructing clienthood in treatment programmes for male perpetrators of domestic violence. Positioning has significant consequences for the course of the treatment process. In the whole body of our data (30 sessions) the male participants apparently construct their victim positioning by appealing to various kinds of victimizing circumstances, such as: their own 'irrational feelings' (helplessness), women's verbal or emotional violence (nagging), biology (genetic heritage of violence), outside circumstances (work stress) and their own childhood experiences (parents' or significant others' violence, i.e. social heritage). The strongest possible victim construction tends to be positioning themselves as a victim of their own childhood. Especially in a therapy context, the men offer childhood trauma as a credible way of accounting for their own behaviour.

In our detailed analysis we addressed the difficulties and conflicts arising out of therapeutic interactions in which a participant aspires to construct a victim position for himself. We showed in detail some discursive practices used in these interactions between therapists and clients. Usually the participant, without any invitation from the therapist, recounts an episode or a recurring pattern that, either directly or indirectly, creates an image of him as a victim. The therapists' method of dealing with these situations is typically either to ignore or confront this victim positioning. In the first extract, when the client aimed at a victim position, the therapist clearly ignored the speaker's offer of himself as a victimized client in need of understanding and support. By ignoring this position the therapist was clearly morally judgemental. In the second extract, the therapist responded to the speaker's construction of a victim position by openly confronting it. Again, the therapist refused the offer of this client construction and took a clear moral position in relation to it.

The third interaction showed a more complicated co-construction of the speaker's position as a client. Although it included the features of the basic grammar of both interactions, that is, the therapist neglecting and confronting the speaker's depiction of himself as a victim, it was however more complicated, with the therapist occasionally confirming the client's victim positioning and occasionally disconfirming it, depending on the complexities of the conversation. The therapeutic context of the conversation here became more accentuated. The therapist took more of a psychological position in addition to a judgemental one and went back and forth between the two positions, maintaining the tension between the psychological and moral discourses.

Placing himself in a victim position has obvious advantages for the participant in this kind of treatment. It is an efficient way to avoid active agency and responsibility for one's violent deeds. It is a rhetoric that distances and depersonalizes the agent from the speaker's actions (Hydén 1994). The victim position can be understood as a very strong position in therapeutic conversations or in conversations in which it is possible to be accused of something. A victim has weak agency and thus has none or little responsibility for his deeds, but is entitled to be the object of sympathy and understanding of others.

The male participants in the treatment groups appeared to be familiar with the theories of modern psychology. They used this repertoire actively in constructing their client position, which supposedly would entitle them to expect understanding and empathy from the therapists. However, as seen in the data we have offered, the therapists did not subscribe to these expectations. By not complying with the 'client-as-victim' construction, the therapists offer themselves as performing a different institutional task than that called for by a 'traditional' psychological point of view. The rejection of the victim positioning, either by ignoring it or by confrontation, allows one to view violence as a way of controlling and dominating other people and as the consequence of an 'active choice'. The therapists were offering this 'violence as a choice' viewpoint actively in the group and it became problematic for the male participants to maintain the positions of active agency and victimization simultaneously. Negotiating a victim position is actually negotiating responsibility and agency.

What are the practical implications of these findings? From a treatment process aspect, victim positioning is problematic for the therapists to confront. The dilemma and the challenge for the therapists arises in terms of how to encourage the male participants to take responsibility for their violent deeds and at the same time to take account of, accept and offer empathy to them in regards to their individual and also possibly painful experiences. The challenge for the therapists is to manage a co-ordinated use of the psychological and moral discourses, as could be clearly seen in the third interaction we analysed. Therapists have to take an active role and take responsibility for the moral side of treatment. From a moral position the therapists' duty is to identify the use of violence as a primary treatment issue and not as a symptom of something else (Adams 1988). As Goldner (1999) sees it, psychological and moral discourses are put up against each other and in psychotherapeutic treatment the questions of morality are not considered relevant. But when the overall goal of treating male perpetrators is to encourage them to take responsibility for their violent actions, the moral issues emerge differently than in traditional therapies.

From a psychological position the therapist can offer understanding and support to the individual client. The therapists must confront the men's violence openly and hold them accountable for their actions, and yet at the same time try to make these actions psychologically meaningful to each particular man. The therapists' way of not supporting and deconstructing the clients' victim positioning seems to be a clear consequence of how the institutional task is defined in this kind of 'specialised violence work'. The challenge is to offer a client position based on a more responsible stance without invalidating the clients' experiences.

Note

1   This research is funded by the Academy of Finland within the scope of a research project, 'Why men batter their partners – a narrative and discourse analytic study'. We thank Juha Holma, Aarno Laitila and the staff at the Mobile Crisis Center.

PART III

Client Work
in Professional Contexts

9

Trafficking in Meaning

Constructive Social Work in Child Protection Practice

Ah Hin Teoh, Jim Laffer, Nigel Parton and Andrew Turnell

We thought long and hard how to present this chapter, conscious that it is quite different in style and presentation from the others in this book. However, we all felt that by offering our material in the form of our four stories we were best able to capture and represent what we wanted to say. It is to the story rather than its analysis that we want to give priority.

Ah Hin is a Chinese Malaysian man whose brother came to Perth (Western Australia) in 1980, formed a relationship with an Australian woman and they had three children. His brother committed suicide in 1987 due to the shame he felt about his family life and his belief that the youngest was not his child. In Chinese culture these circumstances suggest the next brother should take over the responsibilities of the deceased. What follows is Ah Hin's story, an edited version of three hours of taped conversation between Ah Hin and Andrew Turnell.

Ah Hin's story

After my brother's suicide I came to Australia to help my brother's wife re-establish her family. After a few months we got married. Things were good for a while but then went downhill. Things were further complicated because we added two children of our own to the family. I was dependent on my wife; I was on a visitor's visa and not allowed to work or eligible for any kind of assistance. My wife was involved with people using heroin, she was dealing and using, but my commitment was to the children. My wife got busted twice and the second time I went down with her. I was found guilty in 1990 of drug trafficking and sentenced to prison.

Once I was in jail my wife said she couldn't cope any more. She went to the department, they assessed the situation and the children were placed in emergency care. After this the department decided they couldn't return the kids to her, and their Care and Protection (court) application contained 12 pages of allegations against my wife and myself dating from 1984 to 1991. They referred to me as 'the second defendant', called me a drug dealer and said my care of the kids was as bad as the mother's. They also said in about 1984 I'd been involved in ten allegations involving negligence of the children, and teachers reporting bruises on them. Now I didn't exist (in Australia) in 1984. They didn't check their facts and decided that my brother and I were the same person. I guess what made me most angry was that they didn't treat me like the children's father. They treated me like a complete stranger.

Then I had another problem, because the Immigration Department notified me that my application for permanent residency had been refused. At that time I couldn't read or write English. When I spoke to the prison social worker about my problem he just laughed at me and said 'I'm sorry I can't help you'.

The first case conference was held in April 1991; I was excluded from the process, other than to mention that I was incarcerated and likely to be deported. A decision was made to place all the children in residential care. They should at least have sent me a copy of the conference notes automatically but they didn't. I learned that if I didn't request a copy, they'd just ignore me.

(Reading the notes) from this conference I first heard the phrase 'working in the best interests of the children'. I don't like that phrase at all. I was doing research while I was in prison. So I wrote to them: 'Can you clarify what you mean by working in the best interests of the children?' They said they don't have a specific policy. And as far as I can see they were only interested in how they saw things.

About that time I rang the worker in charge of my case and asked to meet her. She was very direct. She said, 'You've committed drug offenses and I don't see why I should help you'. I thought, does that mean that everyone who commits this is not fit to be a parent ever again? This actually happened twice with two different workers. I felt they were not willing to talk sense or to look at the real issues about how we could address the problem, even though I kept hoping each new worker would be more open to me. That's why I took the adversarial approach.

But I still kept requesting that the social workers come and see me in prison before a review or conference. Sometimes they'd turn up and sometimes they wouldn't. When they did turn up they didn't take my view into account at all. They discriminated against me, they simply had the view that I was a big drug dealer and they weren't open-minded enough to find out what sort of care I had given to the children. I know this from reading their reports and case notes. Also they always used my immigration status against me. I asked them for help and they said, 'We are not in a position to support your immigration application'. They thought I wanted to use the children so that I could remain in Australia. There was one worker who had a different attitude to the others. She questioned the department about why they didn't support my application to the Immigration Department. She wrote to the Immigration Department and outlined the important role I could play in the family.

I also asked for weekly access to the children to maintain our relationship. They refused, saying they didn't have the resources, that it would cost $75 per visit for the transport. So I arranged for someone that was willing to bring them to the prison, and then the story changed. I was told 'the children have other commitments'. With all my asking, eventually they gave me access every three weeks.

About the end of 1991 my wife went to prison for more drug offences. After 10 months she was released and the department made a two-week trial to return the children to her. They gave her all sorts of support but the trial didn't succeed. So they decided to hold a case conference, aiming to place the children in permanent foster care, I requested to attend that one personally. I asked the welfare department to help me with the prison authorities. They said, 'No, that's up to the prison'. As far as I was concerned they were simply saying, 'We don't want you here'.

Anyway, after that I asked to be linked up by a teleconference. The prison authority granted that and set it up. In the conference I said, 'I disagree with your plan to place my children in permanent care. You don't know when I'm going to be released from prison, do you? I know that my residence status is uncertain but either way I want to care for my children. I want you to leave it open.' They said, 'We'll take that into consideration', but what sort of consideration they give it, who knows. I was saying, 'OK, my life is uncertain, so can we come up with some plan to accommodate that uncertainty?' But I won a little bit because the children didn't go into permanent foster care.

Then the next worse thing happened. They said, 'We're sorry we can no longer bring your children to visit you in prison', even though the visits were in the conference plans. The prison decided to have random strip searches because someone overdosed. The department used that to say, 'We're not going to jeopardise the children's wellbeing like that'. I had a long fight about this, writing to the Minister for Justice, the Welfare Minister and so on. What annoyed me most was that the department was supposed to want me to see the children but they never tried to help me sort this out. That went on for more than three months and I didn't see my children again until I got out.

When I was released, after two years and nine months, I had no money and nowhere to go. I'd decided not to get involved with my wife again so I contacted a Christian activist, Peter Stewart. He immediately invited me to stay with his family. I was very touched that someone like him who hardly knew me offered me his family home to share. He became the core of the network of my support group.

Then I contacted the worker. I will never forget how shocked she was: 'Are you out already?', I said 'Yes I'm out, can you believe that? But I haven't seen the children for three months, when can I see them?' She was reluctant, saying, 'You would upset the process we have in place.' She told me I should contact the residential care agency worker. The residential worker told me that I shouldn't let the children know I was out because they might be upset. To me her real worry was whether my presence would make things harder for her and the cottage parents. So I held my breath. I said 'I'll wait.' I got to see them eight days later.

It was a very emotional visit. I had to control myself because I was always very concerned about how the supervisor was going to view me. I had in mind if I am not controlling myself emotionally then they could use that to say he's not stable, mentally or psychologically. It was very hard. I was afraid that the children might reject me because from their point of view it's like 'How come we've not seen dad for three months?'. I don't know if someone explained to them why suddenly the prison visits stopped.

The visits were a big disruption to the cottage parents. The residential institution was very defensive and hostile towards me. The direct carers felt threatened by me because after four-and-a-half years, they had developed a close relationship with my children.

I felt that the department and the residential home saw me as a useless person, just out of prison. They had decided I was some sort of Asian drug lord criminal, but they were not going to come out and say it openly, instead they hid behind talking about 'the best interests of the children'. They were scared I was using my children to stay in the country and that feeling of theirs messed everything up, but we could never get to talk about it. It always felt like they had a hidden agenda because they'd get me to do one thing, then they wouldn't be certain that that was enough so they'd come up with another thing. And they were really creative in a way because they would try to find something impossible for me to achieve. To me that was not in the children's best interests, because they were working towards nothing, towards the hope that I fail.

Sometimes when I asked for support they would actually say they had tried that already with my ex-wife, it failed and the kids were disappointed. So in that I was seen as the same as her, they were not seeing me as a different person.

I had to rely on people's generosity and gifts, it was the only way I could survive, I had to borrow cars or get lifts and that meant others had to fit around my schedule and the department's arrangements for me. The department did increase my access over time, up to twice a week, because I kept asking, but they didn't help me to get there. Funnily enough, sometimes as they saw me jump all their hurdles they would say to me, 'Actually we're doing this to help you, you're only just out from prison you have to have a chance to get yourself settled in society again'.

After all this, about 14 months, it seemed like they ran out of ideas. So they passed the whole thing to someone from their head office, who'd worked for the department for many years. He was going to chair a new case conference.

He talked to all the children and he went through all the files. He interviewed me and the people supporting me and talked to my lawyer, particularly about the immigration issue. I think he also talked to the immigration department. He talked to my ex-wife and to the residential institution people. He talked to everyone involved in the case. I think he came with a clear mind, and looked at the situation afresh and started to work from there. He actually asked, 'Are we seriously working towards the best interests of the children?' He stipulated that we would be reunited, and that the immigration issue was a separate matter. He said the department could not rely on someone else's decision before it made its move.

In the end the worker I'd been involved with since I got out took her own view on things more, she did back me up and that took courage on her part. I think she hadn't come across someone so determined. When the kids did come back to me the department organized a house for me near the children's school, and they also provided me with income equal to supporting parent benefit until I finally won my fight with Immigration (see Austlii 2001). But it was never easy between the department and me because we'd been in this fight for so long.

I've had the children with me now for over six years. It's tough sometimes, particularly at the beginning, because we'd been apart so long, but I know I did the right thing fighting so hard to get them back.

Jim's story

I am a middle-aged social worker who has had an interesting but not particularly illustrious career in the Western Australian child welfare department. At the time of this episode I was working in head office on various policy initiatives including updating case conference guidelines. When asked to chair the Teoh case conference I could hardly refuse an opportunity to put the 'guidelines' into practice.

The case was highly political as Ah Hin had a powerful support group which opposed the department's plans for the children. At the same time the residential child care agency who were accommodating the children had expressed strong opinions opposing Ah Hin's efforts to reunite with his children. Realizing there were clearly defined and opposing views, I decided the process must be ethical and fair to all concerned.

What I brought to the conference were skills, albeit a bit dulled by head office; experience a-plenty; an awareness of departmental resources and a certain bloody-mindedness. I think it important to hear the voices of the participants: the children; department and residential agency staff; blood relatives; and the support group. Experience suggests reading the source material is imperative, as front-line workers, for whom time is of the essence, tend to rely heavily upon the representation of previous representations. I see the focus of my bloody-mindedness is to be true to the voices and not to be dissuaded by the power and language of the profession or by organizational defensiveness.

Upon reading the file, two things became evident. First, a worker had misread a 1989 police statement that said 'Mr Teoh was the only person in the household who showed any semblance of care for the children' and wrote instead that the police had found that Ah Hin was 'unable to care for the children'. This misreading had been continually quoted and repeated as independent and vital proof of Ah Hin's parental inadequacy and evidence to support the department's case.

Second, the files showed the manner in which value judgements of staff became inculcated in the 'case culture' and in the views and writing of other workers. Thus it became conventional wisdom that Ah Hin was using the children as a vehicle to stay in Australia. It was a crucial task for me to sift fact from opinion and to ensure the clear separation of the two. That Ah Hin was a convicted drug trafficker added extra spice to the tale. One of Ah Hin's disarming characteristics was his insight into the concerns the department had about his parenting and character, and yet he still sought help from those authorities that opposed his aspirations – this was actually seen by most departmental staff as a clever manipulation on his part.

Ah Hin's support group comprised social rights activists who uncondi-tionally championed his cause. I met with them twice. I attempted to establish my credentials as an 'honest broker' who was of independent mind and could be trusted. I also met with the children, their mother, their carers and the social worker from the residential agency. Again, it was essential to confirm the view that all players would be engaged and their positions con-sidered. Having established my credentials with all players and determined their views, the main task was to manage the case conference to provide maximum benefit for the children. The children were my primary clients and their well-being was my first concern. This perhaps is one of the paradoxes of child welfare work since claiming to act in 'the best interests of the child' is so often the first refuge of defensive practice. Trying to avoid the high moral ground, I was none the less focusing on and listening to the children as my primary method for organizing my decisions.

A difficult task of this conference was to manage the juxtaposed views of participants, particularly since there was a deal of antipathy. In my experi-ence there is a fine line between allowing all parties an opportunity to express themselves and anarchy. Further, to expose the children to what is an impersonal if not depersonalizing intellectual debate (objectification is almost inevitable) arguably creates powerlessness, alienation and confirms a view – often expressed by the 'subjects' of a conference – of being pawns in an adult game.

The conference became the culmination of the review process. There were to be no surprises. The family and supporters were provided with an opportunity to express their views, to participate and then to withdraw. The children had the right to attend the conference in its entirety and did so until they became bored. In the final analysis the decision to place the children with Ah Hin was not too difficult. The children wished to be with their father; there was evidence of the negative impact of their institutionalization and it was clear Ah Hin had a desire to care for the children. Finally, there was no compelling information or evidence that suggested the children would be harmed by the move. The alternatives were either long-term institutional care or a decision to leave them in limbo until such time as there was clarification of Ah Hin's overseas conviction and his Australian residency status. Both of these issues had the potential to drag on interminably and to forestall a decision on the basis that either was giving in to an overly defensive notion of managing the risks of this case.

However, the culture of defensiveness raised its indomitable head again when a senior officer attempted to intervene and impose an embargo on the return of the children until Ah Hin's Malaysian 'criminal' record was clarified. I knew, and so did the department, that clarification was almost impossible, but such a simple and arguably defensible act would be difficult to challenge and could sabotage any attempt to place the children with Ah Hin.

To me this was evidence of the old child welfare maxim, 'the standards of return are always higher than standards of removal'. In my view there was no substantive basis on which to criticize Ah Hin's parenting, particularly once the reality of the initial police statement came to light. Many people who have criminal convictions care for their children, as do parents whose residency status is indeterminate. It also seemed to me that if Ah Hin had somehow taken up the care of his children upon release from prison my department would not have been considering an investigation, let alone removal. Thinking this way, combined with the process I had undertaken and the children's expressed wishes, led me to my decision of reunification. To undertake such a process and make such a decision required in my view a measure of courage to confront the biases, prejudices and the conservatism of the organization. My guess is that any half-decent social worker could achieve the same results on a good day.

Although departmental staff and the residential child care agency objected to my decision, it was a rearguard action, based upon their notions of the children's long-term best interests coloured by the longstanding negative sentiment towards their father. However, when it became obvious the decision would not be reversed, all parties worked collaboratively towards implementation.

It might seem that the front-line social workers and the residential child care facility were intractable. I do not believe this to be the case but simply they could not see the bush for the trees – a position I have been in all to often. Also, the department had had several 'duty of care' scares, combined with a renewed interest in 'risk management'; these undoubtedly contributed to conservative practice. In my view the key elements for good child welfare practice remain: an enthusiasm for the task; the pursuit of source material whether it be written or human; listening but not relying upon the opinion of others and, finally, confronting the biases, prejudices and the conservatism of organizations.

I understand the return of the children has been successful and this provides me with some gratification. It is not often that I get things pretty well right.

Andrew's story

I had been a social worker for 13 years when I first met Ah Hin in 1995. At the time, I was actively involved, as I still am, in child protection work as a family therapist and also in the development of a safety-focused, partnership-based practice framework with front-line statutory workers (see Turnell and Edwards 1999). Ah Hin was never my client, rather I was part of his support group. Peter and Maria Stewart were the key organizers of this support group and were also friends of mine. They knew of my child protection experience and brought Ah Hin to meet me. This placed me in an awkward situation. At that particular time I was working closely with Ah Hin's caseworker in the developmental work I was leading. I knew from the caseworker that she and others in the department felt threatened and worried by the involvement of such strong activists, and some felt that Ah Hin was skilfully manipulating his supporters. When I declared my connections to both the department worker and to Ah Hin this created a little unease in both directions.

The efforts of the support group were extensive and included providing accommodation for Ah Hin, supervising access, and providing transport and financial help, as well as lobbying politicians and any others who might have influence. The group also found a lawyer, who worked *pro bono* to fight Ah Hin's immigration case – which ultimately was heard in his favour in the Australian High Court.

My main input was to provide 'tactical' advice, and I suggested the support group tone down their level and style of opposition as it seemed to me it was escalating the department's defensiveness. Ah Hin in particular was very mindful of the need to maintain pressure but also be able to work with the caseworker. Fortuitously, the efforts of the support group had led to the situation where Jim Laffer was to undertake a review process. I knew Jim fairly well and suggested in the strongest terms to Ah Hin and the support group that Jim was open-minded and would review the case fairly and justly. I crossed my fingers and hoped that this would prove to be the case.

There are many stories that could be told but several subsequent events stand out for me. Once Jim had decided Ah Hin and the children would be reunited he informed everyone in advance of the case conference. I was present with two other members of the support group when Jim told Ah Hin his plans. Before finishing the meeting, however, Jim asked to speak to we three supporters while Ah Hin waited outside. Jim told the three of us that many in the department viewed Ah Hin very bleakly, but part of the reason he had decided to return the children was because of the integrity of those of us supporting him. Jim then said that he wanted us to continue to support Ah Hin since the hardest work lay ahead, given these children had been institutionalized for almost five years. Finally Jim commented that if the reunification failed he would not blame Ah Hin, rather he would want to talk to us. Suitably excited and challenged, we left the meeting. I have observed in my work and writing that good child protection work involves skilful use of authority; I had witnessed that first hand in this meeting.

Jim also acted as a catalyst for another outcome. Jim had commented to Ah Hin that his experience should be written up so others could learn from it. Ah Hin was immediately enthusiastic and it certainly interested me to enable professionals to hear the voice of service recipients. However, I suggested that going public was a task for the future, first the family needed to be reunited and stabilized, and this would better establish Ah Hin's credibility to tell the story. Two years later Ah Hin and I started to prepare his story and I supported Ah Hin to present it at the Australasian Conference on Child Abuse and Neglect held in Perth in 1999. Subsequently, Family and Children's Services invited Ah Hin to come and present his story at its head office. Many of the caseworkers who had been involved with Ah Hin heard one of these presentations. I know for some of the workers this was a challenging experience, but it was also a very productive process in revisiting the issues and bringing some closure to a very high-profile case in our community. The memory of Ah Hin presenting in the main lecture theatre of Family and Children's Services head office, with his mother and sister alongside him, to an audience of forty or fifty including a director and many other senior staff, is an image I will never forget. A remarkable turnaround from Ah Hin's circumstances five years previous.

When I first met Ah Hin I was open to him, but I also wondered about his story. I have known Ah Hin now for seven years and, like all of us who supported him, I have marvelled at his strength and calm determination in the circumstances he endured. Sharing Ah Hin's journey has been a powerful experience for me: I have seen professional child protection behaviour through the eyes of someone on the receiving end.

Nigel's Story

I first met Jim Laffer in November 1995 when I was invited to Western Australia to discuss some of the changes then being introduced by the Department of Family and Children's Services, and subsequently met Andrew Turnell at the 1999 Australasian Child Abuse Conference where he and Ah Hin first presented their paper. I have spent much time with both Andrew and Jim since our first meetings. In November 2000 Andrew introduced me to Ah Hin and the four of us met up to discuss and plan this chapter. I was very interested in what all had to say in that it seemed a very optimistic and hopeful story, in which, against many odds, some very positive developments had happened. Not only did it seem to be a very powerful representation of 'the human spirit', it also seemed to capture many of the elements I had been trying to illustrate with Patrick O'Byrne in *Constructive Social Work Towards a New Practice* (Parton and O'Byrne 2000) and which had been published a few months previously. Before I say more about that I would just like to underline some themes evident in the three earlier stories that have potentially wide resonance with other chapters in the book.

The importance of the written records, reports and files are crucial to the way 'cases' are constructed. After a while a file takes on a life of its own, and it can be very difficult to question what it appears to represent. Jim Laffer spent much time deconstructing the files. He argues that it became clear that in this case a worker had misread a police statement from 1989, but that this (mis)representation was regarded by the department as independent and vital proof of Ah Hin's inadequacy and was provided as evidence to support the department's case in respect of the future care of the children. The key thing is not whether this is 'true' or not. What it does do is to dramatically shift the way Ah Hin was characterized and categorized while at the same time undermining a whole variety of different assumptions which had seemed to underpin the way the department was handling the case. The latter was reinforced when Jim argues that the files show the manner in which judgements of staff become inculcated into the case culture and became reflected in the views and writing of other workers. In this way it became conventional wisdom that Ah Hin was using the children as a vehicle to stay in Australia. He was characterized as jailed and criminal; an Asian drug lord; an illegal immigrant; a man unable to care for his children who was manipulating them to get residency in his new country. When someone is categorized by such negative characteristics it becomes very difficult for that person to behave in ways that might be perceived in anything other than a negative light. This reflects a more general tendency that once judgements have been made, subsequent information and developments are invariably organized to confirm these original assessments. It is also apparent that Ah Hin felt dehumanized, marginalized, misunderstood and continually ignored.

As already suggested, however, I found the stories fascinating exemplars of some of the characteristics that we have come to associate with constructive social work in practice. The term 'constructive social work', when it was first coined (Parton and O'Byrne 2000) had been chosen for two reasons. First, 'constructive' was chosen to reflect the wish to try to provide a perspective that was explicitly positive in building on what is distinctive about social work and what could be seen as its major strengths. While the term is used metaphorically, it was important not to lose its literal meaning, for the core idea of construction from the Latin to the present day is that of building or putting together. The notion of 'constructive' was meant to reflect a positive approach both to social work and towards the users of services. The *Oxford English Dictionary* defines 'construction' as 'the action or manner of construction', while 'constructive' is defined as 'having a useful purpose; helpful'.

Second, the term 'constructive social work' was chosen to reflect the more theoretical concerns associated with social constructionist, narrative and postmodern theoretical developments. In such perspectives an understanding of language, listening, talk and meaning are seen as central. The idea of understanding as a collaborative process is a core one in social constructionism. Constructive social work emphasizes process, plurality of both knowledge and voice, possibility and the relational quality of knowledge. In doing so constructive social work is concerned with the collaborative narratives of solutions to problems. Instead of providing the practitioner with information about the causes of problems, so that he or she can make an expert assessment and prescribe a 'scientific' solution, the service user is encouraged to tell their story of the problem in a way that externalizes it, giving more control and agency in creating a new perspective on how to manage or overcome it.

Constructive social work is not simply concerned with deconstruction but with reconstruction and the ability to work with a multiplicity of voices in a context of ambiguity, uncertainty and complexity. In doing so, it is argued, practitioners should not see themselves as the experts in problems and should be clear about the boundaries of their knowledge. The primary expertise for understanding and solving problems lies with the users of services.

These are many of the qualities and characteristics which I felt were reflected in the stories outlined by Ah Hin, Andrew and, particularly, Jim. Jim's contributions seemed to capture some of these key elements in terms of:

- listening to a range of different voices and being able to hold multiple stories including going back to written source material via the files

- attempting to 'review' (in the sense of viewing again) rather than blame, and being compassionate for different positions, including those of the different social workers and residential care staff

- being able to negotiate or to try to find new understandings or solutions

- limiting the focus on blame, analysing causes and/or determining who is right or wrong and, rather, concentrating on the present and what might be done in the future

- being willing to make judgements and exercise authority but in a way which attempts to be as transparent as possible and, crucially, tries to be serious about taking the views of the children themselves into account

- judgements and authority, however, being situated rather than seen as being absolute and totalized and thus reified and beyond negotiation. Barbara Herrnstein Smith (1997 p.4) makes the case for 'non-objectivist judgements'. While Jim is quite clear about his responsibility to make judgements, he attempts to situate these within the particular circumstances of the case

- not taking himself or his judgements too seriously and not seeing them as set in stone. There is a sense of humility about what he thinks and what he knows and a recognition that while one might get it right sometimes this might be as much to do with contingency as being an expert

- the style of practice seeming to demonstrate that knowledge is created interactionally rather than being absolute and given from on high; as a consequence it becomes important to talk with as many stakeholders as possible and canvass their views, and to make the processes involved as overt as possible and in doing so endeavour to keep everyone involved in what is going on and why. It recognizes that knowledge and solutions are generated mutually.

It seems to me that such an approach is affirmative and positive about the possibilities of practice, and while the role of the professional is in many respects understated it also recognizes that normative choices and trying to build practical and political coalitions and collaborations lie at the heart of everyday life and professional practice. In identifying that subject(s) can only be understood in context(s), it recognizes the importance of interdependence and the way social and political cultures in which we live are becoming increasingly relational. Far from being nihilistic or negative, such an approach recognizes that there can be an opening up or widening in the constructability of identities so that it is not so much that persons have to struggle to find meaning within a *mélange* of meaninglessness but that they are placed at the centre of reality, actually constructing and creating reality.

It is in this context that I feel the stories outlined here show how the different authors have tried to bring about change and invent options in ways that make them real. Similarly, the invention of 'constructive social work' can be seen as an explicit attempt to open up the spaces – both practically and conceptually – whereby such possibilities might be realized in other situations in the future.

10

Complicated Gender

Tarja Pösö

Playing around with gender

If truth be told, this chapter began as a bit of play. This play was suggested by social workers in probation work, who took part in a study conducted by us, by recording encounters with their clients and by discussing and analysing transcriptions of them together with the researchers. Our study looked at how clienthood and social problems were constructed in the practices of probation work and, in particular, in face-to-face encounters during the assessment of suitability for community service. At some stage in the discussion, gender was brought up as an interesting topic and, on the suggestion of the social workers, we met for one afternoon to see whether and how gender was visible in the encounters between social workers and their clients. Our discussions were playful in tone, for gender as a theme to be analysed awoke arguments on the conditions under which gender could be identified and with what certainty.

However, this playfulness carried a serious message: in the event, gender could not be identified on the basis of the anticipations and reconnoitring practices most immediately accessible to us. This observation sends me back to examining this discussion in order to analyse the dimensions which position gender in a discussion and thus to examining the possible relations between gender and clienthood in social work.

Starting out from 'doing gender'

Gender is a serious social theme and category. It is seen to place men and women, girls and boys, in differing social positions and as different actors, and to create expectations and norms for gender-consistent behaviour.

For social work as well, gender is a significant topic. Professional social work has become differentiated as paid work mainly carried out by women. Social work as a social and professional institution is encountered by both women and men. Depending on the sector, however, there are great differences as to whether social work is carried out more with men or with women, since gender is also intertwined with circumstances and processes regarded as social problems (e.g. Davis 1985; Farmer and Boushel 1999). In female-dominated social work both workers and clients are women; the male social workers are a minority and mostly seek male-dominated sectors such as work with intoxicant abusers or offenders, or move away from work with clients to administrative tasks.

Even though gender results in differentiation and positioning, it has been very little studied and discussed. In 1992, Hannele Forsberg, Marjo Kuronen and Aino Ritala-Koskinen (Forsberg *et al.* 1992) wrote an exploratory article on feminist social work; at the time they identified only a few existing Finnish texts on social work and gender. After that, the topic of the gender of social problems or the social worker (Granfelt 1999; Petrelius 2002) has been of more interest to research than, for instance, the gendering of client work in social work.[1] This can hardly be considered a Finnish speciality, but even in a broader sense, gender makes only a tangential or occasional part of social work research.

The debate on feminist social work is a notable exception to this. In this context, gender forms the basis of an ideological examination and penetrates the interpretations of social work as regards both the actors and the structures and institutions of social work (e.g. Dominelli and McLeod 1989; Langan and Day 1992; Cavanagh and Cree 1996). To exaggerate a little, one could say that knowing the gender, we know a lot of the situation and opportunities of the client or the social worker. However, social work analysis which combines postmodernity and feminism is not based on an essentialist concept of gender, knowledge and power, but stresses that they are situational and thus pluralist (Rossiter 2000; Fawcett and Featherstone 2000).

Recently, more and more analyses have also been published on the effect of the researcher's gender on knowledge and the way it is constructed in social work research. Jonathan Scourfield from Britain (2001, pp.62–64) and Leo Nyqvist from Finland (2001) analyse their actions and reception as male interviewers. For them, gender was one of the factors guiding the construction of knowledge, even if it did not unambiguously set up certain kinds of interview relationships. Leo Nyqvist (2001, pp.62–65) states that against his original assumptions, his gender did not guarantee that his relationship with the male interviewees would be direct and informative. According to Nyqvist, one explanation could be the topic under research (violence in intimate relationships) defined the research relationship strongly, perhaps even more strongly than the researcher's gender, as a discrete characteristic. Suvi Keskinen (2001), in her turn, considers that, as a researcher of violence in intimate relationships and a woman, she encountered a special set of ethical questions. It was particularly difficult to solve the question of how a researcher, committed to feminism, avoids making use, in the situations which she studied, of the position of women subjugated through violence, in which women were seeking professional help for their problem. In situations of this kind the relationship between the researcher and the subject is not unidirectional, nor is it the only relationship eventually involving power or exploitation.

Even though gender is a serious topic in the contexts of society, social work or research policy, one can also see it as a category to be constructed, thus not only as social characteristics, significances and destinies accumulating on a biological base. Gender is constructed through behaviour and speech patterns, facial expressions, gestures and styles which we begin to learn during the early stages of socialization and uphold continuously throughout our lives (Sipilä 1998). Gender is made, as has been aptly said by Candace West and Donald Zimmermann (1987) among others. The conventions, expectations and norms related to gender can also be broken. A man dressed as a woman and gesturing like a woman is one instance of this. One of the classical texts of ethnomethodology deals precisely with the maintaining of the gender order (Garfinkel 1967, pp.116–185).

This chapter is informed by the thought that gender is something which must be identified as gender. I shall look at the identification of gender in a situation where the social work actors, talking to and with each other, attempt to identify gender in the interaction of a client encounter presented as a written text. The text does not contain the bodies, voices or gestures, held to be so typical of one's gender, and the identification can 'only' proceed on the basis of words and the way the turns are constructed.[2]

Examining the analyses of assessment encounters

The data used in the article is derived from a male-dominated sector of social work: the assessment and implementation of community service in probation work. On a rough estimate, about 90 per cent of the clients are male, as are almost half of the workers in the relevant unit. As mentioned above, at the end of the 1990s the workers participated in a research project which examined the construction of social problems and clienthoods in the practices of client work (e.g. Juhila and Pösö 1999; Jokinen and Suoninen 1999; Jokinen and Suoninen 2000). The data for this article consists of a tape-recording of one joint analysis session. The question presented for discussion was whether the speakers were men, women, or both. The aim was to examine jointly whether an oral – or, in this case, written – encounter can serve as the basis for identifying the genders of the social worker and the client.

The session was arranged in the same way as previous joint analysis meetings: the researchers, Kirsi Juhila and myself, had selected a number of transcribed passages from the recorded client encounters of the social workers, and these were studied by the group. Hoping to be able to examine the issue of gender, we had selected four passages which we assumed would spark off a discussion. In the passages the workers and clients discussed intimate relationships, housing, how to fit in the eventual community service with family obligations; in other words, themes which the workers were expected to address in their report on the client's suitability for community service. The passages represent fairly conventional stretches of conversation. The speakers were not identified and, in addition to first names, other identifying factors immediately linked to gender (such as naming the spouse as either wife or husband) were omitted.

The session was attended by 13 of the 21 workers in the unit and by the two researchers. No roles had been clearly defined in advance. As researchers we strove primarily to elucidate – to present questions when new angles were opened – or to bring balance to the discussion so that everyone could participate.[3] The meeting was very intensive and involved all participants very deeply.

The data describes an oral interpretation of gender in social work, delivered by workers speaking among themselves in an atypical situation. One may ask whether an analysis of this kind has any significance. I claim that it does; I will go as far as to claim that data of this kind can capture very well the meanings which gender may receive in interactive social work. The workers speak not only of the passages selected but also of their experiences and strategies in their work in general, and comment on each other's representations on these issues. In a way, we are dealing with a verbalization of tacit knowledge, although one must remember that the talk is only about things which are recognized as existing. In this particular situation, the playful atmosphere supported the presenting of counter-interpretations, which is why the talk occasionally turned into an argument, thus revealing and making audible many different views.

I would also like to claim that 'client work' detached from the face-to-face encounter, as it was here, presents a new kind of challenge to research and practice. Let us take, for example, the effort to strengthen the expertise in social work by means of various virtual forms of consultation. Even though face-to-face encounters continue to form the core of social work, other ways of 'dealing with the clients' are coming up in parallel. Through the social workers' interpretations, the client's talk is transmitted to other workers for assessment, which may take place in a virtual web environment, for instance. In these cases the issue at stake is generally the client's life situation, so the situation is not the same as in this chapter. However, this is also a case where direct interaction with the client as actor is not present; instead, clienthood is being 'represented', in these cases by the means used by the social workers in their descriptions.

Analysis of the data

Even though the audio recording of the joint analysis provides a rich interactive process,[4] I shall use the data very pragmatically in my analysis. I shall confine myself to a thematic analysis. My first question to the data is, how were men and women identified? Second, I shall ask what things were linked with the gender, i.e. what facts were used in constructing the assumption of whether the actor was a man or a woman. The third and last theme is to read the data through the question of what the many uncertainties of identification mentioned above were linked with. I have selected passages from the transcribed discussion which, according to my interpretation, are linked with these themes.

I read gender as a complex and multiple issue. This is an understanding of gender which has been called for in social work by Sven-Axel Månsson (2000) and Margareta Hyden (2000), among others. In my data, complexity and multiplicity are revealed in that gender is situated expressly in the interaction and the collaboration constructed between the worker and the client.

As far as this goes, the definition of clienthood is interactive, as can be seen from the following.

How were women and men identified?

In general the participants took their time identifying the gender of the speaker in a text documenting the worker–client interaction. Especially at the beginning of the joint analysis session, many workers rapidly claimed this speaker to be a woman or that to be a man, but others would claim otherwise. The workers suggested many codes for identification, but another participant would contradict them. As the discussion proceeded, the ease of identification became less clear cut, and towards the end almost all workers were reserved in their opinions on gender identification. Since the participants had different assumptions on the gender of the actors in the passages, the group adopted the suggestion of one of the workers and voted for the genders of the client and the worker in each case. The votes were never unanimous, which was one reason why as a rule they did not lead to the correct alternative.

In one case only was the client's gender identified during a brief discussion, after which it was felt to be absolutely certain (thus, no one contradicted the opinion) – and it was proved correct. The identification was easy because of the single sentence 'looks like you[5] got busy at once', which the social workers felt could only be addressed to a man. There were attempts to come up with an alternative that could be said to a woman in a similar situation, but this expression was felt to be impossible in speaking to a woman. The expression 'looks like you got busy at once' was linked to sexuality and directly to biological reproduction, so in that sense it was linked to the active role of a man. The worker used the words when talking about the caring for a small baby. The baby had been born about nine months after the client came out of prison. Other sets of codes, such as those linked to child care or the support systems for it, were clearly more ambiguous as regards gender identification than was this sentence, which was interpreted as referring to the biological conception of the child.

What type of man, what type of woman?

I asked the data about the things which were linked with gender, in other words what factors served as the basis for the assumption of the actor's gender? For the analysis, this meant that I looked for the descriptions presented by the workers as supporting evidence for their guesses during the discussion. These justifications were required by the other workers and, at times, by the researchers as well. The following things were presented as reasons for choosing a gender.

1. *Female client:*

- when speaking of her life, highlights particularly events related to relationships (such as moving in with partner)
- speaks of emotions (and/or continues the emotionally charged talk started by the worker)
- commits certain types of offences.

2. *Male client:*

- speaks objectively, clearly regulates the level of personality
- does not speak a lot
- commits certain types of offences.

3. *Female social worker:*

- speaks of happiness and other emotions
- speaks more easily of love, children and other relationships than a man would, especially with female clients
- uses certain methods, such as solution-oriented, to orient the work, more often than a male worker.

4. *Male social worker:*

- speaks less than a woman would
- speaks in a more objective manner and uses more objective words than a woman.

These were characteristics which came up in the discussion: some participants may have shared them, but they were again contradicted because they were not felt to be universal.

To identify the client's gender there was an interesting discussion on a topic essential for probation work, i.e. crime and criminality, which proved that such things as categories of offence – which in themselves are generally fairly well segregated according to gender – do not provide criteria for identifying the gender. On this topic there was a discussion in which a female worker described why she thought the client speaker to be a man. As the basis of the discussion, a passage was pointed out in the original worker–client encounter in which the social worker says the following to the client.

> At this stage we could take a look at your criminal record here, which is a document which we always request when community service is contemplated, to see what it contains. And it's got your data for ten years, you've got theft, vandalism. And you've got a conditional sentence for that. Then the next entries are from early 1996, that's drunken driving, driving without a licence, such things. Then you've got…breach of peace at domicile, mugging, and there's even an attempted manslaughter. So these are what took you to prison. And then, then you came out in February…

The passage generated the following discussion among the workers.

Extract 10.1.1

(FSW1 = female social worker 1, MSW1 = male social worker 1, FSW2 = female social worker 2)

FSW1: I deduced from the form that it'd be a man.

MSW1: Well yes, sharp instrument and… Women do use sharp instruments.

FSW1: Yes, but then…since there were several.

FSW2: But women often have that, attempted manslaughter. So generally you couldn't get by with less.

The discussion continues and moves on to other themes, but then comes back to the extract from the Criminal Records.

Extract 10.1.2

(MSW2 = male social worker 2, MSW3 = male social worker 3)

MSW2: The form shows that the interviewee at least is a man.

MSW3: It could be a girl now.

And again, later.

Extract 10.1.3

(R = researcher, MSW = male social worker, FSW2 = female social worker 2)

R: Most of you bring up this that the client has a lot of form. This list that is given here is a masculine one.

MSW: You're accustomed to thinking of it like that since there are so few women.

FSW2: And then since there are theft, vandalism, and then drunken driving and driving without a licence, so this just shows that it can be a woman too.

Once more, the extract from the Criminal Records comes up when the talk turns to the interview perhaps having been conducted in prison, which in itself was assumed to affect the interview talk. At that point one of the male workers deduces that on the basis of the extract the client would have been placed in the Riihimäki prison, which only takes men.

The positioning of gender on the basis of offences committed shows how difficult it is to use facts known as general rules in social work. On the individual level there is always the possibility of an exception to the rule, which is why the knowledge must be constructed case by case. Positioning the speaker's gender on the basis of what is said makes no exception to this.

What were the uncertainties in identification linked with?

To answer the question of the speaker's gender, the social workers explored replies following the essentialist gender interpretation but, as has been noted, these did not work. The explorations were generally contradicted by the fact that in an individual interactive situation a given fact may work in a different manner. The workers read the data as interactive data in which the discussion was guided by the worker's attempt to construct a well-functioning interaction. That in its turn was seen as an essential requirement for achieving the actual task, a report on the suitability for community service. This could be called a strongly interactive gender interpretation.

The interactivity emphasized by the workers was primarily manifested in three ways. First, the workers stressed that a smooth interaction is so important that, to safeguard it, you can play around with gender in the interaction (I shall return to this later). Second, they stressed the location of the assessment interview. This refers to the discussions on whether the interview was conducted in the probation office or in prison. The latter was assumed to change the way in which men in particular speak. In prison, speaking of interpersonal relationships is possible in a way which is not possible outside it. This is why it was more difficult to identify gender in interviews made in prison as opposed to the probation office. Thus, location broke the universally acknowledged gender code of the speech pattern. Third, the workers referred to the client's age. They said that young clients talked in a way which was different from older clients, among other things because different things would come up. With young men, they would speak more like with women, but not in the way that they would talk to older men. The combination of age and gender was primarily considered to change the way in which the worker acted.

The interactively constructed gender interpretation was discussed intensively in a situation where the participants felt that the assessment interview did not proceed smoothly. In general, the safeguarding of a smooth interaction came up as important for the worker's action. There were many references to the fact that the worker is prepared to 'stretch' his or her way of speaking in order to get the ball rolling. Concerning the episode under discussion, the workers felt that the stretching 'had gone too far'. They considered that the worker had used humour as a means of stretching. This did not work; in other words, it was interpreted as having failed to carry the interaction forward. During the joint analysis the explanation was gradually constructed that the worker was using a humorous manner of speaking which was unfamiliar to his or her gender.

In the recorded episode the worker leads the talk on to the family situation. The client is married. On hearing this, the worker asks about children. After the children have been discussed the worker asks, 'Were you ever married before?' This leads to the following.

Extract 10.2

(C = client, SW = social worker)

C: No.

SW: So now you've found the right one and are going to hold on to it?

C: Yes.

SW: Well are you two happy?

C: Yes.

SW: Well I just thought, seeing the way you talk.

C: But see you should ask see this if you ask me whether we're happy then I'm not the best person to answer for (the other) I can only speak for myself.

SW: That's true. I already noticed, that was last time, that you are pretty smart that way, but right now you're the only person I can ask.

C: Yes.

SW: Besides I'm not asking you about it so I could write it down here.

C: Hmm.

SW: But simply because I want to ask, I always like to see people happy, well, but I suppose what you could do is ask about it sometime.

C: Hmm.

SW: Because you already know?

C: No need to ask. You can see it in (the other's) face.

SW: Well that's true. What I was thinking, I thought of course it is important for you, but for me it's just something extra, sort of all right. What about the family situation otherwise? Are there, how should I put it, I mean your mother and father, do you have contact with them?

C: Hmm.

SW: Have you got many siblings?

C: Hmm.

In the social workers' discussion, this episode was felt to be going nowhere: the client gives up answering, the worker is floundering about, he or she explains the questions and yet fails to elicit a response. The workers described the collaboration as a dance, a waltz which either works or does not work. The metaphor is based on dance, which is what Eero Suoninen (2000), for instance, has used in describing the interactive processes of helping on the basis of a detailed analysis of empirical data. According to him, the dance metaphor stresses the fact that interaction is always about a joint production which requires a genuine participation. Dances come in different styles, and this is why speaking of styles of dance in analysing interaction refers to our understanding of what the interaction is about and what the interactive framework observed 'here and now' is (Suoninen 2000, p.70).

The awkwardness of the dance generated a long discussion during the joint session. The opinions all come back to the fact that the worker acts – above all, uses humour – in a manner which is not consistent with his or her gender. Striving for a smooth interaction, he or she tries to use masculine humour and language, and fails because the client does not like the worker's humour.

Extract 10.3

(FSW1 = female social worker 1, MSW1 = male social worker 1, R1 = researcher 1, FSW2 = female social worker 2, MSW2 = male social worker 2, R2 = researcher 2, MSW3 = male social worker 3, MSW4 = male social worker 4)

FSW1: Well I started out thinking it's two men but then I thought that this being the beginning then maybe it's a woman trying to woo the man and then sort of changing tack when it is not working. In the beginning she's trying to be like the man.

MSW1: I have the opinion, although I don't know this field much at all, but isn't all of this community masculine, so as far as I see it couldn't women just use the same method, even though I am of the opinion that there are no women here.

R1:   Or then it could be a bit of humour or something, I mean consciously using it even if you don't approve of it personally, but it can also be used for this type of.

FSW2: Now that's true. I think, I've been told at home that my language has gotten much worse, that my humour is different, I use stronger language, so that is what happens, I've noticed it in myself.

MSW2: So what was it that you wanted to say?

FSW1: Well I just started to say but got side-tracked, that I kept thinking that it's two men, but then I began to think that maybe it could still be a woman who is just trying to talk a bit like a man, to establish contact in that way.

R2:   In that sense the waltz metaphor is very good, I think, because everybody here has somehow identified this humour as masculine, meaning there is something here that is linked to how men talk with one another, but do we have here, is this worker a woman.

MSW2: Did you say that it's a woman?

R2:   Oh yes, it is.

MSW2 Do you mean really? How many of us thought that? But of course afterwards when you learn this, then that sort of explains why it fails, why it's so awkward, because it sort of falls down flat. At first it sort of goes, but...

MSW 2: So the role is not played all that successfully. Of course, the role is all right, but... You're funny people, you women. Meaning you can simply take up a man's role just like that.

MSW 4: But that's, this could work somehow, I mean this is exactly the kind of situation that could come up just as easily in a man/woman situation. I mean if you start constructing something which is not that familiar to you, you start from the assumption that this is what you should do and you're not familiar with it, your client will spot it at once.

This discussion continues at several other instances. The themes that emerged included not only the interaction between the worker and the client in the passage but also the changes in the worker's speech during the encounter and partly also the relationships between the workers. There was an interesting overlapping discussion on behaviour according to essentialist gender (especially as regards the worker's gender) and the interactive interpretation of gender. Gender can be played around with during interaction, but the play is only justified when it works. If the worker receives no response for the action (speech) which goes counter to his or her biological sex, they must return to a manner of speech compatible with it. The client and the client's reactions are the determining factor here. It is the worker's duty to be sensitive to the client's reactions. This is the strong norm which is used to specify gender in this data.

The many 'But' questions

As Sven-Axel Månsson (2000) calls for social workers to understand gender as a complex and multiple issue, he takes up a position which protests against categorizing clienthood on the basis of gender. There does not exist a category of girl clients, for example. There are always 'only' girls, and in certain situations each of them is something more and something less than the category which is constructed by assuming something on the relationships between girlhood and clienthood as such. Thus, the perspective on gender is pragmatic and situational. Complexity and multiplicity are manifested in this data so that gender is positioned expressly in the interaction and the collaboration constructed between the worker and the client. To this degree, the definition of clienthood is strongly interactive, and the meanings and contents of gender vary with it.

The data describe an oral interpretation of gender in social work constructed between workers in an atypical situation. In the context of the data passages the workers speak of their experiences in general and their work strategies, and comment on each other's representations on these things. This may contain a lot of idealized descriptions of how workers or clients act, but ideal descriptions have always been a part of talk on social work. However, one must be cautious as to how widely an image of social work emphasizing the smoothness of interaction corresponds to social work in general. The primary data for this study was collected for the purposes of a report about the client's suitablity for community service. It follows a form which needs to be filled in with data elicited from the client, and at the end the worker must present his or her assessment of the client's suitability. Detailed and truthful entries are in the interest of both the client and the worker, which is why it is evident that they both strive for a synchronized interaction. In probationary supervision or in problems encountered during community services, the basic set-up could be very different – not to mention interventions in child protection, generally charged with many oppositional critical concerns.

Thus, gender is fragmented in a way which shares many views with the gender interpretation regarded as postmodern (e.g. Butler 1990). This observation is strongly linked with the data used: the positioning of gender was attempted with a text, and the corporeality of the actors was present only as far as it was manifested in the speech. Speech itself is not gender-marked, as is stated by Tainio (2001), although speech situations may be (Coates and Cameron 1988). The uncertainty experienced by the social workers and their exploratory behaviour and emphasis on interaction would seem to support the view that corporeality is an important dimension in identifying gender. The body mostly fixes the gender identification as more or less certain. The social workers seem to speak for the fact that the body is given a strong significance.

Suvi Ronkainen (1999) criticizes the gender interpretations considered postmodern and constructionist for the fact that, due to their emphases, they come to construct a repeated freedom of opting for a gender or a given gender representation. This simultaneously leads to a Utopian freedom of opting out from gender. She writes:

> Is it possible to commit acts without them having any links with the corporeal I or the I in general? Can you de-select your previous selections? If

you think of performativity as an activity of the corporeal subject, we are not dealing only with innocent play, but a play where the markers are already determined and where we receive significations on the basis of rules which we ourselves do not govern. Performance is more than performance, but less than a destiny. (p.66)

The fact that, in this data, the links between gender and clienthood proved complex and multi-dimensional gives rise to several questions. Of primary importance is the tension inherent in the issue of how situational and, so to say, case-specific clienthoods and genders are. On the basis of this analysis, ought we to think that such gendered social positions as care and maintenance obligations, and low pay, are not visible in the clienthoods constructed in social work encounters? Or if, in the domain of male-dominated crime and violence, the deed itself cannot be used to predict gender, does this mean that the relationships between gender, violence and crime are not actualized in social work? In each client encounter, do we select the freedom to interpret gender and its social meanings and impacts?

My proposal is that the relationships between gender, clienthood and social work should be studied on the basis of practice, more than has been done so far. This is the clearest view which I consider myself able to present on the basis of this analysis. We need more information on how the different institutional situations in social work and the researcher's different data sets and analysis methods create a picture of the relationships between the phenomena mentioned. This is particularly important and topical because the observance of the gendering of social problems has strengthened the creation of social work programmes directed specifically to either gender. This is true, for instance, of violence in close relationships. Thus, at the moment, it is important to ask what kind of masculinities – or, correspondingly, femininities – are being constructed in men- or women-specific social work programmes (Nyqvist 2001) and in which contexts does gender come secondary to some other dimension. In my opinion, the ideological angle must be paralleled by an angle which provides an empirical analysis of practices and thus provides resources for these practices. For social constructionism, this creates the challenge of specifying how it is possible to speak of gender, clienthood and social work in a way which transmits both the generation of universal categorizations and continuous uniqueness. Meanwhile, when speaking of the gender of clienthood, I think one must approach with scepticism all statements which assume the relationship between clienthood and gender as self-evident. Likewise, we must be careful in the face of opinions which exclude gender from the elements of social work.

Notes

1   The situation is different for the study of care giving and caring work, as in this context the influence of the care giver's gender on caregiving, its financial support and its content has been analysed.

2   In the Finnish language gender is less visible than in most other European languages, since the personal pronoun corresponding to 'he/she' does not reveal the gender of the person referred to. This is why, in the translations of the data passages below, the words 'the other' have been substituted for the English pronoun where the gender could not be known.

3   At the beginning of the research process we had briefly explained to the social workers the commitments to social constructionism which formed the basis of our attitude towards the data. The joint discussions revealed clear influences of these commitments, but the workers also analysed the passages on the basis of other assumptions. Thus, it was not expected that a systematic, scholarly method would be used in these discussions.

4   Another interesting analytical dimension could have been constructed out of the way in which the workers played around their own gender and its influence in interpreting the data. They also commented on their own action during the joint analysis through gender expectations. As an example, overlapping speech was common, and in this particular discussion some men apologized for it as masculine behaviour. In this chapter I have omitted the analysis of the interaction between the workers (and the researchers).

5   Note that in Finnish the pronoun is in the singular, thus only referring to one person.

11

The Social Worker as Moral Judge

Blame, Responsibility and Case Formulation

Sue White

> It is essential that practitioners and their managers ensure their practice
> and supervision are grounded in the most up to date knowledge… The
> combination of evidence based practice grounded in knowledge and
> finely balanced professional judgement is the foundation for effective
> practice with children and families. (Department of Health *et al.* 2000,
> p.16)

The quotation above is taken from the *Framework of Assessment of Children in
Need and their Families*, designed to be a systematic guide which social workers
in the UK must follow in making their assessments. The Framework is
intended to standardize practice and ensure rigour in the assessment process.
The quotation illustrates the primacy of evidence-based practice in current
government thinking, but it also stresses the importance of 'balanced
professional judgement'. This chapter will argue that, while a good deal of
attention is currently being paid to accumulation of evidence about the
efficacy of various interventions, the nature of professional judgement
remains underexplored and is poorly interrogated.

The development of a systematic, research-based knowledge base seems
to promise welcome reassurance to the range of constituencies concerned
with the provision of social care services. Consistency and precision, it is
argued, will replace the *ad hoc*, arbitrary and 'commonsensical' processes
which allegedly have applied in previous decision making. Up-to-date factual information and more rigorous procedure replace outdated knowledge,
lack of knowledge and outmoded practices (Taylor and White 2000). For

example, the function and purpose of the recently established Social Care Institute for Excellence (SCIE) has been described as follows:

> SCIE [Social Care Institute for Excellence] will create a knowledge base of what works in social care and the information will be made available to managers, practitioners and users. It will rigorously review research and practice to provide a database of information on methods proven to be effective in social care practice. Using this information, SCIE will produce guidelines on Best Practice... The guidelines will also feed into the standards set by the Social Services Inspectorate, and ultimately those produced by the General Social Care Council and the National Care Standards Commission, to monitor performance. This will mean users can then be confident that the services they receive have been tested against the best and most up-to-date knowledge in social care. (Department of Health 2001)

Laudable aims indeed. Yet, by situating knowledge outside of the practitioner, EBP effectively brackets out the 'balanced professional judgement' that clearly is so important. There is a substantial literature, for example, from within sociology (e.g. Atkinson 1995; Hall 1997; Latimer 2000; Taylor and White 2000; White and Stancombe forthcoming) to show that in producing formulations for the cases they confront, professionals rely on a range of warrants for their opinions with personal anecdotes, appeals to 'common-sense', professional identity and moral judgement playing their part. These kinds of common-sense and often taken-for-granted ways of thinking can affect practitioners' use of evidence, as Green (2000) notes:

> Evidence does not speak for itself, but must be spoken for, and the skilled use of devices, such as personal experience and appeals to common sense, is needed to establish its relevance and credibility. (p.473)

If we want professional judgements to be 'balanced', and this seems to be a highly desirable aim, we need to find methods for interrogating some of the more subtle ways in which social workers make sense of cases and what are their preferred formulations.

Looking, hearing, seeing and understanding

When professionals, or indeed human beings in general, seek to understand and make sense of a situation, they do so in the context of particular frameworks of understanding. This is as true of natural science as it is of social and behavioural observations. In the quotation below, the microbiologist and sociologist of science, Ludvik Fleck (1979), suggests that there are some popular misconceptions about our ability to access unvarnished truth.

> Observation and experiment are subject to a very popular myth. The knower is seen as a kind of conquerer, like Julius Caesar winning his battles according to the formula 'I came, I saw, I conquered'. A person wants to know something, so he makes his observation or experiment and then he knows. (p.84)

Fleck argues that in order to produce an observation, people must first learn how to observe within their own particular domain. They must learn what serves as a competent observation or formulation of reality. In natural science this may involve the use of technologies or formulae which reduce complex questions to 'yes' or 'no' answers. However, this chapter will argue that child care social workers have their own preferred 'prototypical causal *Gestalt*' (Bull and Shaw, 1992, p.640) which is historically and morally situated.

In the analysis that follows I look at some of the tacit dimensions of practice in social work with children and families. I examine extracts from social workers' case files, transcripts of interviews and interprofessional talk. The data are taken from a corpus derived from a multi-method discourse analytic ethnography of child care social work which was completed in 1997 (White 1997). The study involved two years of participant observation, the audio-taping and transcription of agency meetings and interviews with professionals and the analysis of a sample of case files. In particular, I want to illustrate how social workers in the UK tend to prefer hearing children's stories as more revealing of the family reality. This privileging of the child's voice, combined with ironizing parents' versions, results in social workers working up versions of the troubles which tend to exculpate children while inculpating parents. Parents who explicitly blame their offspring for family problems are often perceived to be particularly suspect and blameworthy. These formulations are often supported by complex characterizations of family members which do particular moral work. This *modus operandi* appears to have an uncontroversial, intrinsic correctness and seems to be in keeping with the paramountcy principle (the child's welfare is paramount) in the Children Act 1989. However, it may carry some unintended consequences, not always conducive to the production of 'balanced judgements'. It may, for example, presuppose that the best interests of a child are to be served by disbelieving its parents.

Parents, children, blame and responsibility

Ethnographic work in health settings has shown that children appear to be a social category exempt from classification as 'bad patients' (Dingwall, Eekelaar and Murray 1983). Dingwall and Murray, in their study of an accident and emergency department, found that moral judgement did not routinely pass to parents. However, Strong's (1979) earlier work in the more holistic domain of paediatrics found that normative judgements about parents were a regular feature of the work. In paediatric and child psychiatry settings, the possibility that a child may have some embodied medical condition is a routine consideration. Thus, clinicians are oriented to deciding between a number of competing aetiological accounts of the troubles with which children present. My own recently completed ethnographic study of paediatrics confirmed that, while children or young people may be described as difficult, sensitive, challenging or damaged, they are exempted from blame using one of two devices. Either their problems are attributed to their medical or psychiatric condition (e.g. they have autism), or to their parents' or carers' (mis)management, or some traumatic aspect of their biography (White 2002). This includes those children and young people whose behaviour breaches moral codes, for example, those who self-harm or engage in behaviour dangerous to others and those whose chronological age places them very close to adulthood. In categorizing cases either as 'medical' or 'psycho-social' moral judgements about the appropriateness of parental responses are vital.

The literature on parent–professional interaction in medical encounters provides compelling evidence of parents' sensibilities to the potential that they may be blamed by clinicians in some way. Parents must present their actions in the context of moral versions of responsible parenthood. For instance, in his work in a paediatric diabetic clinic, Silverman (1987) notes that moral evaluations of parenting depended on the extent to which parents were able to demonstrate that they managed and took responsibility for the child's condition, by monitoring blood sugar, administering or supervising insulin injections and providing a suitable diet. Decisions became more complex with older children, in relation to whom parents had to demonstrate that they were also encouraging autonomy. Stancombe's (forthcoming) work on family therapy comes to a similar conclusion. He shows that the successful production of a moral account by a parent involves the use of one of the following sequences:

1. parents present themselves as 'good' parents who have done everything they can to ensure the welfare of their child and are continuing to act as a 'good' parent by seeking expert help for their child

    or,

2. parents may confess irresponsibility, admit to blame and seek absolution and so seek guidance, in the form of expert intervention, to ensure that they become 'better' parents.

Stancombe's data provide evidence of a tacit rule which therapists follow in producing formulations in this tricky moral domain – 'produce versions of the troubles in which children never deserve blame or moral censure'. Moreover, there is a corollary to this rule – 'even if they seem culpable it is because parents have been, or continue to be deficient in meeting their emotional needs', or, 'identify those features of the parents that have produced the troubled child' (see Gubrium 1992 for further 'rules' and White and Stancombe forthcoming, for empirical data which illustrate these processes).

Social work with children and families involves the use of a similar set of rules. Judgements must be made about children's and parents' blameworthiness and creditworthiness. In this chapter, I examine how these are constructed by child care social workers and argue that there appears to be a tacit hierarchy of credible accounts. In this hierarchy, the membership categories, e.g. father, mother, child, professional (see Sacks 1972; 1992), to which the sources of stories are assigned, and the differential moral weights which seem to be attached to those categories, appear to be crucially important.

Before embarking on the analysis, it is important to stress that I use the words 'culpability' and 'blame' to mean 'attribution of responsibility' (see Pomerantz 1978). This particular definition is crucial, as social workers frequently offer mitigating statements for parental 'failure' (e.g. by invoking the past – 'she was brought up in care and suffered dreadful abuse as a child', 'he's a very damaged person') which imply that the individual is somehow *not* to blame. However, these mitigations simultaneously preserve the rhetorical force of the 'blaming' as an attribution of responsibility for causing a particular problem in the present. That is to say, notions of causation and culpability are inextricably bound together in work with children and families.

Parental culpability and the tacit dimension

The problem with tacit moral rules is that they are rarely explicitly articulated. Rather, they are treated as the only right and proper ways to think. However, they may be rendered visible on occasions when they are breached. New recruits and novices who are unaware of the dominant professional mores are clearly more likely to perform these breaches. During my fieldwork, an experienced social worker was transferred from adult services into a child care team. In the first few weeks the kinds of breaches to which I have referred were a frequent occurrence. On one such occasion she was asked to assess a family in which the teenage daughter had recently taken an overdose of paracetamol. On returning from her first encounter with the family, she remarked:

> That was hard work. That mother's got her hands full. She says Lisa took the overdose because her mum refused to let her stay out until 3 o'clock. Little madam.

This comment, which takes the mother's version on face value, provoked censure from a more experienced member of the team who admonished the new worker with the following statement:

> There's usually more to it than that when young people take overdoses. If everything was OK at home she'd never have done it. (Field notes, March 1995)

These kinds of exchanges quickly induct novices into the established taken-for-granted ways of ascribing culpability and acquaint them with the imperative to 'believe the child'. Parents who present their child as the problem are likely to be faced with a rapid redefinition of the situation using the aforementioned rule or 'identify those features of the parents that have produced the troubled child'. This is illustrated in the following extracts from interviews.

Extract 11.1

(I = interviewer, SW = social worker)

I: Parents will often say, at least in my experience, that problems that children are exhibiting are to do with the child, that 'he's just like his dad' or whatever. What do you think about that explanation?

SW: I think that says more about the parent than the child and what we are most often dealing with is young parents who've been cases themselves been neglected or abused or whatever in their own...they even when they think they are doing a good job they are comparing it against their own experience, so I think those sorts of things say more about the parents.

Extract 11.2

(SW = social worker)
(In response to similar question.)

SW: Well, if the parents are saying that's how they experience it then it's true to the parents. Whether that is the reality is a different matter and I think it's unhelpful to poo poo it because if that is how the parents experience it then it's worth trying to understand why the parents experience the child's behaviour in that way, rather than just saying no child acts like that. So it's about understanding the reasons for the parents attributing the behaviour, often it's not about the child it's about the parents about their perception of situations or understanding of child development that is skewed or the way it is because of their parenting and childhood.

Writing blame – examining case records

In order to make a more thorough assessment of the generalizability of the tendency to ironize parental versions of events and also to look for some disconfirming cases, an analysis was undertaken of a sample of case files ($n = 72$) and child protection case conference minutes ($n = 45$). Like social workers' talk, the descriptions in case records of the accounts of others and of the social work assessment process itself can be read as struggles to assign culpability to a particular individual or individuals within a family. Again, although the child is frequently presented as the 'problem' by the referrer, there is a clear preference for causal accounts which ascribe *parental* culpability. Challenges to this preferred and privileged way of understanding rely on 'expert' invocation of the biological medium through clinical diagnosis. In cases where a child is seen to have 'intrinsic' medical problems (i.e. those which can be named and identified by paediatricians or child psychiatrists) causal accounts more frequently imply that the child is the 'problem'. In such cases, stories affirming the parents' moral worth are often an accompaniment.

Within the records, 'blame' often transfers from one person to another as information unfolds; this is particularly evident in the example below.

> B. [child aged 19 months] has had several breath-holding attacks and has been in hospital twice. Hospital wish him to attend playtherapy. Father works long hours . Mother has children 24 hours a day with no break. (Extract from original referral from the health visitor)

The initial referral form was completed by the social worker as follows:

> Request for financial assistance with 1x session per week childminding fees. Child with medical problems, mum needs respite. B. experiences some problems with breath holding – deliberate and manipulative catching of breath during temper tantrums. This has necessitated two hospital admissions because of convulsions. Father works long hours – he clearly sees his role as provider for the family and does not help out much with the children. The health visitor feels that mum is overwhelmed by the difficulties entailed in managing B.'s behaviour and desperately needs some respite.

Here, B has become more clearly defined as a 'problem child'. This is necessary rhetorical work in situations where a child is being held responsible for family problems. Furthermore, although the father has conformed to certain normative expectations (breadwinner), he is still subjected to professional censure. Textual devices are employed (describing his lack of availability at home) in order to assign culpability to him. However, as the case progresses things quickly change.

> B. is now 20 months old and stronger than ever. Mum finds him very overpowering… I felt mum does not help. She is quite anxious and shouts quite a bit… I felt a child minder was not going to help B. I felt from what she had been saying, he would feel rejected by her and it is his mother's attention he seeks. I explained that we do not just pay for child minders and asked about an FRW [Family Resource Worker].

Here there is a clear shift away from a 'service delivery' construction, where the parent's account is accepted, to a 'sceptical professional' position, in which the problem is redefined as mother's 'fault'. The parent's request for day care is, for the time being, denied and the need for more of the mother's attention asserted.

The example illustrates the tendency for social workers to inculpate parents, even when the initial referral suggests that some particular characteristic of the child is the cause of the problem. The ascription of 'problem' status to children relies, as I have said, on the medicalization or psychiatrization of the presenting problem. Although there were few examples of such cases in the initial sample, I undertook a further analysis of cases involving a child with a disability or clear diagnosis ($n = 12$) and, in such cases, the social workers' accounts of their involvement are more service delivery focused and tend to be accompanied by references to parental moral worth. The following case has this typical service delivery focus and contains explicit references to the parents' moral worth.

(E. has Down's Syndrome.)

> E. came home from school very high and noisy, insisting on being fed immediately. At first he seemed a little shy but soon came round. He constantly made demands, mostly on his father, to provide food and drinks. It appears father does not enforce such rigid boundaries as his mother does, consequently E. has learned to make more demands on him. He [E.] showed very short concentration span, but enjoyed talking about his videos. When there was not a positive response to his demands, he either cried or sulked and lashed out. He responded very positively and almost immediately when his mum made a request... There appears to be a very caring attitude to E. by his parents, perhaps a little overprotective at times. However, he did make great demands on them and they expressed concern not only for his physical development, in terms of strengths, but also about his social networks and emotional growth.

The trend continues in a subsequent referral, dealt with by another social worker. The referral states:

> The hospital had received a telephone call from J [mother]. She is not sleeping due to E.'s pump going off 8–10 times a night. Dr thinks Mrs H. [mother] is in danger of cracking up. Dr feels they should have a nurse available to sit up with E.

The outcome was allocation to a social worker, who arranged respite care and made applications to charities for financial support.

Causation is not always easy to ascribe and, in the following case, the struggles involved in constructing causal accounts for 'disturbed' behaviour in children are clearly demonstrated. The account is something of a roller coaster ride, with blame settling from time to time upon the mother, but with frequent reference made to M's problems. The sections which appear to question the mother's parenting capacity are shown in italics and the phrases which reconstruct her as a morally worthy, struggling parent are depicted in bold. The initial referral sheet, completed after the child's mother had made contact with the service, states the following.

(Request for urgent assistance with child.)

> *Mrs T. brought M. [child, 9yrs] into the office threatening him with a children's home.* M. attends B. school and has special needs. Headteacher told mum to come in if in difficulty. M. behaved badly in the supermarket and ran off – mum had to drop her shopping and jump on top of him to stop him. She was distressed saying she could not cope, *but really was using us as a threat.* She regained composure very quickly. *M. goes to a childminder after school as mum works. He also goes to an aunt and father every Fri– Sun. So mum has quite a lot of respite.* [Educational psychologist] is involved. There is a special education meeting next week. I suggested we wait until that meeting to see recommendations. Mum felt sure she could manage until school began. M. promised not to misbehave in shops and not to run away.

The difficulties the worker was experiencing in constructing a consistent account are understandable when one considers the content of a referral made the previous month by the headteacher.

(Concern for child who is beyond parental control.)

> M. is in a special needs unit at school – behaviour is aggressive and is deteriorating. Ed. Psych. is involved and a referral to [Child and Adolescent Mental Health Service] for assessment has been made. School feels M. is 'out of mum's control' and she is at the end of her tether. M. set fire to his bedroom on 27/3/94. 'Very disturbed little boy, but very loving'. M. has drawn a picture at school showing himself watching horror films, through a hole in the door at his uncle's home. Head teacher advised mother to contact social services and thinks she did so and then withdrew request some months ago.

This account displays similar ambivalence, and leaves the social worker struggling to decide on an appropriate response. The outcome was a referral letter to the Child and Adolescent Mental Health Service. Assessment procedures rest on the assumption that parenting skills, or the lack of them, will be *embodied* in the child. That is, good enough or bad enough parenting is assumed to be measurable using standard measurements and yardsticks (height, weight, growth, development, psychological adjustment). Where an intrinsic problem appears to exist and in the absence of a clear medical opinion suggesting inappropriate parenting, social workers are pushed towards a service delivery response as the dominant sceptical professional response (parent as culpable for problems in the child) cannot be straightforwardly authorized and authenticated using the temporal markers of 'normal' development (White 2002).

A hierarchy of accounts?

I have noted that in constructing a competent interpretation, social workers are often exposed to competing accounts of events. It appears that there is a hierarchy affecting the attribution of truth status to a particular version, with professional accounts generally privileged over lay accounts. In situations where members of a family offer different versions of events, a mother's version is usually treated with less scepticism than a father's unless she belongs to a deviant category (e.g. she is mentally ill). As I have said, children's accounts are treated as 'true' unless they can be discredited by the presence of 'intrinsic' disturbance or where abuse is suspected but denied by the child.

Based on my reading of the case files a clear hierarchy emerges, which can be depicted as follows:

1.   the child

2.   professional staff (usually, in this instance, health visitors)

3.   mothers

4.   fathers living in the household

5.   estranged fathers and other male caretakers (e.g. stepfathers).

I have illustrated the privileging of the child's voice above, so it will be heuristic to consider a case involving two incommensurable, competing parental versions. The case was referred by the Court Welfare Service after an application for a Residence Order under the Children Act 1989 had been made by the child's estranged father. The reasons given by the father in his statement were as follows.

> I have arranged contact and have been concerned that D. has bruises on his body and, on the weekend of 18th/19th June, had burn marks to his arm and his eyelashes.

There were further concerns expressed by the father:

> Mr S. and his family believe that D. is living in an incestuous family and is in potential danger. They have no concerns about J.'s [mother] ability as a

mother. She is loving and caring towards D. However if J. were to leave him in the care of certain members of the family…this may place him at risk.

The case was allocated to a social worker who interviewed Mr S. in the office in the company of his brother, who reiterated their concerns about the burns, bruises and risk of sexual abuse. Later, the social worker spoke to the health visitor and recorded the following.

> Health Visitor saw D. and his mother on 21st July (first meeting), she said she was staying with her parents at [address] but due to move to [ ]. She said she had met the previous H.V. there. D. was up to date with immunisations and was up to milestones. Looked happy and healthy. Bright and intelligent and active. J. said she was having trouble with her boyfriend over access.

This was followed by a visit to the mother.

> Visit to J. and D. D. looked well and lively and cheerful. J. friendly and willing to talk. She showed me a mark on D.'s arm (an old and small scar). She said this had happened when D. was playing at her mother's in a red toy car which had fallen off the concrete path onto the garden… She also said she did accidentally singe D.'s eyebrows when she lit a cigarette and D. was standing beside her on the couch and made a grab for the lighter. She says D. was a very active child and she tried to be careful with matches, lighters and cigarettes. She showed herself to be conscientious and careful of D. She had taken D. to the doctors the day before, he had diagnosed slight asthma and given syrup for this. She intends to visit the clinic frequently now she has registered with Dr…

Obviously, we do not have the data to adjudicate on the correctness of the social worker's interpretation, but the way that it is formulated is quite revealing. The social worker's evaluation of the mother is explicit here, but there has been no neutral way for her to adjudicate on the veracity of the father's original account. The child has injuries consistent with his version, but she treats the mother's account as more true although she does not produce any rhetorical work to support the formulation. It is treated as self-evidently correct and is supported only by the mother's reported speech. The case was closed.

Scepticism about fathers' accounts is also illustrated in social workers' interprofessional discussions. The following extract is taken from a transcript of an allocation meeting.

Extract 11.3

(TL = team leader, OS = others)

TL: One [case] that Deborah's been out on today with Bev, and Deborah and Sally are going to finish it off this afternoon was a family called [name] where there's a sort of marital conflict and where father's made allegations about mother's treatment of the children which [does appear to be over the top]

O: [uuuuurgh] *laughter.*

TL: I know, I know… Deborah is either trying to see Mum this afternoon or she and I will try to see them together tomorrow, but it just is possible that this is one that will appear again and I just think that I want people to be aware. There are four children in the family and there's been a marital dispute, mother left and dad said the children had made allegations which sound (0.9) a bit over the top (0.5) so that's one that may be coming back to us I suspect, but at the moment we're trying to deal with it very clearly as a one off and getting them to get legal advice.

The team leader explicitly categorizes this case as a 'sort of marital conflict', which implies that the father's account may be subject to bias or partisanship. This in effect ironizes the father's version and trivializes any risk to the children. By the collective exclamation 'uuuuurgh', followed by laughter, social workers display their shared knowledge that allegations of abuse made by estranged partners are problematic.

Thus, case formulation in child care social work can be shown to depend on moral evaluations based on membership categories and also on rhetorical work undertaken by social workers in their oral and written accounts.

Disconfirming cases

I have said that social workers privilege the child's voice. However, a child's account may not be believed if they are asserting that all is well at home when social workers' suspicions have been aroused that it is not, either by a referral or by a previous statement from the child. Under these circumstances, questioning whether the child has been silenced or 'forced to retract' by a parent is deemed imperative. The scepticism usually reserved for parental versions is reinstated and the child's account loses its privileged status. This is illustrated in the following extract taken from a transcript of an allocation meeting in which a social worker is recounting a recent interview with a ten-year-old girl, Sophie Byrne, who is suspected to have been sexually abused by an older boy and who has recently been found alone in a local shopping precinct in the early hours of the morning. Sophie's father's version is that Sophie is really a rather naughty girl who had sneaked out on her own without the parents' knowledge, and is a bit of a handful. This version is not pursued by the social workers.

Extract 11.4

(SW = social worker)

SW: ...and Sophie isn't actually saying, well it was a very brief interview with Sophie. Basically Sophie erm wasn't giving any information over at all... She was still maintaining that Catherine felt unwell, erm so she took her home and we said that left her on her own to come home and that's very dangerous, etc. etc. and she said erm she said oh yeah but she said she didn't meet any friends erm. She says, she was very emotional because she thought we were there to tell her off and erm the usual and erm it was quite obvious erm she did say she can't talk to anyone, she didn't have anyone to talk to. But with regards to the older boys playing with her she's going to be told that they don't collect her from school.

We can see that the social worker has taken the view that Sophie is failing or refusing to produce an account of the abuse and distress which professionals have decided has taken place. The social worker's account is clearly linguistically coded to convey doubt and to imply that Sophie is reluctant to tell the full story or has not had the opportunity to do so. The use of the phrases, '...and Sophie isn't actually saying, well it was a very brief interview' and 'she was still maintaining' situates Sophie's version (or lack of it) as a contestable account, not as fact or her subjective experience.

Social workers' reluctance to accept a simple denial from a child obviously has some value, since children sometimes are frightened to tell the truth about abuse. However, unless they are using this scepticism self-consciously and carefully, it may well get in the way of 'balanced judgements'.

Discussion

In this chapter I have argued for the practical utility of ethnographic and discourse analytic work in interrogating the tacit dimensions of professional practice. In its current form, EBP depicts professional judgements as objectified, internal, cognitive actions informed by a stable knowledge base. But, before deciding 'what works', social workers must first decide 'what's wrong?'. They must decide exactly what sort of trouble they are dealing with and what has caused it. It seems that they do this using a range of preferred formulations. These must be seen as a product (at least in part) of social processes, such as the circulation and reproduction of dominant ideas (or discourses) about parenthood and childhood and about the right and proper way to classify cases and intervene in particular problems. The local nature of these formulations can be illustrated by comparing and contrasting the data in this chapter with those presented by other contributors to this volume whose work was undertaken in other countries (see for example, van Nijnatten and Hofstede; Hall, Jokinen and Suoninen; Ah Hin, Laffer, Turnell and Parton).

We have seen that the accounts of certain categories of person appear to carry more moral weight than others. For example, through their practices, social workers invoke and reproduce a dominant cultural notion of childhood as an age of fragility, passivity and precarious *potential* personhood (Burman 1994; Marks 1995; Rose 1989; Stainton Rogers and Stainton Rogers 1992; White 1998) but also of truthfulness and reliability. This appears to be challenged only when a child has a documented and named medical or psychiatric condition, or when he or she is denying abuse. There is an interesting paradox in social workers' use of biological explanatory frameworks, in that the notion of development – as an absolutely age graded pre-programmed process – is clearly a profoundly materialist, biological concept. However, as I have illustrated above, there is a manifest preference for 'deviant' behaviour and/or development in children to be constructed as an avoidable consequence of individual parenting styles (nurture). In explaining a particular behaviour or individual difference, biology and genetics have become deeply unfashionable and have come to be defined as 'oppressive' explanatory models. Biology is thus held responsible for similarity but not for difference.

If social workers are to operate in a reflexive and rigorous manner to produce 'balanced judgements', these common-sense, preferred formulations must be rendered more explicit, because:

> Common sense…creates a sense of shared values between speaker and audience, which is difficult to resist without explicitly rejecting these values. It is also a device which constitutes expert knowledges as redundant, simply because what is said is self-evident and known by everybody. (Green 2000, p.470)

Thus professional common-sense must be defamiliarized. Not so that social workers can reject it and replace it with some ideal-typical uncontaminated objective alternative, but so they can decide whether it applies to *this* case at *this* time and so that they may debate its contradictions. Preferred models of causation and assumptions about the trustworthiness or otherwise of parents' or children's accounts need to be made explicit, available and reportable so that practitioners can debate them properly. They cannot do this, however, while presuppositions and shortcuts remain taken for granted. By making use of and debating detailed ethnographic data, social workers can be helped to become more reflexive, analytic and systematic in their sense-making activities and so may be helped to further develop their capacity for 'balanced judgements'.

12

Writers', Clients', Counsellors' and Readers' Perspectives in Constructing Resistant Clients

Gale Miller

This chapter focuses on what might be called 'troubles in counsellor–client interactions'. The troubles consist of times when counselling sessions and relationships do not proceed as counsellors expect or wish. Troubles are a potential aspect of all counsellor–client interactions. Even the most competent counsellors must deal with such troubles from time to time. Counsellors sometimes discuss troubles in their relationships with clients as evidence of client resistance. Signs of client resistance may include overtly threatening behaviour by clients, not adequately answering counsellors' questions (from the counsellors' perspective), client refusals to acknowledge that they have problems, and/or client refusals to follow counsellors' recommendations.

Troubles in counsellor–client interactions might be described as discontinuities or ruptures in routine and expected counsellor–client interactions. It should not be surprising, then, to find that writings on different counselling approaches include explanations for why and how clients resist and how counsellors should respond to client resistance. The counselling literature also includes texts that reject the concept of client resistance all together. Indeed, the latter writers often portray the concept itself as a source of troubles in client–counsellor relationships. These troubles are created by counsellors, not by clients.

I see the concept of client resistance as one way in which counsellors 'make up people' (Hacking 1986). We make up people by classifying others and ourselves into abstract person categories. The categories include official classification schemes (such as government census categories and crime categories) as well as such everyday distinctions as age and gender classifications. Hacking explains that making up people involves more than simply noting and describing people's observable features and actions. Person categories are social constructions that are based on and express our 'theories' about why people do what they do and about our relationships with others. As Hacking (1986, p.229) explains, making up people is, in some ways, similar 'to making up gloves, because we manufacture them. I know not which came first, the thought or the mitten, but they have evolved hand in hand. That the concept of 'glove' fits gloves so well is no surprise; he made them that way. My claim about making up people is that the category and the people in it emerged hand in hand'.

Counsellors' classification of some clients as resistant is one part of developing and justifying changes in their relationships with clients. The changes that accompany counsellors' classification of some clients as resistant have implications for both clients and counsellors. Counsellors assume new professional responsibilities in dealing with their resistant clients and may hold clients accountable to new expectations and responsibilities within their counselling relationships. Thus, counsellor debates about client resistance are also debates about what it means to be a responsible and effective professional.

This chapter addresses the issues raised above by considering aspects of three orientations to constructing counsellor–client relationships. The approaches are psychoanalytic therapy, strategic therapy and solution-focused brief therapy. Each of these counselling approaches has been adapted to and used in social work settings. Psychoanalysis is central to many diagnostic approaches in social work; strategic therapy is associated with systems approaches; and solution-focused brief therapy complements strengths-based strategies. Psychoanalytic and strategic counselling represent two different approaches to assessing and treating some counselling clients as resistant. Solution-focused counsellors, on the other hand, reject the idea that clients are – or even can be – resistant.

I should add two points before moving on to these counselling approaches. First, my comments are limited to how clienthood and professionalism are socially constructed in counselling texts. I do not assume that these texts necessarily tell us what actually goes on in counselling sessions. Second, the paper is about more than how clienthood and professionalism are socially constructed in counselling texts. It also addresses the relationship between the readers and writers of counselling texts, including how readers might become better questioners of the texts that they read. Thus, it is important that I offer the following caution. Because this chapter is itself a social construction, I ask that you read this text with the same questioning orientation that you bring to the reading of the texts discussed here.

Clients as patients

We usually associate the social role of patient with medicine. The patient role is central to the so-called medical model which emphasizes assessment and classification (diagnosis) of the patient's symptoms and problems by a professional expert. The medical approach to problem solving also involves developing treatment plans that are designed to manage – if not eradicate – the patient's problems. Professional experts are responsible for directing their interviews with patients towards professionally useful topics and activities. Patients are responsible for providing professionals with useful information and for following the recommendations of the professionals.

Parsons (1951) discusses these aspects of the medical approach to problem solving as bases for the sick role. The sick role is a cultural category that is associated with a social and moral exchange between people classified as sick and others in the society. 'Sick' people are granted various levels of exemption from 'normal' social expectations, such as exemption from some family obligations and work responsibilities. But this exemption is contingent on sick people trying to get well by seeking the assistance of and co-operating with appropriate professional experts.

Of course, the professional experts are expected to provide competent advice and assistance to their sick clients. Collaboration in medical settings, then, is achieved when both medical professionals and patients fulfil their obligations within their exchange relationship. Medical professionals often classify patients who are unable or unwilling to provide requested information or to follow prescribed treatment plans as resistant.

Psychoanalytic counsellors understand their patients by observing the patients' behaviour and by noting symptoms of underlying intrapsychic processes and disorder (Herson and Turner 1994). Psychoanalytic counsellors use this information in assessing their patients' mental statuses (Akisal and Akisal 1994; Sommers-Flanagan and Sommers-Flanagan 1999), and in fostering insight in patients (Othmer and Othmer 1994a). Insight is achieved when patients understand that their perceptions of reality are distorted and that patients' inappropriate behaviour is related to their distorted senses of reality. The distortions are revealed in the gap between patients' and psycho-analytic counsellors' senses of reality. Patients' distorted perceptions are also related to deep-seated conditions that patients cannot recognize – much less understand – without the guidance of professional experts.

These issues are central to understanding the meaning of client resis-tance in psychoanalytic counselling. Othmer and Othmer (1994b) define resistance as patient actions that interfere with the interviewing process. Resistance is a symptom of the disorder from which the patient suffers.

Psychoanalytic counsellors also take account of patients' resistance in assessing patients' mental statuses and levels of insight about their lives and problems. While patient resistance is a roadblock in developing patient insight, it is a common and even expected aspect of many psychoanalytic counselling interviews. As MacKinnon and Michels (1971, p.16) state, 'the patient is motivated to resist the therapy in order to maintain repression, ward off insight, and avoid anxiety'.

Patient resistance is an observable part of psychoanalytic counselling interviews (Shea 1998). It may be expressed in a variety of verbal and non-verbal ways. For example, Morrison (1995) states that any of the following patient behaviours may be evidence of resistance and that the 'interview might be in trouble': tardiness, forgetfulness, changing the subject, leaving out information, exaggerations, diversionary tactics (such as telling jokes), silence and hesitating prior to answering counsellors' questions (p.172). Shea (1998) explains that these and other expressions of patient resistance are related to the 'core pains' from which patients suffer. The pains include patients' fears and devaluation of themselves, as well as from their feelings of isolation, meaninglessness and powerlessness.

Once they have observed evidence of patient resistance, psychoanalytic counsellors classify and treat it. For example, Othmer and Othmer (1994b) classify patient resistance into four categories. The categories are resistance caused by stress and trauma, delusions, cognitive impairment and patient deceptiveness. Psychoanalytic counsellors differ in their responses to patient resistance.

Some counsellors (such as Othmer and Othmer 1994b) use the same general strategies in responding to all forms of patient resistance, whereas other psychoanalytic counsellors vary their responses depending on the context and kind of resistance expressed by patients. According to Shea

(1998, p.583), counsellors may 'go with' the resistance, 'go against it', or may choose strategies that involve aspects of both strategies.

Clients as system members

Strategic counsellors address their clients' problems by creating changes in clients' family systems (Haley 1963; Watzlawick, Beavin and Jackson 1967). They use the concept of 'family system' to highlight how family members are interrelated, particularly how the actions and interactions of any one family member may have implications for other family members. Strategic counsellors portray themselves as experts at assessing clients' family systems and in creating change in the systems. Strategic counsellors explain that their expertise is vital to the success of counselling because clients caught in dysfunctional family relationships are incapable of solving their own problems.

An important factor affecting strategic counsellors' ability to create change in clients' family systems is the level of therapist manoeuvrability that clients are willing to grant their counsellors (Fisch, Weakland and Segal 1982).

Therapist manoeuvrability refers to the extent to which counsellors are free to define clients' problems as they see fit and to create whatever changes in clients' family systems that they deem appropriate. Fisch *et al.* (1982) explain that in the ideal (collaborative) strategic counselling interaction, the client would say to the counsellor, 'I will give you all the information you request, in a form you can understand clearly, seriously entertain any new ideas you have about my problem, try any proposed new behaviours outside the therapy hour, and work hard to bring into treatment any of my family or friends who might help solve my problems' (p.21).

Strategic counsellors stress the centrality of communication in family systems. The diverse actions and interactions that make up family systems are sources of messages and meanings that may or may not be recognized by family members (Madanes 1984; Watzlawick *et al.* 1967). Clients' inability to recognize what they are communicating to one another is to be expected since system members' actions and interactions often involve multiple – even contradictory–messages. Clients only focus on the most obvious meanings of their communications and miss the less visible meanings. Strategic counsellors' interest in looking past obvious meanings in clients' communications is also related to their orientations to client resistance.

The following statement is a beginning for considering how client resistance is defined and explained in strategic counselling discourse. '…quite a few people seem not to enter therapy for the purpose of resolving a problem and being themselves changed in the process; they behave as if they wanted to defeat the expert and presumably 'prove' thereby that the problem cannot be solved, while at the same time they clamour for immediate help' (Watzlawick, Weakland and Fisch 1974, p.133). Watzlawick *et al.* further explain that the common-sense response to this situation is to focus on the content of their clients' complaints. For example, counsellors often suggest concrete ways in which their clients might change their situations. Clients resist the advice by responding with 'yes but' statements that emphasize how the counsellors' advice might be reasonable under other circumstances but not in the current situation.

Watzlawick *et al.* (1974) stress that a more effective response is for the counsellor to focus on the counsellor–client relationship. The new focus alters the 'rules' of the strategic counselling 'game' and it greatly reduces resistant clients' ability to respond with 'yes but'.

Watzlawick *et al.* suggest that a useful way of responding to resistant clients is to ask the clients to explain why they should change. Few clients are prepared for such a request from their counsellors, since most counselling interactions rest on the assumption that change will be useful for clients. The response also changes the counsellor–client relationship by placing the resistant client in the position of explaining to the counsellor that change is needed and is possible. We might even say that, in asking resistant clients to explain why they should change, strategic counsellors take their own resistant position with clients.

The 'why change' response to client resistance is part of the general strategy of strategic counsellors to utilize the clients' resistance to foster change (Erickson, Rossi and Rossi 1976). The response is designed to turn client resistance into a counsellor resource. As with asking clients to explain why they should change, many strategic counsellor responses to client resistance involve indirect and paradoxical problem-solving strategies (Haley 1976).

Watzlawick *et al.* (1974) note, for example, that strategic counsellors may respond to resistant clients by telling clients to slow down the rate at which they are changing their lives, pointing out the dangers of improvement to clients, and giving advice that will clearly make the client's problem worse. A related response is to encourage resistant clients to do more of the behaviour that they see as their problem. Each of these responses creates a choice for the client. The client may choose to take the counsellor's advice (not resist) and maintain the problem, or the client may choose to resist the counsellor and initiate change in the client's family system.

Clients as consumers

An important way in which strategic and solution-focused counselling differ is in their orientations to problem solving. Strategic counselling rests on the assumption that change requires that clients' problems be solved. Solution-focused counsellors reject this assumption, stating that change is more easily and quickly created by building solutions (de Shazer 1994). Solution building involves focusing on the times when clients are more effectively managing their lives and identifying resources already present in clients' lives that clients might use to create other desired changes (Berg and Miller 1992).

Solution-focused counsellors assume that change is an ongoing and ever-present aspect of people's lives. Solution-focused counsellors encourage their clients to notice how their lives are changing by asking them to describe the times when their lives have been better. Solution-focused counsellors also assume that clients' lives will change in the future by asking 'not if change will occur, but rather when, or where, or what type of changing will occur' (de Shazer 1989, p.16). A related theme in solution-focused counselling, then, involves counsellors' encouragement of clients to expect change in the future. Solution-focused counsellors explain that this expectation makes it more likely that clients will notice when, where and what changes happen in the future.

The emphasis on solution building in solution-focused counselling has important implications for how clienthood and professionalism are defined in this counselling site. Solution-focused counsellors stress that solution building requires that counsellors treat their clients as consumers of their counselling services. Thus, solution-focused counsellors have a professional obligation to take their clients' concerns and desires seriously. Solution-focused counsellors use the metaphor of client as consumer to reverse the professional-first and client-second hierarchy associated with the professional as expert imagery.

Solution-focused counsellors further explain that, in solution-focused counselling relationships, clients are responsible for making the most important decisions about how their lives should change. They state that clients know better than counsellors about what is possible in clients' lives and about the best ways of achieving their goals.

Solution-focused counsellors foster change by supporting and assisting clients in identifying existing resources that clients might use in changing their lives. Perhaps the most important way in which solution-focused counsellors assist their clients is by asking questions which help clients to better use their expertise in describing what they want from life and what they are already doing to achieve their goals.

An influential early statement by a solution-focused counsellor about client resistance is de Shazer's (1984) paper, 'The Death of Resistance'. The paper is a critique of the concept of client resistance in strategic counselling. The argument has since been extended and applied to medically oriented counsellors' orientations to client resistance (Bohart and Tallman 1999; Duncan and Miller 2000). De Shazer states that strategic counsellors create client resistance as a problem by focusing on clients as members of homeostatic family systems. Such systems respond to changes in their environments by restoring the status quo. Thus, family systems that are organized around problems will resist external sources of change.

De Shazer (1984) adds that this orientation to family systems separates clients and counsellors from each other by assigning different – even opposed – goals to each party in the counselling relationship. Further, the separation between counsellors and their clients is not based on clients' interest in resisting counsellors; rather, it rests on strategic counsellors' assumptions about and interpretations of clients' behaviour. Solution-focused counsellors reject these assumptions and interpretations along with the concept of client resistance. Indeed, solution-focused counsellors state that clients always co-operate with their counsellors, even if the counsellors do not always see how the clients are co-operating.

De Shazer (1984) further explains (p.14) that in assuming that clients are always co-operating with their counsellors, clients and counsellors may be seen as 'like tennis players on the same side of the net' who share the same goal of defeating a common opponent. Thus, he rejects the assumption that solution-focused counsellors are to blame when troubles emerge in solution-focused counselling sessions. De Shazer (1989, p.231) states that 'attributing blame to either party of an interaction is theoretically unsound. Such a split between members of a system inevitably creates imaginary oppositions. But clinically, both therapists and clients are in it together and co-operation is what we want'.

Duncan and Miller (2000) further develop this orientation by describing how clients and counsellors might work together to challenge and subvert practices of other mental health professionals that they see as ignoring and devaluing clients' concerns, desires, experiences and perceptions. These practices may be based on many factors, including organizational, professional, economic and political interests that do not put clients first. Duncan and Miller (2000, p.215) state that 'escape from such a quagmire lies in one avenue, the true partnership and collaboration, in both research (action research), theory building and practice'.

Textual dynamics of clienthood

I have no interest in taking sides in the debates that I have described. Nor do I intend to mediate between the debaters' positions in order to construct a consensus that all of the debaters can agree about. I do not see the value of such a consensus for psychoanalytic, strategic solution-focused or other counsellors. Disagreement can be very useful. Rather than getting directly involved within the debates, I wish to examine them as textual realities and as social contexts for constructing clienthood and professionalism in counselling. The examination requires that I move away from stressing the differences that separate psychoanalytic, strategic and solution-focused counselling texts from one another. Instead, I focus on their textual similarities.

A useful starting-point for discussing these similarities is to note that the debates discussed here are counsellor constructions. They involve issues of primary interest to professional counsellors. The debates are not client initiated, although proponents of differing counselling approaches often suggest that they speak for their clients' interests. It should not be surprising, then, to find that clients' interests vary depending on the author's preferred counselling approach. What counts as clients' 'true' interests is itself a matter of contest and social construction in counsellor debates about client resistance. I see counsellor debates about client resistance as one part of what Bazerman and Paradis (1991, p.4) call the textual dynamics of the professions, that is, 'once established, professions maintain their organization, power and activity in large part through networks of texts. As these professions increasingly form the frame of modern existence, their texts set the terms of our lives'.

Viewed from this perspective, counsellor debates about client resistance are aspects of contests about the purpose and character of the counselling profession. Psychoanalytic, strategic and solution-focused counsellors write texts to advocate for their preferred images of counselling as a practical and as a moral activity. The texts cast psychoanalytic, strategic and solution-focused counsellors' preferred techniques and strategies as both effective responses to clients' needs and as morally appropriate responses. This is one way in which counselling texts attempt to assert authority over their readers. The texts construct images of proper professional conduct that counsellors may use in assessing others and themselves as competent psychoanalytic, strategic and solution-focused counsellors. Thus, we might portray debates about client resistance as contests about what will count as genuine professionalism in counselling.

This brings us back to the social construction of clienthood in counselling texts. The texts socially construct clients as characters within counsellors' stories about proper professional conduct, attitudes and values.

Within the texts, clients are cultural symbols that align advocates for different counselling approaches with their preferred social values. I see this as an important factor in explaining psychoanalytic, strategic and solution-focused writers' proclivity for defining and speaking for clients' interests in counselling. We have seen how: psychoanalytic texts link counsellors with the social value of health by constructing clients as suffering from illnesses which counsellors diagnose and treat; how strategic texts cast counsellors as expert problem solvers by constructing clients as trapped in dysfunctional system patterns that keep clients from solving their own problems; and how solution-focused texts align counsellors with the social value of co-operation by constructing clients as consumers of counselling services.

We also see how counselling texts socially construct clients as symbols of preferred social values in psychoanalytic, strategic and solution-focused writers' descriptions of preferred counsellor–client relationships. An example is the earlier quote from Fisch *et al.* (1982) in which they describe the ideal counselling interaction as one in which the client gives the counsellor all requested information and the client fully complies with all of the counsellor's recommendations. A similar image of counsellor–client collaboration is central to the sick role and to psychoanalytic counselling. For strategic and psychoanalytic counsellors, then, client resistance refers to departures from the ideal. Client resistance is a practical problem that strategic and psychoanalytic counsellors must solve in order to solve clients' systemic and medical problems.

Solution-focused writings about client resistance also include images of ideal counsellor–client interactions and relationships. We see this in de Shazer's (1989) rejection of the suggestion that solution-focused counsellors might be to blame when troubles emerge in solution-focused counselling sessions. He explains that blaming the counsellor is theoretically unsound because it creates an 'imaginary opposition' between the counsellor and client. De Shazer (1989) concludes that counsellor–client opposition is not 'what we want'. Duncan and Miller (2000) further develop this image of the ideal solution-focused counsellor–client relationship by casting clients as heroic figures and as victims of 'planet mental health', that is, as victims of counselling approaches based on the medical model.

Clearly advocates for psychoanalytic, strategic and solution-focused counsellors socially construct clients and counsellor–client relationships in ways that fit with their assumptions and preferences. The counsellors also use these constructions to confer preferred identities on themselves. These aspects of counsellors' social construction of clienthood and professionalism remind us of Hacking's (1986) discussion about how making up people is similar to manufacturing gloves.

Questioning textual authority

Some readers may assume that I am preparing to tell them about what 'actually' goes on in psychoanalytic, strategic and solution-focused counselling sessions. After all, I have stressed how writers of counselling texts use idealized images of clients, counsellors and counselling interactions in pressing their claims. Surely, I know something that these writers do not know or that they are not willing to admit. I might also highlight the contrast between my 'great' expertise about counselling or about clients' 'real' interests with other writers' 'mere' claims about these issues. I could describe my knowledge as 'objective' and label my claims as 'the truth'. In using this language I would also be suggesting that the other writers' knowledge is not objective and that they do not know truth.

There are several problems with these assumptions. First, I do not know more about psychoanalytic, strategic and solution-focused counselling or about clients' 'real' interests than do the writers of the texts discussed in this chapter. Nor would I call my knowledge about counselling objective or *the* truth. Any generalizations that I might make about what 'actually' goes on in counselling sessions would also be idealizations. I do not see the usefulness of adding yet another set of idealizations to the counselling literature. I am also not going to suggest that counsellors stop writing and reading texts about counselling or that the texts be written in different ways. Counselling texts are filled with useful ideas, suggestions and social constructions. Their popularity among practising counsellors attests to the usefulness of the texts.

The issues that interest me focus on readers' participation in the textual dynamics of the counselling profession. Readers may participate in several different ways, including as largely passive consumers of counselling texts and as committed proponents for their preferred counselling approaches. Another way that readers may participate in the social construction of the counselling profession is by questioning texts representing different counselling approaches. I hasten to add that asking useful questions does not necessarily mean that the questioner is hostile to the approach represented in the text. Some of the most useful questions asked about counselling texts come from readers who are sympathetic to the texts and their authors. I have found that confused readers often ask useful questions about texts. Confused readers ask for greater clarification, explanation and/or elaboration of the concepts, principles and applications discussed in counselling texts. A related set of useful questions asks that writers of counselling texts clarify the connection between their texts, on the one hand, and the diverse practical realities of counselling settings and relationships, on the other. This brings me to my own confused question about the counselling literature on client resistance.

My question asks for greater clarification about what writers of counselling texts mean when they use the word 'client'. The writings about client resistance discussed here consistently define the client as the person or group with whom the counsellor meets to discuss aspects of the client's life. This is the client whose best interests are being served by the counsellor. There is no conflict of interest between the counsellor and client. Clients are not put at a disadvantage in collaborating with counsellors. Thus it makes sense for psychoanalytic and strategic counsellors to define client resistance as symptomatic of clients' problems and for solution-focused counsellors to deny the possibility that clients might resist.

But aren't there times when the people who meet with counsellors are put at a disadvantage in these meetings? Do counsellors sometimes knowingly or unknowingly align themselves with groups that oppose what these clients consider to be their best interests? The opposed interests with whom counsellors might be aligned include parents and schools (against children), adult children (against their aged parents), courts and correctional agencies (against law offenders), social service agencies (against their clients) and employers (against their employees). Each of these groups may compel others to participate in counselling and they often pay for counselling services given to others. Further, governmental, professional and insurance regulations with which counsellors must comply may sometimes conflict with clients' interests.

Several other questions come to my mind when I think about these counselling situations. For example, is it possible for counsellors to have two different and opposed clients, that is, a client who makes the referral and pays the counsellor's fee and another client who meets with the counsellor? If this is possible, then should one client's interests be given precedence over the other client's interests? Would it be ethical to accept one client's money and then to ignore that client's interests in the counselling session with the other client? Would it be ethical for a counsellor to meet with a client (such as a child) and not tell the client that the counsellor is orienting to the interests of another client (such as a school or the child's parents)? Is it possible that, in this situation, the child's 'co-operative' behaviour might also be called acquiescence to the authority and power conferred on the counsellor by the referring client? Might resistance be a rational response for a person in this situation? I believe that these questions are useful to counsellors for at least two reasons. First, the questions remind us that counsellor–client interactions are associated with diverse social contexts. We should expect to see a greater variety of social constructions of clienthood and professionalism in these interactions than we see in texts written about the interactions. Certainly I have observed a wider variety of therapy contexts than I find described in counselling texts. Second, I believe that these questions are particularly useful for solution-focused and other so-called collaborative counsellors to consider. The questions point to some of the practical difficulties of enacting the social value of counsellor–client co-operation in concrete counselling interactions. The difficulties involve both the diversity of social contexts under which clients and counsellors meet, but also the matter of counsellor power within the interactions.

The possibility that counselling involves the assertion of professional power over clients is much less problematic for counsellors who define themselves as experts than it is for counsellors advocating for collaborative counselling approaches. Expert counsellors know what is best for their clients and might even be said to have a professional responsibility to sometimes impose their will on clients. Power is not a word that solution-focused and other collaborative counsellors like to use in writing about themselves as professionals or their approaches to counselling. It might, however, be an issue that collaborative counsellors need to talk and write about.

While I am not yet ready to advocate for it, I am intrigued by the possibilities of adapting Fiske's (1989) approach to resistance in popular culture to solution-focused counselling contexts. Fiske socially constructs resistant consumers in making sense of the distinctive situations of socially marginalized groups in dealing with mainstream, mass-produced popular culture. This situation is loosely similar to that of clients who are compelled to participate in counselling. In both cases, the consumer lacks the power to define the situation to fit with her or his self-interests. Popular culture consumer resistance centres in accepting mainstream popular culture objects (such as blue jeans) but in ways that transform their meaning to better fit with the consumers' interests, identities and circumstances. As Fiske (1989) explains:

> If today's jeans are to express oppositional meanings, they need to be disfigured in some way – tie-dyed, irregularly bleached, or, particularly torn. If 'whole' jeans connote shared meanings of contemporary America, then disfiguring them becomes a way of distancing oneself from those values. But such a distancing is not a complete rejection. Wearing torn jeans is an example of the contradictions that are so typical of popular culture, where what is to be resisted is necessarily present in the resistance. (p.4)

It might be useful for solution-focused counsellors to explore whether and how some of their clients might use counselling sessions to construct oppositional meanings, meanings that are now rendered invisible to the counsellors because they have socially constructed their clients as people who are incapable of any type of resistance.

Solution-focused counsellors might also ask, 'How respectful is it to deny clients the ability to resist their counsellors?' A related question asks, 'Is it an assertion of professional power over clients when solution-focused counsellors deny that their clients are incapable of resisting?' Finally, solution-focused and other collaborative counsellors might ask about the contradictions associated with diverse counselling contexts and how these contradictions might make consumer resistance sensible for clients.

Practical implications

It is now time to consider some of the practical implications of the chapter. First, I should say that I do not see any major practical implications for how most counselling sessions are done. Most of the counsellors that I have observed and talked with over the years are quite adept at adjusting to the diversity of clients and contexts that make up their professional practices.

Thus, I believe that the main practical implications of this chapter centre in how counsellors are trained. These are sites for asserting authority over counsellors in the name of proper professional practice. One way that trainers assert authority is by insisting that trainees strictly follow the teachings of counselling texts. My point is not to deny the authoritativeness of trainers or the authors of counselling texts. Rather, I ask that trainers consider exercising their authority in ways that recognize the limiting assumptions and images of counselling texts. I have already indicated some of the questions that trainers and the people they train might ask in critically examining counselling texts. These questions are intended to encourage discussions about the relationship between counselling texts and professional practice. The issue for me is not whether to accept fully or reject the authority of counselling texts, but how to make them useful within conversations among counsellors. Specifically, I find it useful to treat training as opportunities to talk about the variety of contexts of counselling. Based on these discussions, we can begin to develop multiple – perhaps even contradictory – constructions of clienthood and professionalism that fit with the various contexts of counsellor–client interactions. I see this approach to training as solution-focused. It is consistent with solution-focused counsellors' claim that 'one size does not fit all people' and that there are always exceptions to dominant patterns.

13

Client, User, Member as Constructed in Institutional Interaction

Søren Peter Olesen

Unemployed people have a marginal position. The role of public service as part of their treatment, their interaction with public service and the roles and identities they take and get in public encounters may be of crucial importance as regards their inclusion in social life. Activation and workfare schemes in employment policy, like other aspects of social and labour market policy, have focused increasingly on adaptation of policy aims to the premises and qualifications of individuals, making negotiations at the front-line of welfare systems strategically important.

To illuminate such negotiations this chapter analyses similarities and differences between talks about individual action plans at the ground level of Danish social and labour market policy. Extracts from three selected cases of public encounters in different institutional settings, a public employment office, an unemployment insurance office and a social activation project are presented.

The presentation focuses on three aspects (separable analytically only) of the encounters:

1.   What is the talking about? Content of the talks and action plan talks as activity type. (Levinson 1992)

2.   How are they managed? The way action plan talks are handled by participants, including forms of talk or discourse type. (Sarangi 2000)

3. Accomplishing the institutional task, how are roles and identities presented and constructed in the interaction (Antaki and Widdicombe 1998)? Reproduction as well as softening and loosening of structural traits. (Goffman 1983)

The talks about activation represent the overall shifts from 'welfare' to 'workfare', in a specific Danish version, however. Improving the qualifications of the unemployed to some extent is emphasized, even if the political rhetoric expresses a neo-liberal, 'work first' strategy (Lødemel and Trickey 2001; Peck 2000; Torfing 2000). The purpose of the talks as regulated by law is the making of individual action plans (Olesen 1999). The institutional task at action plan talks, according to a thorough Danish labour market reform in 1994 and a reform of social policy in 1998, is to balance individual wishes and qualifications with demands in the labour market and in society.

Danish social and labour market policy, including the activation system, is organized as a two-tier administrative system aimed at the insured and uninsured unemployed respectively. Unemployment insurance funds build on voluntary membership. You get entitled to benefits after one year of work and membership. Historically funds have been organized as part of trade union activity and most of them are still organized along trade union lines (the so-called Gent-system is well known for example in Belgium, Sweden and Finland; see Ploug 1992). Often membership of a trade union and the unemployment insurance fund appear as one membership, and you are talking about withdrawing benefits from the union. Although funds get most of their finances from the state, it is considered less stigmatizing to receive unemployment benefits than to get social assistance.

Public employment offices administer activation schemes, including the obligation to make individual action plans, for insured unemployed people. Extract 13.1 below illustrates this. Unemployment insurance offices take part in the administration and, among other things, prepare the insured unemployed and control availability as a precondition for payment of benefits. Extract 13.2 represents a case of that. Social assistance recipients, in contrast, get their assistance from local authorities, which also administer activation schemes for the uninsured. Excerpt 13.3 is from a follow-up talk at a municipal social activation project about the individual plan of a young female client.

Analytical frame

The analytical frame covers the wider social and political context, the institutional task at action plan talks, forms and modalities of talks and, finally, participation structure, including roles and identities constructed at the talks (Layder 1993). It draws on Sarangi's integrated model of activity analysis (Sarangi 2000, p.4). Meetings between unemployed citizens and the state involve an official party vested with legal and organizational powers and professional methods as well as a lay party representing a life-world. Analytically separate, but in practice overlapping, processes could be isolated (Olesen 1999) policy implementation (Winter 1994) ending up with the application of professional counselling methods. Further, service seeking with thresholds and barriers to pass for the unemployed is taking place (Bleiklie 1996). Finally, institutional interaction as such (e.g. Drew and Heritage 1992a) is fundamentally characterized by structural asymmetry, eventually although not always and with necessity appearing as linguistic dominance (Sarangi and Slembrouck 1996).

Institutional interaction is close to a 'public encounter' – a dyad of two people, an official with 'authority and vested with legal powers' and a citizen 'standing alone before the sovereign state' – (Goodsell 1981, p.5), 'institutional gate-keeping' (Erickson and Schultz 1982) or '*Alltagskontakte mit der Verwaltung*' (Grunow 1978). It represents 'street-level bureaucracy' and dilemmas of the individual in contact with public authorities (Lipsky 1980). As indicated with the three aspects listed above, the main focus is the interaction process.

Looking at the first aspect, the content of the talks, activation is about unemployed people getting (back) into work. Constraints on participants and the settings and kind of contributions considered allowable in this activity are of interest. Levinson's (1992) definition of activity type focuses on 'goal-defined, socially constituted, bounded, events with *constraints* on participants, setting, and so on, but above all on the kinds of allowable contributions' (p.69). The activity type, among others, helps to determine how what one says will be 'taken' (Levinson 1992, p.97). It connects talk with setting and wider social context, and offers a way of interpreting which of a number of meanings is relevant regarding a specific utterance at a specific talk.

As regards the second aspect in focus, the forms of talk, action plan talks might represent a monological (Linell 1998) casework structure with more or less outspoken asymmetry and dominance as well as a dialogical balancing of considerations through negotiation as intended by regulation, thus leading to the question, how are new activities handled with existing forms of talk? Sarangi (2000, p.2) applies activity type as characterizing settings, whereas the notion of discourse type is used to characterize forms of talk. Discourse type, however, is a broad category (Fairclough 1992, p.124), including a range of concepts such as genre, style, register, talk, and social practice. Discourses and social practices draw on discourse types rather than mechanically implementing them (Sarangi 2000, p.12; Fairclough 1989, p.39).

Activity types and discourse types may overlap. Sarangi suggests that 'activity types and discourse types (re)configure in various ways and that various modes of talk mix as "interactional hybridity"' (Sarangi 2000, p.2; Sarangi and Roberts 1999, p.62). Some cases of social change, following the idea of 'interactional hybridity', appear as (new) applications or recontextualizations of (elements of) existing discourse types in emerging activity types. For instance, a teaching discourse (as in Extract13.3 below), a discourse of casework (Extract 13.2) or counselling (Extract 13.1), a discourse of interrogation or other discourse types, including balanced negotiation, may appear in or as part of talks about activation. As a relatively new field of social work practice, variety and interactional hybridity can be assumed to characterize workfare and activation, including talks about individual action plans.

Specific activity types will seldom, if ever, appear in pure form. Especially in cases of highly contradictory or dynamic or quite new types of activity, interactional hybridity may occur. Discourse types from other settings get mixed up with the activity type in question. For instance, in a corpus from 1996 of 32 activation plan talks at Danish employment offices the talks tend to have an asymmetric casework structure of information gathering, 'social diagnosis' and unilateral planning of activation measures. According to policy intentions, however, they should have represented a dialogic balancing of interests through negotiation and contracting (Olesen 1999).

Finally, regarding the third aspect, role identities as managed in interaction (Antaki and Widdicombe 1998b) appear in face work (Goffman 1967) and politeness strategies (Brown and Levinson 1987). Identities as underlying cultural and psychological patterns, are further situated in the interaction, closely related to the aspects mentioned above. Unemployed people may appear as humble, complying individual subjects before representatives of the sovereign state. Others may have the gumption to stand forward with a developed public identity based on their legal rights and on their earlier experiences as regards contacting public services, altogether forming their 'public identity' (Hetzler 1994). Differences between the institutional settings referred to in the cases below are manifest. At public employment offices users are seeking service as citizens, users or even 'customers'. At unemployment insurance offices the unemployed act, and are treated, first of all as union members, even if subject to availability control routines. Finally, at social activation projects (uninsured) clients were perceived as (mostly young) persons, entitled to, but also dependent on, help, training and education, on learning something in order to behave (especially in educational and work settings) and maybe even in need of further social treatment.

Cases selected for analysis

The three cases selected represent variations in the way counselling is brought into being across different institutional settings. In the 1996 corpus, mentioned above, different types of encounters were identified: client compliance, resistance, co-operation and users getting helped (Olesen 1999, 2001a, 2001b). The first excerpt is from this corpus, while the others are from a corpus collected in 2000–01, covering activation more broadly. Each of the three extracts has been selected as illustrative and crucial regarding the detailed balancing of individual and labour market considerations taking place at the single encounter; and the three encounters have been selected as cases of relatively 'successful fulfilment' of the institutional task (balancing of considerations) across various institutional settings. Participants were satisfied with the talks and referred to them in a positive way in interviews immediately afterwards. The analysis indicates some of the reasons why.

The talks were tape-recorded, and while the recording took place they were observed. Afterwards the parties at the talks were interviewed about their experience and their attitudes towards these kind of talks. In advance regulation by law, institutional setting and societal context as well as a number of theoretical approaches were analysed as constituting the field. In the extracts unemployed people are coded U and counsellors C. Turns are given numbers. Backchannellings are shown in brackets: < >. Transcripts are with few details. Most of the analysis was based directly on the soundtracks.

Support through resistance to troubles telling at an employment office

The first extract is from an employment office. The content clearly has to do with activation issues. It is characterized by the counsellor trying to 'convince' the unemployed person, an unskilled woman in her thirties, about her ability to handle a possible ordinary placement in the near future. She has wanted more training, although she has just left a 13-week course aiming at the tree industry, where she explicitly wished to become employed. She expresses the aim of getting an unskilled industrial job. The talk is also a matter of indicating to her that receiving benefits means being available for the labour market, so she needs to be able to take jobs at some distance and to have organized day care for her children. Thereby it is making distinctions between 'allowable' and 'unallowable' as regards activation as activity type. The counsellor is characterized as a thorough and careful 'craftsman' (Olesen 1999), trained in classical vocational guidance. He tries to convince her both that it is quite realistic to get an ordinary industrial job and that she will be able to manage this.

Extract 13.1

(C = counsellor, U = unemployed person)

1   C: <after having checked the immediate placement opportunities> ... We haven't got anything right now.

2   U: No, I thought so.

3   C: Yes, but we'll get that, I believe. But-uh, one of the places where production is booming just now is at C <a big factory in a small town about 10km away>.

4   U: Well, but that's then too far on a bicycle. I only have my old bike.

5   C: Well, that's a matter of – there are indeed a lot of people in this town working at C. You might find somebody, make an arrangement with somebody about driving together.

6   U: <pause> It may then even, it may even get too much bother <thick voice>. It is something like…the nursery has to open first, before you can get out of the door.

7   C: It isn't far to C. It is somewhat like a suburb to this town, isn't it?

8   U: That's of course quite right.

9   C: Well, even I would say it's too far to go by bike. I would say that also. Especially in wintertime. However, it is then somehow part of this town.

10   U: But C, isn't it more like so to speak-uh...

11   C: It is a very modern factory, big. They make fine products. There is...

12   U: You shall not make me believe, that you just can drop in there and then believe that you are something.

13   C: Well, that is the tree-industry. Whether you make coffee tables, or you make kitchens. That's completely the same. That is, actually I believe that.

14   U: Well, it might then be, that just, just, just for instance kitchens, right, that it maybe would require, that you knew a little about it on beforehand.

15   C: Well, it's blockboard, isn't it, and veneer, and maybe even somewhat solid wood.

16   U: Yes-yes, it's just that I don't know anything about it, isn't it. I have only worked with chest-legs.

17   C: That's the tree-industry. And my point of view is in principle that it doesn't matter whether you make chests of drawers or you make kitchens <a lengthy argumentation>. It is the same. I believe that.

18   U: I just do believe, it should rather be inside this town, shouldn't it. That is, children, you know, they get ill and things like that <tells a story about being recalled by the nursery from a training course>. And I'm alone, you know, with the children. I haven't got anybody to bring them home to. I have neither parents nor siblings or someone, who might step in and bring them home, so I'm not too enthusiastic about getting outside the town. That is, I think it's going to be too much stress...

19   C: Well, I can see that. It's just that, C you know, that is something like, that is something like the neighbourhood, isn't it...and...but, well, I can see that it may be kind of a problem. However, I believe, in case of, if you are there, then I don't believe, there would be any problem, because there are so many, with whom you might make an arrangement, drive together with and something like that. There is then a stream of traffic out there to the factory in the morning. How far is it, 10 km?

20   U: Is it? Well, I don't even think there are 10 km.

The content of this talk is characterized, among other things, by a number of negotiations. This one is initiated by the counsellor's information that there are no current opportunities for ordinary placement (turn 1) and her understatement (turn 2) probably meaning 'this is hopeless!'. It is followed by a number of moves, indicating that the place suggested by the counsellor as a possible opportunity (turn 3) is too far, too much trouble, above her level and on the whole overwhelming (turns 4, 6, 12, 16 and 18). Besides 'convincing' remarks (e.g. turns 5, 7, 9 and 19) the counsellor, keeping the talk on track of the institutional task given, is showing resistance to the troubles telling of the unemployed (Jefferson and Lee 1992; Vehviläinen 1999). He is, however, taking the time necessary to listen to her and explain demands and possibilities in a supportive way.

The form of talk thus combines authority and empathy (Shulman 1991) on behalf of the official. He seems to categorize her as competent and available, willing and able to work although surprised that job openings might be just around the corner, and maybe in doubt whether she is still qualified after a period away from the labour market during childbirth and divorce. At the end of the extract she seems to show alignment to this (turn 20). There are only a few minimal responses and a few strong initiatives in the extract. His moves are formed as and met with prolonged responses (Linell and Gustavsson 1987). Additionally there is a close to equal distribution of interactional space. Thus, the level of linguistic dominance is low.

The unemployed person is categorized as competent and available, and belonging to the active, industrial labour force through negotiation. The negotiation is characterized among other things by her counsellor combining authority with empathy and keeping up demands on her as available for the labour market as well as by lack of linguistic dominance. The underlying asymmetry, associated with institutional interaction as such, obviously still is there. However, lack of linguistic dominance, authority combined with empathy in resistance to her troubles talk, and lack of face-threatening acts in the counsellor's professional style are important aspects of the talk. They make it a case of supportive co-operation, satisfactory to the unemployed person according to the interview after the talk.

Negotiating compliance while protecting member status at an unemployment office

The second extract covers a case of controlling availability as activity, a rather well-defined institutional task at unemployment insurance offices. The control routines develop into a negotiation about burnout. The talk is taking place between a service-oriented official (with an education as a clerk and supplementary experience and training in counselling) and an unemployed woman in her forties. This activity is preliminary to activation planning at the employment office. The woman has given up her work as a social pedagogue and moved to a rather isolated place on an island to live together with her new husband. Her job seeking activity, however, is insufficient, resulting in a written request demanding a higher level of activity over the next three months. The potentially face-threatening discussion about availability, active job seeking and burnout should be seen in the light of exercising availability control as task, but also of the unemployed person eventually getting re-educated as part of an activation plan from the employment office.

Extract 13.2

(C = counsellor, U = unemployed person)

1 C: I'll tell you what, now, when you say, you cover a wide field, don't you <yes I do>, because I think you do that, right? Then we might say, well, why don't you enhance the field of your job-seeking to be wider still <yes>, because I don't know at all, if-uh something like-uh…

2 U: However, I do want to remain a social pedagogue and a member of the Union of Social Pedagogues <yes>, because that's what I am.

3 C: Yes you can <yes>. You can always stay as a member of the union <yes, yes>. You can even, if you end up outside this field <I see> stay as associate member <oh, I see>… That is because, that's what I have written here now, that you want to get a job. However, you are afraid of not being equal to the job, and that's why you haven't applied <yes> for advertised jobs, isn't it <yes>. And there has only been a few of them, I write, because you can't endure work that strains your back and neither, mentally, can you stand to work with psychotic children and so on. But grown up people you are able to work with, aren't you, and you think <yes> you are burned out without having known that, owing to hard work in 6 years <yes>, when…

4 U: I _was_ at that time.

5 C: …out of which one year…yes <yes>, didn't I formulate it that way?

6 U: No, I think you…

7 C: BB is burned out without…

8 U: No, I don't think I am now.

9 C: But you just said, that you were, however, that you didn't know.

10 U: Yes at that time. I knew it – I didn't know it<no>, it was at that time.

11 C: But then, what is it then, you say, you are now in relation to that kind of…clients?

12 U: Then I go right back in the same – that is, then…

13 C: That is, then you still are.

14 U: Then something happens…

15 C: Then you still are.

16 U: Yes that's right.

17 C: Is that, what we come up with?

18 U: Then I go by routine <yes>, that is-uh…

19 C: But don't you think you might overcome that?

20 U: Then I go straight back.

21 C: Do you think you would do that, also, if you were in the situation at a workplace?

22 U: Yes, I know that.

23 C: With good colleagues?

24 U: Yes.

25 C: Well, then-uh, I think, I have used the right formulation.

26 U: Well, so you have.

27 C: That you shouldn't try to seek jobs in this field again <yes>. Isn't that correct?

28 U: Yes, so, you have <pause>. It isn't, because I don't like them.

29 C: No, of course not. That's neither the reason why you get burned out. On the contrary <no>. People who get burned out, they are always enthusiastic people, aren't they <yes>, as a rule at the least.

30 U: Yes that's right.

31 C: But, but that's to say, you agree on, what I write.

32 U: Yes.

33 C: That you are burned out without having known that, owing to hard work during six years <yes> with this.

34 U: In this area.

35 C: Yes, I have to write 'in this area' and that's the one we mentioned <yes> with
          psychotic and autistic children, isn't it <yes> …and then I write 'only burned
          out in certain areas'.

36 U: Yes that's right.

The first half of the extract (turns 1–16) is the crucial part. It ends up with
the member changing her resistance (turns 4, 6, 8 and 10) to compliance
with the burnout categorization (turn 16). A supplementary and specifying
negotiation about the current interest of the categorization (turns 17–20)
releases a check of the conclusion from the counsellor (turns 21 and 23). The
next sequence (turns 25–29) specifies and confirms the conclusion. A last
check from the counsellor (turn 31) provokes a final renegotiation that specifies burnout and limits on availability as a distinct part of her professional
field. She ought to enhance her job seeking. It is, however, considered allowable that she is unable to deal with certain types of pedagogical work.
Burnout is even connected with enthusiasm.

The form of talk is characterized by casework routines and negotiation
with recontextualizations of written sentences from a journal documenting
the counselling and guidance measures as well as the control routines
applied. Extracts from the case record are made subject of part of the
negotiation (e.g. turns 3, 5, 7 and 25). Interactional asymmetry is outspoken.
The counsellor has more than 75 per cent of the words. Out of her 18 turns
12 are strong initiatives and none are minimal responses, while the member
has 13 prolonged responses and 5 minimal responses. The member,
however, clearly shows resistance before complying with the evaluation of
the counsellor. This sequence is potentially 'face' threatening for the
member. Her 'face', however, is protected by the categorization of her as
member (turn 3). And due to that, the talk in the end appears as a case of
co-operation.

Membership status of the unemployed, and neutrality and service-
orientation on behalf of the counsellor, are salient. Availability controls and
the written request demanding active job seeking don't interfere with the
membership status. Although the unemployed person is dissatisfied with the
request, which she considers superfluous and an overreaction, she is feeling
secure coming to the unemployment office because she considers it part of
her own trade union and experiences it as being there for her sake.

Despite asymmetry as regards linguistic dominance and control routines
the unemployed at the unemployment office is categorized and treated,

through a discourse of casework routines, negotiation and agreement, as a member with membership rights, indicating the importance of the institutional set-up surrounding the interaction. Even to the unemployed the experience is one of membership role and identity as such.

Producing alignment through politeness and discursive hybridity at an activation project for social welfare clients

The third extract is from a social activation project for young women. It is about 'hanging on' to activities like education, training and work and about becoming independent through this. It represents a very positive style. Even if potentially face threatening as regards her ability to 'holding on' and her need for help related to that, the young woman in the interview afterwards declares herself very content with the talk. The female social worker is a former teacher.

Extract 13.3

(C = counsellor, U = unemployed person)

1   C: They said you were incredibly good at doing all the jobs you were told to do, and-uh putting things on shelves and things like that, didn't they? It looked pretty nice, when you did something.

2   U: Yes.

3   C: Do you remember that?

4   U: Yes.

5   C: Yes, do you remember something he thought you should work on, do you remember some of it?

6   U: Well, there was something about sticking to things. Things like what we have talked about, VUC (Adult Education Centre), I should hold on to that and keep on sticking to that <yes>, until it was finished. At least he said so.

7   C: Why was it that he said so?

8   U: It was because I had talked about stopping.

9   C: Yes.

10 U: That's what he said, that it's not too smart to do <no>, because you can't just stop – yes you can – but he didn't think it was a good idea to stop in the middle of something.

11 C: Why is he poking his nose in that?

12 U: It was just because we had talked about it.

13 C: Yes, actually I do remember something he said about looking at applications for jobs, do you?

14 U: Just slightly. I don't recall all of it.

15 C: He had been looking at two applicants, and he should choose one of them.

16 U: Yes.

17 C: And then he looked at what they had been doing.

18 U: Yes, and for how long they had been sticking to <yes> different things.

19 C: Yes, and then it was important for him to see that some of them could hold on, wasn't it?

20 U: Well, it is important. I can see that <yes>. Even when, like he said, it is important then, isn't it, that you can hold on, when…and then even finish it.

21 C: Yes that's right. So, this was some of the matters I recall we talked about in the middle of your stay, and even you can by now as you <yes> <not audible> <laughter>. That's right…and the reason I talk about it, Karen <*fictitious name*>, is because, as I said, what I think we are also aiming at with this conversation, that is to find out about your future. How is it going to work out? And then I think it is fine that when this has been said: What was pretty well and what is it that I have to work on…

22 U: Well, at least I know I have to work on holding on to things.

23 C: Yes.

24 U: Because, well I have…I'm fed up with this VUC.

25 C: But you stick to it.

26 U: Yes-yes, I keep at it.

The extract is characterized by the social worker several times asking questions, even if she knows the answers very well herself (e.g. turns 5, 7 and 13). The conversation resembles classroom examination. Other typical turns from her contain bits of information reminding the client about specific points (e.g. turns 15, 17 and 19) and leading or guiding her to specific conclusions about 'hanging on', and finally giving her recognition (turns 21, 23 and 25). This is a display of 'positive politeness' (Brown and Levinson

1987). However, a rather clear distinction is made between allowable (to hold on) and unallowable (to drop out) contributions from the unemployed (Levinson 1992; Sarangi 2000). In turns 20 and 26 the client gives the 'right' answers, showing that she has learned her lesson well. In turn 24, talking about being fed up with the education centre she goes to, she is on the edge of the unallowable but is kept on track by the statement in turn 25.

The counsellor was trained as a teacher. Although the setting is informal and the activity type clearly about activation and opportunities for future education and employment in ordinary jobs (turn 21), it is mixed up with forms of talk derived from a teaching discourse (Linell and Gustavsson 1987). The counsellor, using informal style as if it is a matter of illegitimate curiosity ('poking his nose in that') at turn 11, makes a kind of alignment with the client. The extract is characterized by marked asymmetry. The counsellor makes the agenda and is steering the interaction. She takes eight out of nine initiatives while the client has six out of eight minimal responses. Linguistic dominance of the counsellor is obvious by her occupation of 57 per cent of the space (measured by number of words) as against the client's 43 per cent. Thus, the worker puts up the agenda from the beginning and through the extract (and the talk as a whole). She also, however, leaves some room for the client (turns 9, 15, 17 and 23).

At the activation project social work and the role and identity of being a client is constructed with asymmetry, linguistic dominance and elements from a discourse of classroom examination. The young woman is categorized as a client, drawing on a discourse of teaching, in the sense that she is treated as a student. She even acts as a student who has a lesson to learn. She is reminded about this lesson by the counsellor's questions, communicated with intuition and informal style, however, and with the cessation of clienthood as a realistic perspective.

Conclusion

The analysis has demonstrated how the unemployed at an employment office is actively constructed, through authority, empathy and resistance to the troubles telling, as available, able and qualified, and belonging to the labour force. Further, it has shown how membership status of an unemployment insurance fund and trade union is partly ascribed and partly preserved through negotiation, even if the official is operating casework and control routines regarding availability as entitlement to unemployment benefits. Finally, at an activation project for social assistance recipients, client status is established through alignment and through the practising of a discourse of teaching.

The interplay of different public identities on behalf of the user, member or client, as well as different strategies, professional standards and methods on behalf of the counsellors, results in a wide range of forms of institutional interaction. However, across the three extracts the client party is met with insistence on the institutional task in activation as activity type and with some resistance. Clear distinctions are made between allowable (to be available and actively job seeking, to hold on to an education, etc.) and unallowable contributions. Behind this is the central idea of activation and workfare strategies, that recipients of unemployment benefits and social assistance ought to become self-supportive and independent of income transfers from the public. As a client you have to accept that you are dependent but also that you shouldn't be in such a state of dependency.

The diversity, ambiguity and discursive hybridity of institutional inter-action, as demonstrated in the analyses, show that there is no simple and mechanical reproduction of structural traits and no simple and unequivocal image of how activation emerges in practice. Asymmetry and other structural traits are in some respects reproduced, in other respects softened and loosened (Goffman 1983), depending, among other things, upon the ability to enter into negotiations. Macro social theory is not able to explain this variety of forms and consequences of situated interaction. Situational factors and 'bricolage' play a role of their own, so that institutional gate keeping eventually emerges as a 'wiggle room' (Erickson 2001).

The three cases are at the outset considered relatively successful encounters in activation. Among the implications for practice to be drawn from analysing them is that there is no simple formula at hand for negotiating activation. As a new field of regulation, it is characterized by a mixture of forms – discursive hybridity. Authority seems important on behalf of the official party, but it has to be communicated. Education and training in counselling methods, especially as regards balancing through negotiation and contracting, is needed. Finally, membership status or other kinds of resources on behalf of the unemployed person are an advantage for an unemployed person, indicating the importance of the organizational set-up, specifically the role of unions, around the activation effort as part of public service.

14

Conclusion

Yes, But Is This of Any Use?

*Christopher Hall, Nigel Parton, Kirsi Juhila
and Tarja Pösö*

Making things more complicated

When Michel Foucault (1981) was asked whether *Discipline and Punish* (Foucault 1977) has set back attempts by social workers to reform prisons, he said:

> My project is precisely to bring it about that (social workers) no longer know what to do, so that the acts, gestures, discourses which until then has seemed to go without saying become problematic, difficult and dangerous. This effect is intentional. (p.12)

There is no doubt that it is never easy to clearly identify the implications for policy and practice of any piece of research. More specifically, one response to constructionist and discourse approaches to human services is to be sceptical that anything of substance can be achieved. Constructionist explorations of the backstage and unseen arenas might be heard as ironic and undermining, challenging the very possibility of competent professional practice. Another response, however, is much more vitriolic. Recently, for example, Brian Sheldon has referred to ethnography, discourse analysis and social constructionism as 'not so much a critique, more a fashion statement' (Sheldon 2001, p.806). This has certainly not been our intention in this book, and in this conclusion we wish to explore a number of the themes we feel are illustrated in the preceding chapters. A central theme is that the (social work) world is complex and we feel the approaches adopted here provide positive ways of trying to capture this complexity, which then allows us to intervene in thoughtful, sensitive and productive ways. However, we are not suggesting that this is straightforward – it is complicated – but it does suggest we need to try and adopt a certain 'ethos' towards what we do, how we do it and, crucially, how we think it. The second part of the Foucault quote we began with continues:

> What is to be done ought not to be determined from above by reformers, be they prophetic or legislative, but by the long work of comings and goings, of exchanges, reflections, trials, different analyses…The problem is one for the subject who acts.

Foucault always attempted to introduce an untimely 'ethos' to the present, thereby adding a sense of its fragility and contingency – demonstrating that things do not necessarily have to be like this. In the process we can think about the present differently and act in new and creative ways (Bell 1994). The present is not inevitable or homogeneous but something to be decomposed, problematized and acted upon. The purpose is to bring into the open the problems that have relevance for our current experiences and, in doing so, uncouple our experiences from their conditions. Destabilizing and fragmenting the present opens up a space for change. The ethos is thus one of a permanent questioning of the present and a commitment to uncertainty, not to establish the limits of thought and action but to locate where they might be transgressed and thus arrive at novel ways of thinking and acting. The ethos is not concerned with relativizing – a common critique of constructionist perspective – but with 'destabilizing' in order to open up possibilities for change (Parton 1999). In the spirit of this 'ethos' we have tried to show how the studies reported here offer greater insights into the 'what-ness' of everyday action (Garfinkel 1967) than has been possible by traditional research methods. At the same time, these studies point towards different approaches to what counts as knowledge and evidence for both researchers and practitioners. In doing so, it promotes a more 'constructive' (Parton and O'Byrne 2000), 'reflexive' (Taylor and White 2001) and even more 'social' (Saleeby 2001) form of professional practice located in the everyday life-worlds of clients and professionals.

Such an approach, while located in research and exploring evidence, does not however draw on simplistic notions of scientism – science as a practice 'distinct from and superior to common sense' (Silverman 1993, p.5). It questions whether it is possible or appropriate to justify social research and professional practice on the basis of quasi-experimental methods – that family problems can be easily identified and labelled, that interventions can be provided in a uniform and consistent manner and that outcomes and effects can be measured. These are all social processes and therefore available to social scientific study. These studies have shown that it is more complicated than that: professional and researchers' problem categories are complex and jointly produced in institutional processes. Interventions are unlikely to be 'the same' in any meaningful sense (see, for example, Heritage and Sefi 1992 on approaches to advice giving), and measurement is also a social process (Porter 1995).

Studying practices rather than beliefs

There are several alternatives to the quasi-experimental view of research, which seek to ask what counts as knowledge and evidence. One approach often favoured by qualitative researchers is to claim authority on the basis of developing personal involvement with the research subjects and seeing the social world through their eyes (Bryman 1988, p.61). In such approaches the researcher aims to become immersed in the subjects' world through, for example, depth interviews and participant observation. It involves taking the actors' point of view (Denzin 1970) and searching for the 'meaning and essences of experiences' (Moustakas 1994, p.21). Halfpenny (1979) sums up:

> In the interpretivist approach, 'understanding' the action and interactions of respondents, by virtue of grasping and comprehending the culturally appropriate concepts through which they conduct their social life is the way in which explanation is achieved. (p.808)

The researcher, through involvement with the subjects, is able to understand their interpretation of the social reality and provide evidence of their perceptions and concepts.

While there is some sympathy with such approaches and support for a view that understanding contexts and interpretations of subjects is an important component of analysis, there is a danger in merely treating the actors' point of view as explanation. Silverman (1993) notes, 'Naïve interviewers believe that the supposed limits of structural sociology are overcome by an open-ended interview schedule and a desire to catch "authentic experience"'.

The chapters in this book have developed approaches to analysis that are concerned less with how speakers explain their point of view than with an exploration of the verbal, rhetorical and literal methods used to make social work possible; as Silverman (1985) puts it, less a concern with what people are thinking than an interest in what they are doing (p.96). To this extent the work is empirical, displaying data in the form of talk and writing and identifying patterns. It is even scientific. Silverman (1993) notes how 'Sacks wanted to do better science' (p.52) – a concern for what is observable, avoiding abstractions and generalizations, and providing the reader with transcripts of naturally occurring activities.

What do we mean by evidence-based practice?

A theme which runs through the book, but which is most explicitly discussed by Sue White, concerns the nature of evidence and its usefulness, particularly in the context of the increasing prominence given to the notion of evidence-based practice (EBP) in policy and practice debates about social work and human services work more generally. It is important to emphasize that we are not unsympathetic to these developments and in many respects see this book as making a positive contribution to them. However, we are concerned at the way EBP is often interpreted and implemented. We are concerned that it is often conceived narrowly, of a top-down nature, and seen as unproblematic. The approach adopted is often excessively utilitarian and instrumental in intention. We feel the messages of the research discussed in this book are much more complex than social scientists telling politicians, managers and professionals 'what works', and 'why' and what policies and practices are likely to be most 'effective'.

There are two approaches which tend to dominate debates about EBP. The naïve rational approach that research *leads* practice (knowledge-driven model) and which places the researcher in a very powerful position; and the problem-solving approach where research *follows* policy and where practice issues shape research agendas. Here the researcher is much more at the behest of the policy maker.

Both models assume a linear relationship between research and practice, however; the difference is in the posited direction of the influence. It is only more recently that we have come to recognize the much more uncertain and sometimes contradictory messages for practice of scientific evidence. In Britain the impact of the BSE scare and arguments about genetically modified crops have had political as well as social implications well beyond their research and professional communities. Increasingly it has been recognized that the relationships between research and decision makers – whether they be politicians, policy makers or practitioners – is much more subtle and complex than might previously have been assumed. Research is better understood as just one of the factors which might play a role in decision making so that the relationship is much more nebulous and interactive in nature. Weiss (1979) outlines at least six models for the way in which research might be conceptualized as impacting on decision making.

Researchers who are trying to take thinking forward in these areas (see, for example, Young *et al.* 2002; Packwood 2002) have argued that it is much better to talk in terms of 'evidence-informed' practice, rather than 'evidence-based' practice, and see the most appropriate approach as being characterized as an 'enlightenment model'. Here research is seen as standing a little distant from immediate policy and practice concerns; the relationship is much more indirect. The focus is less likely to be the decision problem itself than the *context* within which the decision might be taken, providing a frame for thinking about it. Research aims to illuminate the landscape for decision makers and actors more generally. The role of research becomes one of primarily clarifying issues and informing debate and less one of problem solving. Research takes on the role of aiding the democratic process rather than being part of a narrowly focused decision-making process and recognizes that evidence is likely to be contested and subject to debate.

However, such debate is likely to be more reasoned than if research were not available in the first place. Research on process as well as outcomes is equally, if not more, relevant in these circumstances. The prime focus of the research in this book has been on 'how the work gets done'. More specifically, the researchers have rarely been concerned with normative issues and with the efficacy or otherwise of particular techniques or approaches (although the chapter by Ah Hin Teoh *et al.* is something of an exception as it is written primarily from the perspective of the client and the social worker). They have been primarily concerned with providing detailed, qualitative descriptions, reports and analyses of what is going on in the client–worker interactions. In doing so the research is able to reveal some of the limits of purely theoretical accounts of social work(ing). The research is very empirical and thus provides a range of different pieces of 'evidence' of social work practices with a range of different clients. In doing so the nature and content of the work becomes more transparent, so that research can make a contribution to debates about what is 'really' going on and the nature of the processes and outcomes involved. Primarily, however, it aims to inform those debates rather than direct or circumscribe them.

Things are not what they seem

Importance of language and interaction

These studies have been concerned with language and interaction, a view that entities and action are constituted in language. Common to the chapters is a rejection of the notion that language corresponds in a direct way with the 'real' world and an emphasis on the way language functions in social life. There is a recognition that the relationship between language and things in the world is much more undetermined than is often assumed; that is, that there is no necessary connection between objects, actions and states and what they are called. Rather than reflecting the world, language generates it in the contexts of human and material interchanges. In effect, the metaphor of 'language as a mirror' is replaced by that of 'language as a tool'.

When professionals and clients talk to one another there is not a transparent exchange of information but the very process of communication creates realities. What this suggests is that any concept needs to be explored for how it is talked about rather than assuming it exists unproblematically. Kirsi Juhila discusses the process and criteria involved in *creating* good and bad clients. Based on her detailed case analysis she argues that the construed characteristics of a good client include:

- taking on the client identity and accepting the help offered by the social workers

- showing good motivation to be helped

- accepting the social workers' suggestions as competent

- not criticizing the policy and conduct of the agency or the worker.

The more a client contravenes these criteria the more likely they are to be deemed a bad client. Perhaps most crucially the disalignment of identities creates trouble in conversation and the original reason for the encounter can be lost. Carolus van Nijnatten and Gerard Hofstrede also comment that the family supervisor in the case they present became so concerned with the mother's (in)capabilities that little attention was given to the condition of the child, which was the original reason for contact. The chapter by Søren Olsen demonstrates that, in practice, authority and empathy can constitute complementary, as well as contradictory, aspects of professional social work and counselling.

In a rather different way Tarja Pösö, by excluding specific references to the gender of clients in the transcripts discussed with probation officers, demonstrates how situational and case-specific clienthoods and genders are. Her suggestion is that the relationship between gender, clienthood and social work should be studied empirically in the contexts of practice rather than the characteristics attributed to it normatively being assumed. She also points out that the workers who were shown the transcripts described the interactions between the workers and the clients as a 'dance', and in fact she describes the whole exercise as 'playing around with gender'. The metaphors of play, dance and stage are often drawn on in research of this sort. This is not to underestimate the seriousness of many human situations but it does recognize that the way these are represented can have many of the characteristics of a drama.

Emotions are a key element in much of the work and it is clear that the interactional devices are not only concerned with words themselves. This is demonstrated in the chapter by Katja Kurri and Jarl Wahlström. What they also demonstrate is the importance of 'negotiations' in the process of establishing a social and moral order of the relationship between couples. The role of the therapist in couple therapy is key, they argue, for if the therapists they studied had missed the meta-level of clienthood and joined in the conversation with their own understanding of emotions, the voices of the spouses could have been obscured. The discursive moves of the therapist were important for countering blame constructions and introducing alternative constructions of the relationship.

The emphasis throughout the book, on the importance of the concrete and the real rather than the general and the normative, demonstrates how such approaches are thoroughly grounded in practice and can make a direct contribution to practice itself. Researchers often comment how merely showing research subjects the transcripts of their talk with colleagues or clients causes them to question their communication (see, for example, Silverman 1997 ch. 10). It suggests that professionals could gain by examining their language use and considering the ways in which language both imprisons them and offers the opportunity for liberation. It points towards, for example, the sort of brief therapy discussed by Gale Miller, which uses language to explore solutions to problems and which is an important part of the constructive approach discussed by Nigel Parton in the chapter with Ah Hin Teoh, Jim Laffer and Andrew Turnell (see also Parton and O'Byrne 2000).

More specifically, such research can help practitioners identify facets of their practice of which they were previously unaware, or only partially aware, as well as reframing what they 'know'. However, it should be noted how important it is that practitioners have the time, space and techniques available for taking stock of these issues. The sort of transcript used by the researchers – a verbatim audio- or videorecording of session – is likely to prove invaluable. However, we should not underestimate the resource, ethical, and potentially legal, implications involved. While there are increasing expectations that clients have 'access to files' in health and welfare agencies, it is also the case that most agencies are wanting to keep these as brief and 'factual' as possible. The time and space for recording process is becoming very limited in many institutional contexts. This issue is currently receiving little attention in mainstream social work. For example, the recent *Blackwell Encyclopaedia of Social Work* (Davies 2000) has no entry on either 'recording' or 'process recording'.

Categories are always more complex than at first sight

The human services rely for their processing on being able to identify what sort of case they are dealing with. Is it urgent or can it wait? Is it family support or child protection? Is this patient depressed or neurotic? Such categories work to enable professionals to identify the characteristics of families, link them to decisions made with similar cases and suggest possible interventions, and as a shorthand for colleagues. As Spencer (2001) says, 'Institutional selves are needed to conduct institutional business' (p.158). However, the danger is that, once categorized, the label attached to a case becomes fixed and client identities established.

A number of studies have investigated how professional categories are applied and maintained, often in a deterministic way, and how clients attempt to resist the categorizations (Silverman's 1987 work on 'neurotic mothers'). Chris Hall, Arja Jokinen and Eero Suoninen look at how social workers and parents negotiated the category of the 'rejecting mother' in social work meetings – one meeting where the mother wanted custody transferred to the father and the other where the mother asked that the child remain in care. In both meetings, the category of the 'rejecting mother' proved to be difficult, almost anomalous for the social workers to accept. Each meeting spent considerable time negotiating a more complex notion of how such a state of affairs was acceptable and what constituted the identity of a rejecting mother. However, once established, what to do next was relatively straightforward; that is, category negotiation is central to the practice of social work, not a precursor to it.

Similarly Pirjo Nikander demonstrates the importance of establishing acceptable categories between professionals when making decisions about resource allocation. This is, however, a complex process since placing clients into categories means some clients are denied services. It points towards enabling professionals to work towards greater heterogeneity of clienthood.

Moral formulations are inevitable

We have already noted a number of examples which illustrate that the moral construction of clients is a central feature of both how clients are categorized and how they are responded to. It is sometimes suggested that in identifying this the purpose should be to expunge such moral constructions from practice. This is not our position, as the data clearly demonstrates morality issues are inherent in the work. The issue becomes much more about trying to make this explicit and so ensure there is some consistency between what is intended and what is actually going on in practice; that there can be as much coherence between the normative and the practical, between the theory and the practice.

This is very evident in the chapter by Terhi Partanen and Jarl Wahlström which looks at how male clients who have been violent to their female partners, and therapists, negotiate clienthood in group therapy conversations. A key issue for the therapists was to try to ensure that the men took responsibility for their actions while offering empathy to their experiences and situations. Responsibility was key to the moral dimensions of the treatment, while the men invariably tried to take a position of victimhood and thus deny responsibility for their actions. Similarly, Sue White notes how parents are treated as culpable for their child's behaviour where their child does not have a clear medical diagnosis. Where there are clear medical diagnoses, parents' moral worth is more likely to recognized.

Clients too are concerned about the nature of their moral character and act to protect themselves against criticism. Stef Slembrouck and Chris Hall explore how excuses are used to defend a potentially damaged identity. Using the formulation 'caring but not coping' they work to re-establish themselves as caring parents despite their children being in public care.

How the work gets done

Social work has been described as 'an invisible trade' (Pithouse 1987), the encounters between professionals and clients taking place in interviews and meetings away from the public gaze. Most of the chapters have made available talk and writing from these unseen arenas. However, the analysis is concerned with aspects of the encounter which the participants themselves do not see. Garfinkel (1967, p.36) talks of the 'seen but unnoticed' features of everyday interaction which actors manage without thinking. Apart from on training courses, the actual management of such activities is rarely discussed, as if the way social workers communicate with the client is straightforward. This is in contrast with, for example, teaching, where observing lessons is central to assessment and inspection processes.

Most research and professional scrutiny takes place at a level above the everyday – generalizations about people's attributes, the aims of interventions, overall plans and intentions. Pirjo Nikander investigates how the abstract and theoretical notion of interprofessionalism is carried out in practice. She shows the tensions when professionals are forced to make decisions about allocating resources to clients and how they draw on moral and categorical formulations, obligations and responsibilities.

Katja Kurri and Jarl Wahlstrom's detailed analysis of couple therapy displays the skill of the therapist in formulating questions and problems, and thereby enabling the spouses to move from blame to negotiation. As they point out, an analysis which ignores the turn-by-turn structure of therapy would miss the subtlety of this work. Similarly Sue White's chapter shows how case files are more than merely reports of people, events and action; they display tacit assumptions about parents and children which become embedded in the accounts. If taken at face value as evidence of accurate (or inaccurate) assessments of parents and children, the constructive nature of professional accounting practices is missed.

And finally...

Social constructionism has at its core the notion of reflexivity (Taylor and White 2000); that is, the continual attempt to place one's premises into question and to listen to alternative framings of reality in order to grapple with potentially different points of view. Reflexivity is not necessarily a prelude to rejecting the present or the past, but it does underline the importance of entering into dialogue in order to clarify what might lead to improvement and to recognize that there may be differing points of view as to what 'improvement' might mean. It is thoroughly consistent with the ideas associated with 'evidence-informed' practice which we outlined earlier and which aims to illuminate the democratic process.

We see many of the themes identified here as having relevance for both practitioners and researchers, and in many respects would argue that many of the ideas relevant to the research process run in parallel with the processes of practice. A major part of this involves questioning the texts relevant to professional practice, whether these are generated by researchers, practitioners, administrators, academics or clients. As Gale Miller has argued, it is important to read all texts with the same questioning as we hope you have brought to the various chapters assembled here. To do so requires us to: treat the taken-for-granted as strange; try and hold opposing points of view without losing the ability to make judgements and take action; locate our actions in our diverse but everyday dialogues and relations. To do so requires us to identify the spaces – both in time and place – which allow us to reflect and think critically, which is no easy matter in the contemporary hubbub and demands of everyday practice and research.

References

Abell, J. and Stokoe, E. (2001) 'Broadcasting the royal role: Constructing culturally situated identities in the Princess Diana Panorama interview.' *British Journal of Social Psychology 40*, 3, 417–435.

Abrams, P. (1968) *The Origins of British Sociology 1834–1914*. Chicago, IL: University of Chicago Press.

Adams, D. (1988) 'Treatment models of men who batter. A profeminist analysis.' In K. Yllö and M. Bograd (eds) *Feminist Perspectives on Wife Abuse*. Newbury Park, CA: Sage.

Akisal, H.S. and Akisal, K. (1994) 'Mental status examination.' In M. Hersen and S.M. Turner (eds) *Diagnostic Interviewing* (2nd edn). New York: Plenum Press.

Aldridge, M. (1994) *Making Social Work News*. London: Routledge.

Andersen, T. (ed.) (1990) *The Reflecting Team. Dialogues and Dialogues about Dialogues*. Kent: Borgmann.

Andersson, G. (1992) 'Social workers and child welfare.' *British Journal of Social Work 22*, 3, 253–269.

Antaki, C. (1994) *Explaining and Arguing. The Social Organization of Accounts*. London: Sage.

Antaki, C. and Widdicombe, S. (eds) (1998a) *Identities in Talk*. London: Sage.

Antaki, C. and Widdicombe, S. (1998b) 'Identity as an Achievement and as a Tool.' In C. Antaki and S. Widdicombe (eds) *Identities in Talk*. London: Sage.

Atkinson, M. (1984) *Our Masters' Voices: The Language and Body Language of Politics*. London: Methuen.

Atkinson, M. and Drew, P. (1979) *Order in Court: The Organisation of Verbal Interaction in Judicial Settings*. London: Macmillan.

Atkinson, M.A., Cuff, E.C. and Lee, J.R.E. (1978) 'The re-commencement of a meeting as a member's accomplishment.' In J.N. Schenkein (ed.) *Studies in the Organisation of Conversational Interaction*. New York: Academic.

Atkinson, P. (1995) *Medical Talk and Medical Work*. London: Sage.

Auburn, T., Drake, S. and Willig, S. (1995) 'You punched him, didn't you?': Versions of violence in accusatory interviews.' *Discourse and Society 6*, 3, 353–386.

Austin, J.L. (1961) 'A plea for excuses.' In J.D. Urmson and G. Warncock (eds) *Philosophical Papers*. Oxford: Clarendon Press.

Austlii (2001) Minister for Immigration v. Ah Hin Teoh F.C. No. 95/013 (1995) available at http://www.auastlii.edu.au/cases/cth/high_ct/183clr273.html

Baker, C.D. (1997a) 'Membership categorization and interview accounts.' In D. Silverman (ed.) *Qualitative Research: Theory, Method and Practice*. London: Sage.

Baker, C.D. (1997b) 'Ticketing rules: Categorization and moral ordering in a school staff meeting.' In S. Hester and P. Eglin (eds) *Culture in Action: Studies in Membership Categorisation Analysis*. Lanham, MD: International Institute for Ethnomethodology and Conversation Analysis & University Press of America.

Bakhtin, M. (1986) *Speech Genres and Other Last Essays*. Austin, TX: University of Texas.

Banks, S. (1995) *Ethics and Values in Social Work*. Basingstoke: Macmillan.

Barker, C. and Galasinski, D. (2001) *Cultural Studies and Discourse Analysis. A Dialogue on Language and Identity*. London: Sage.

Bazerman, C. and Paradis, J. (1991) 'Introduction.' In C. Bazerman and J. Paradis (eds) *Textual Dynamics of the Professions*. Madison, WI: University of Wisconsin Press.

Beattie, A. (1995) 'War and peace among the health tribes.' In K. Soothill, L. Mackay and C. Webb (eds) *Interprofessional Relations in Health Care*. London: Edward Arnold.

Beck, U. (1992) *Risk Society: Towards a New Modernity*. London: Sage.

Beck, U. (1994) 'The Reinvention of Politics: Towards a Theory of Reflexive Modernisation.' In U. Beck, A. Giddons and S. Lash (eds) *Reflexive Modernisation: Politics, Tradition and Aesthetics in the Modern Social Order*. Cambridge: Polity Press.

Beck, U., Giddens, A. and Lash, S. (1994) *Reflexive Modernization*. Cambridge: Polity Press with Blackwells.

Bell, V. (1994) 'Drawing and time in Foucault's philosophy.' *Theory, Culture and Society 11*, 2, 151–163.

Berg, I.K. and Miller, S.D. (1992) *Working with the Problem-Drinker: A Solution-Focused Approach*. New York: Norton.

Bergmann, J.R. (1998) 'Introduction: Morality in Discourse.' *Research on Language and Social Interaction 31*, 3–4, 279–295.

Bernardes, J. (1997) *Family Studies: An Introduction*. London: Routledge.

Billig, M. (1985) 'Prejudice, categorization and particularization: From a perceptual to a rhetorical approach.' *European Journal of Social Psychology 15*, 79–103.

Bleiklie, I. (1996) *Service Regimes in Public Welfare Administration. Case Studies of Street-Level Bureaucrats as Decision Makers.* Bergen: Department of Administration and Organisation Theory, University of Bergen.

Boden, D. (1994) *The Business of Talk: Organizations in Action.* Cambridge: Polity.

Boden, D. (1995) 'Agendas and arrangements: everyday negotiations in meetings.' In A. Firth (ed.) *The Discourse of Negotiation. Studies of Language in the Workplace.* Oxford: Pergamon.

Bohart, A.C. and Tallman, K. (1999) *How Clients Make Therapy Work.* Washington, DC: American Psychological Association.

Brown, P. and Levinson, S. (1978) 'Universals in language usage: politeness phenomena.' In E. Goody (ed.) *Questions and politeness: strategies in social interaction.* Cambridge: Cambridge University Press.

Brown, P. and Levinson, S.C. (1987) *Politeness: Some universals in language usage.* Cambridge: Cambridge University Press.

Bryman, A. (1988) *Quantity and Quality in Social Research.* London: Routledge.

Bull, R. and Shaw, I. (1992) 'Constructing causal accounts in social work.' *Sociology 26*, 4, 635-649.

Burman, E. (1994) *Deconstructing Developmental Psychology.* London: Routledge.

Burr, V. (1995) *An Introduction to Social Constructionism.* London: Routledge.

Butler, I. and Williamson, H. (1994) *Children Speak: Children, Trauma and Social Work.* Harlow: Longman.

Butler, J. (1990) *Gender Trouble.* London: Routledge.

Buttny, R. (1990) 'Blame-account sequences in therapy: the negotiation of relational meanings.' *Semiotica 78*, 3/4, 219–247.

Cavanagh, K. and Cree, V. (eds) (1996) *Working with men. Feminism and social work.* London: Routledge.

Chambon, A. and Irving, A. (1999) 'Introduction.' In A. Chambon, A. Irving and L. Epstein (eds) *Reading Foucault for Social Work.* New York: Columbia University Press.

Chan, J. and Sigafoos, J. (2001) 'Does respite care reduce parental stress in families with developmentally disabled children.' *Child and Family Forum 30*, 5, 253–263.

Coates, J. and Cameron, D. (eds) (1988) *Women in their Speech Communities.* London: Longman.

Collins, P. (1998) 'Negotiating selves: Reflections on "Unstructured Interviewing".' *Sociological Research Online 3*, 3 www.socresonline.org.uk/archive.html

Crowe, M. (1996) 'Couple therapy.' In Bloch, S. (ed.) *An Introduction to the Psychotherapies* (3rd edn). Oxford: Oxford University Press.

Cuff, E.C. and Sharrock W.W. (1985) 'Meetings.' In T.A. van Dijk (ed.) *Handbook of Discourse Analysis. Vol. 3. Discourse and Dialogue.* London: Academic Press.

Dallos, R. and Sapsford, A. (1995) 'Patterns of diversity and lived realities.' In J. Muncie, M. Wetherell, R. Dallos and A. Cochrane (eds) *Understanding the Family.* London: Sage.

Daniels, J.W. and Murphy, C.M. (1997) 'Stages and processes of change in batterers' treatment.' *Cognitive and Behavioral Practice 4*, 123–145.

Davies, M. (ed.) (2000) *The Blackwell Encyclopaedia of Social Work.* Oxford: Blackwell.

Davis, A. (ed.) (1985) *Women, the Family and Social Work.* London: Tavistock.

Day, D. (1998) 'Being ascribed, and resisting, membership of an ethnic group.' In C. Antaki and S. Widdicombe (eds) *Identities in Talk.* London: Sage.

Denzin, N. (1970) *The Research Act in Sociology.* Chicago, IL: Aldine.

Department of Health (1991) *The Children Act Guidance and Regulations Volume 2 Family Support, Day Care and the Educational Provision for Young Children.* London: HMSO.

Department of Health (1995) *Child Protection: Messages from Research.* London: HMSO.

Department of Health (1998) *Review of Working Together?* London: HMSO.

Department of Health (2001) 'New social care institute for excellence will raise standards and tackle inconsistencies.' Press Release 0100, 25 February.

Department of Health, Department for Education and Employment, and Home Office (2000) *Framework for the Assessment of Children in Need and their Families.* London: HMSO.

de Shazer, S. (1984) 'The death of resistance.' *Family Process 23*, 11–17.

de Shazer, S. (1989) 'Resistance revisited.' *Contemporary Family Therapy 11*, 227–233.

de Shazer, S. (1994) *Words Were Originally Magic.* New York: Norton.

de Swaan, A. (1988) *In Care of the State.* Cambridge: Polity Press.

Dingwall, R. and Murray, T. (1983) 'Categorisation in accident departments: "good" patients, "bad" patients and "children".' *Sociology of Health and Illness 5*, 2, 127–148.

Dingwall, R., Eekelaar, J. and Murray, T. (1983) *The Protection of Children: State Interventions and Family Life.* Oxford: Blackwell.

Dobash, R.E., Dobash, R.P, Cavanagh, K. and Lewis, R. (2000) *Changing Violent Men.* London: Sage.

Dockrell, J. and Wilson, G. (1995) 'Management issues in interprofessional work with older people.' In K. Soothill, L. Mackay and C. Webb (eds) *Interprofessional Relations in Health Care.* London: Edward Arnold.

Dominelli, L. and McLeod, E. (1989) *Feminist Social Work.* Basingstoke: Macmillan.

Donzelot, J. (1979) *The Policing of Families.* London: Hutchinson.

Drew, P. and Heritage, J. (1992a) 'Analyzing talk at work: an introduction.' In P. Drew and J. Heritage (eds) *Talk at Work. Interaction in Institutional Settings.* Cambridge: Cambridge University Press.

Drew, P. and Heritage, J. (eds) (1992b) *Talk at Work. Interaction in Institutional Settings.* Cambridge: Cambridge University Press.

Drew, P. and Sorjonen, M-L. (1997) 'Institutional Discourse.' In T.A. van Dijk (ed.) *Discourse Analysis: A Multidisciplinary Introduction.* London: Sage.

Duncan, B.L. and Miller, S. D. (2000) *The Heroic Client.* San Francisco: Jossey-Bass.

Edwards, D. (1994) 'Script formulations: a study of event descriptions in conversation.' *Journal of Language and Social Psychology 13*, 211–247.

Edwards, D. (1995) 'Two to tango: script formulations, dispositions, and rhetorical symmetry in relationship troubles talk.' *Research on Language and Social Interaction 28*, 4, 319–350.

Edwards, D. (1996) *Discourse and Cognition.* London: Sage.

Edwards, D. (1998) 'The relevant thing about her: Social identity categories in use.' In C. Antaki, and S. Widdicombe (eds) *Identities in Talk.* London: Sage.

Edwards, D. (1999) 'Emotion discourse.' *Culture and Psychology 5*, 3, 271–291.

Edwards, D. (2000) 'Extreme case formulations: softeners, investment, and doing nonliteral.' *Research on Language and Social Interaction 33*, 4, 347–373.

Edwards, D. and Potter, J. (1993) 'Language and causation: a discursive action model of description and attribution.' *Psychological Review 100*, 1, 23–41.

Eliasson, M. and Lundy, C. (1999) 'Organizing to stop violence against women in Canada and Sweden.' In L. Briskin and M. Eliasson (eds) *Women's*

Organizing and Public Policy in Canada and Sweden. Montreal: McGill-Queen Press.

Erickson, F. (2001) 'Co-membership and wiggle room: Some implications of the study of talk for the development of social theory.' In N. Coupland, S. Sarangi and C.N. Candlin (eds) *Sociolinguistics and Social Theory*. London: Longman.

Erickson, F. and Schultz, J. (1982) *The Counsellor as Gatekeeper. Social Interaction in Interviews*. New York: Academic Press.

Erickson, M.H., Rossi, E.L. and Rossi, S.I. (1976) *Hypnotic Realities*. New York: Irvington.

Ewald, F. (1991) 'Insurance and Risk.' In G. Burchell, C. Gordon and P. Miller (eds) *The Foucault Effect: Studies in Governmentality*. London: Harvester Wheatsheaf.

Fairclough, N. (1989) *Language and Power*. London: Longman.

Fairclough, N. (1992) *Discourse and Social Change*. Cambridge: Polity Press.

Farmer, E. and Boushel, M. (1999) 'Child protection policy and practice: women in the front line.' In S. Watson and L. Doyal (eds) *Engendering Social Policy*. Buckingham and Philadelphia: Open University Press.

Fawcett, B. and Featherstone, B. (2000) 'Setting the scene. An appraisal of notions of postmodernism, postmodernity and postmodern feminism.' In B. Fawcett, B. Featherstone, J. Fook, and A. Rossiter (eds) *Practice and Research in Social Work*. London and New York: Routledge.

Featherstone, B. (1999) 'Taking mothering seriously: The implications for child protection.' *Child and Family Social Work 4*, 43–53.

Ferguson, H. (2001) 'Social work, individualization and life politics.' *British Journal of Social Work 31*, 41–55.

Fisch, R., Weakland, J.H. and Segal, L. (1982) *The Tactics of Change*. San Francisco: Jossey-Bass Publishers.

Fiske, J. (1989) *Understanding Popular Culture*. London: Routledge.

Fleck, L. (1979) *Genesis and Development of Scientific Fact*. Chicago, IL: University of Chicago Press.

Fook, J. (2002) 'Practice and Research in Social Work. Towards an Inclusive Approach for Social Work Research.' *Qualitative Social Work 1*, 1, 79–95.

Forsberg, H. (1998) *Perheen ja lapsen tähden. Etnografia kahdesta asiantuntijakulttuurista*. Helsinki: Lastensuojelun Keskusliitto.

Forsberg, H., Kuronen, M. and Ritala-Koskinen, A. (1992) Feministinen sosiaalityö – kysymyksiä ja uusia kysymyksiä. *Janus 1*, 1, 367–372.

Foucault, M. (1976) *The History of Sexuality: Volume I An Introduction.* London: Penguin.

Foucault, M. (1977) *Discipline and Punish.* London: Allen and Unwin.

Foucault, M. (1981) 'Questions of method.' *Ideology and Consciousness 8*, 3–14.

Franklin, B. and Parton, N. (eds) (1991) *Social Work, the Media and Public Relations.* London: Routledge.

Fuchs, S. and Ward, S. (1994) 'What is deconstruction and where and when does it take place?: Making facts in science, building cases in law.' *American Sociological Review 54*, 4, 481–500.

Gadsby Waters, J. (1992) *The Supervision of Child Protection Work.* Aldershot: Avebury.

Garfinkel, H. (1967) *Studies in Ethnomethodology.* Cambridge: Prentice-Hall and Polity Press.

Garfinkel, H. (1972) 'Conditions of successful degradation ceremonies.' In J.M. Henslin (ed.) *Down to Earth Sociology. Introductory Reading.* New York: Free Press.

Gergen, K. (1994) *Realities and Relationships. Soundings in Social Construction.* Cambridge, MA: Harvard University Press.

Gerlock, A.A. (2001) A profile of who completes and who drops out of domestic violence rehabilitation. *Issues in Mental Health Nursing 22*, 379–400.

Gibbons, J., Conroy, S. and Bell, C. (1995) *Operating the Child Protection System.* London: HMSO.

Giddens, A. (1991) *Modernity and Self-Identity: Self and Society in the Late Modern Age.* Cambridge: Polity Press.

Gill, R., Potter, J. and Webb, A. (1991) *Public Policy and Discourse Analysis: A Rhetorical Approach.* Unpublished paper, University of Loughborough.

Gilligan, C. (1982) *In a Different Voice: Psychological Theory and Women's Development.* Cambridge, MA: Harvard University Press.

Goffman, E. (1959) *The Presentation of Self in Everyday Life.* Garden City, NY: Anchor Books.

Goffman, E. (1967) *Interaction Ritual. Essays on face-to-face behaviour.* New York: Pantheon Books.

Goffman, E. (1979) 'Footing.' *Semiotica 25*, 1–29.

Goffman, E. (1983) 'The interaction order.' *American Sociological Revue 48*, 1, 1–17.

Goffman, E. (1990a) *Stigma. Notes on the Management of Spoiled Identity.* London: Penguin.

Goffman, E. (1990b) *The Presentation of Self in Everyday Life*. London: Penguin.

Goldner, V. (1999) Morality and multiplicity: perspectives on the treatment of violence in intimate life. *Journal of Marital and Family Therapy 25*, 3, 325–336.

Gondolf, E. (1997) 'Batterer programs. What we know and need to know.' *Journal of Interpersonal Violence 12*, 1, 83–99.

Gondolf, E. (2001) 'Limitations of experimental evaluation of batterer programs.' *Trauma, Violence, and Abuse 2*, 1, 79–88.

Goodrum, S., Umberson, D. and Anderson, K. (2001) 'The batterer's view of the self and others in domestic violence.' *Sociological Inquiry 71*, 2, 221–240.

Goodsell, C.T. (1981) 'The public encounter and its study.' In C.T. Goodsell (ed.) *The Public Encounter. Where State and Citizen Meet*. Bloomington, IN: Indiana University Press.

Gorman, P. (1998) *Managing Multidisciplinary Teams in the NHS*. London: Kogan Page.

Graham, H. (1982) 'Coping: or how mothers are seen and not heard.' In S. Friedman and S. Elizabeth (eds) *On the Problem of Men*. London: The Women's Press.

Granfelt, R. (1999) *Kertomuksia naisten kodittomuudesta*. Helsinki: SKS.

Green, J. (2000) 'Epistemology, evidence and experience: evidence based health care in the work of Accident Alliances.' *Sociology of Health and Illness 22*, 4, 453–476.

Griffiths, L. (2001) 'Categorising to exclude: The discursive construction of cases in community mental health teams.' *Sociology of Health and Illness 23*, 5, 678–700.

Grunow, D. (1978) *Alltagskontakte mit der Verwaltung*. Frankfurt: Campus Verlag.

Gubrium, J.F. (1990) *Home Care Experience*. Newbury Park, CA: Sage.

Gubrium, J.F. (1992) *Out of Control: Family Therapy and Domestic Disorder*. Newbury Park, CA: Sage.

Gubrium, J.F. and Holstein, J. (1990) *What is Family*. Mountain View, CA: Mayfield.

Gubrium, J.F. and Holstein, J. (eds) (2001) *Institutional Selves. Troubled Identities in a Postmodern World*. Oxford: Oxford University Press.

Gunnarsson, B.-L., Linell, P. and Nordberg, B. (eds) (1997) *The Construction of Professional Discourse*. New York: Longman.

Haakana, M. (1999) *Laughing Matters. A Conversational Analytical Study of Laughter in Doctor–Patient Interaction*. Helsinki: University of Helsinki.

Hacking, I. (1986) 'Making up people.' In T.C. Heller, M. Sosna and D.E. Wellbery (eds) *Reconstructing Individualism.* Stanford, CA: Stanford University Press.

Hacking, I. (1991) 'How should we do the history of statistics?' In G. Burchell, C. Gordon and P. Miller (eds) *The Foucault Effect: Studies in Governmentality.* London: Harvester Wheatsheaf.

Hak, T. (1998) 'There are clear delusions. The production of a factual account.' *Human Studies 21,* 419–436.

Haley, J. (1963) *Strategies of Psychotherapy.* New York: Grune and Stratton.

Haley, J. (1976) *Problem-Solving Therapy.* New York: Harper & Row.

Halfpenny, P. (1979) 'The analysis of qualitative data.' *Sociological Review 27,* 4, 799–825.

Hall, C. (1997) *Social Work as Narrative: Storytelling and Persuasion in Professional Texts.* Aldershot: Ashgate.

Hall, C. and Featherstone, B. (2002) *Families' Views of the Core Assessment Process.* Huddersfield: Nationwide Children's Research Centre.

Hall, C. and Slembrouck, S. (2001) 'Parent participation in social work meetings – the case of child protection conferences.' *European Journal of Social Work 4,* 2, 143–160.

Hall, C., Jokinen, A. and Suoninen, E. (2000) 'Laugh and you laugh alone: Legitimating parental rejection in a social work meeting.' Paper to 'Text and Talk at Work' Conference, Gent, Belgium.

Hall, C., Sarangi, S. and Slembrouck, S. (1997) 'Moral construction in social work discourse.' In B.-L. Gunnarsson, P. Linell and B. Nordberg (eds) *The Construction of Professional Discourse.* New York: Longman.

Hall, C., Sarangi, S. and Slembrouck, S. (1999a) 'Speech representation and the categorisation of the client in social work discourse.' *Text 19,* 4, 539–570.

Hall, C., Sarangi, S. and Slembrouck, S. (1999b) 'The legitimation of the client and the profession: Identities and roles in social work discourse.' In S. Sarangi and C. Roberts (eds) *Talk, Work and Institutional Order: Discourse in Medical, Mediation and Management Settings.* Berlin: Mouton de Gruyter.

Hallett, C. (ed.) (1989) *Women and Social Services Departments.* London: Harvester Wheatsheaf.

Harré, Rom (1983) *Personal Being.* Cambridge, MA: Harvard University Press.

Harway, M. and Hansen, M. (eds) (1993) *Battering and family therapy: a feminist perspective.* London: Sage.

He, A.W. (1995) 'Co-constructing institutional identities: The case of student counselees.' *Research on Language and Social Interaction 28,* 3, 213–231.

Hearn, J. (1998) *The Violences of Men.* London: Sage.

Heath, C. (1992) 'The delivery and reception of diagnosis in the general-practice consultation.' In P. Drew and J. Heritage (eds) *Talk at Work. Interaction in Institutional Settings.* Cambridge: Cambridge University Press.

Heritage, J. and Lindström, A. (1998) 'Motherhood, medicine and morality: Scenes from a medical encounter.' *Research on Language and Social Interaction 31*, 3–4, 397–438.

Heritage, P. and Sefi, S. (1992) 'Dilemmas of advice: Aspects of the delivery and reception of advice in interactions between health visitors and first-time mothers.' In P. Drew and J. Heritage (eds) *Talk at Work: Interaction in Institutional Settings.* Cambridge: Cambridge University Press.

Hersen, M. and Turner, S.M. (eds) (1994) *Diagnostic Interviewing (2nd edn.).* New York: Plenum Press.

Hester, S. and Eglin, P. (eds) (1997) *Culture in Action: Studies in Membership Categorisation Analysis.* Lanham, Maryland: International Institute for Ethnomethodology and Conversation Analysis & University Press of America.

Hetzler, A. (1994) *Socialpolitik i verkligheten. De handikappada och försäkringskassan.* Lund: Bokbox Förlag.

Hofstede, G., Nijnatten, C. van and Suurmond, J. (2001) 'Communication strategies of family supervisors and clients in organizing participation.' *European Journal of Social Work 4*, 2, 131–142.

Hollis, M. (1985) 'On masks and men.' In M. Carrithers, S. Collins and S. Lukes (eds) *The Category of the Person: Anthropology, Philosophy, History.* Cambridge: Cambridge University Press.

Holstein, J. (1993) *Court-ordered Insanity: Interpretative Practice and Involuntary Commitment.* New York: Aldine de Gruyter.

Holstein, J. and Gubrium, J. (2000) *The Self We Live By: Narrative Identity in a Postmodern World.* Oxford: Oxford University Press.

Holstein, J. and Miller, G. (eds) (1993a) *Reconsidering Social Constructionism. Debates in Social Problems Theory.* New York: Aldine de Gruyter.

Holstein, J. and Miller, G. (1993b) 'Social constructionism and social problems Work.' In J. Holstein and G. Miller (eds) *Reconsidering Social Constructionism. Debates in Social Problems Theory.* New York: Aldine de Gruyter.

Hoogsteder, M., Nijnatten, C. van and Suurmond, J. (1998) 'Communication between family supervisors and mandated clients. An analysis of videotaped interactions.' *International Journal of Child and Family Welfare 3*, 1, 54–73.

Housley, W. (2000) 'Story, narrative and team work.' *The Sociological Review 48,* 3, 435–443.

Hout, A. van and Spinder, S. (2001) *De (gezins) voogd als jongleur. Een methodisch handboek voor het (gezins) voogdijwerk.* Houten: Bohn, Stafleu and Van Loghum.

Howe, D. (1996) *An Introduction to Social Work Theory.* Brookfield: Ashgate.

Howitt, D. (1992) *Child Abuse Errors: When Good Intentions Go Wrong.* London: Harvester Wheatsheaf.

Hyden, L. (1996) 'Applying for money: Encounters between social workers and clients – a question of morality.' *British Journal of Social Work 26,* 843–860.

Hydén, M. (1994) 'Woman battering as a marital act: Interviewing and analysis in context.' In C. Kohler Riessman (ed.) *Qualitative Studies in Social Work Research.* London: Sage.

Hydén, M. (2000) 'Att lyssna till en kör av röster: Den berättarfokuserade intervjun.' *Socialvetenskaplig tidskrift 1–2,* 137–158.

Hydén, M. and McCarthy, I.C. (1994) 'Woman battering and father–daughter incest disclosure: Discourses of denial and acknowledgement.' *Discourse & Society 5,* 4, 543–565.

Jefferson, G. and Lee, J.R.E. (1992) 'The rejection of advice: Managing the problematic convergence of a "troubles telling" and a "service encounter".' In P. Drew and J. Heritage (eds) *Talk at Work. Interaction in Institutional Settings.* Cambridge: Cambridge University Press.

Jokinen, A. and Suoninen, E. (1999) 'From crime to resource. Constructing narratives in a social work encounter.' In S. Karvinen, T. Pösö and M. Satka (eds) *Reconstructing Social Work Research.* Jyväskylä: SoPhi.

Jokinen, A. and Suoninen, E. (2000) *Auttamistyö keskusteluna.* Tampere: Vastapaino.

Jokinen, A., Juhila, K. and Pösö, T. (1999) 'Introduction: Constructionist perspectives on social work practices.' In A. Jokinen, K. Juhila and T. Pösö (eds) *Constructing Social Work Practices.* Aldershot: Ashgate.

Jordan, B. and Jordan, C. (2000) *Social Work and the Third Way. Tough Love as Social Policy.* London: Sage.

Juhila, K. and Pösö, T. (1999) 'Local cultures in social work. Ethnographic understanding and discourse analysis in probation work.' In S. Karvinen, T. Pösö and M. Satka (eds) *Reconstructing Social Work Research.* Jyväskylä: SoPhi.

Juhila, K. and Pösö, T. (2000) 'Auttamisen organisaatiot ja ongelmien tulkinnat.' In A. Jokinen and E. Suoninen (eds) *Auttamistyö keskusteluna. Tutkimuksia sosiaali- ja terapiatyön arjesta.* Jyväskylä: Gummerus.

Julkunen, R. (2001) *Suunnanmuutos. 1990-luvun sosiaalipoliittinen reformi Suomessa.* Tampere: Vastapaino.

Karisto, A. (1997) 'Kaupunkisosiaalityö tulee.' In R. Viialainen and M. Maaniittu (eds) *Tehdä itsensä tarpeettomaksi.* Sosiaalityö 1990-luvulla. Research Reports 213. Helsinki: Stakes, 129–144.

Kelly, L., Regan, L. and Burton, S. (1991) *An Exploratory Study of the Prevalence of Sexual Abuse in a Sample of 16–21 Year Olds.* London: University of North London.

Keskinen, S. (2001) 'Ahdistavien tunteiden äärellä. Tutkijan, väkivaltaa kokeneiden naisten ja kulttuurin kohtaamisia.' *Naistutkimus 3*, 14, 29–40.

Kullberg, C. and Cedersund, E. (2001) 'Images of encounters in social work – with a focus on social interaction, morality and gender.' In M. Seltzer, C. Kullberg, S. Olesen and I. Rostila (eds) *Listening to the Welfare State.* Aldershot: Ashgate.

Kurri, K. and Wahlström, J. (2001) 'Dialogical management of morality in domestic violence counselling.' *Feminism and Psychology 11*, 2, 187–209.

La Fontaine, J. (1990) *Child Sexual Abuse.* Cambridge: Polity Press.

Laitila, A. and Sveins, P. (2001) 'The Jyväskylä model in practice.' In L. Keeler (ed.) *Recommendations of the E.U. Expert Meeting on Violence Against Women.* Helsinki: Ministry of Social Affairs and Health.

Langan, M. and Day, L. (1992) *Women, Oppression and Social Work. Issues in Anti-discriminatory Practice.* London: Routledge.

Lash, S., Szerszynski, B. and Wynne, B. (eds) (1996) *Risk, Environment and Modernity; Towards a New Ecology.* London: Sage.

Latimer, J. (1997) 'Figuring identities: Older people, medicine and time.' In A. Jamieson, S. Harper and C. Victor (eds) *Critical Approaches to Ageing and Later Life.* Milton Keynes: Open University Press.

Latimer, J. (2000) *The Conduct of Care: Understanding Nursing Practice.* Oxford: Blackwell Science.

Latour, B. (1987) *Science in Action.* Milton Keynes: Open University Press.

Layder, D. (1993) *New Strategies in Social Research. An Introduction and Guide.* Cambridge: Polity Press.

Leonard, P. (1997) *Postmodern Welfare. Reconstructing an Emancipatory Project.* London: Sage.

Levinson, S.C. (1992) 'Activity types and language.' In P. Drew and J. Heritage (eds) *Talk at Work. Interaction in Institutional settings.* Cambridge: Cambridge University Press.

Linell, P. (1998) *Approaching Dialogue. Talk, interaction and contexts in dialogical perspectives.* Amsterdam: John Benjamins.

Linell, P. and Gustavsson, L. (1987) *Initiativ och respons. Om dialogens dynamik, dominans och koherens.* Linköping: University of Linköping.

Lipsky, M. (1980) *Street-Level Bureaucracy. Dilemmas of the Individual in Public Services.* New York: Russell Sage Foundation.

Lødemel, I. and Trickey, H (eds) (2001) *An offer you can't refuse. Workfare in International Perspective.* Bristol: The Policy Press.

Losake, D. and Cahil, S. (1984) 'The social construction of deviance: Experts on battered women.' *Social Problems 3*, 3, 296–310.

MacKinnon, R.A. and Michels, R. (1971) *The Psychiatric Interview in Clinical Practice.* Darien, IL: W.B. Saunders Company.

Macleod, M. (1996) *Talking with Children about Child Abuse.* London: ChildLine.

Madanes, C. (1984) *Behind the One Way Mirror.* San Francisco: Jossey-Bass.

Mäkitalo, Å. (2002) *Categorizing Work: Knowing, Arguing and Social Dilemmas in Vocational Guidance.* Gothenburg: Göteborg Studies in Educational Sciences 177, Acta Universitatis Gothoburgensis.

Månsson, S-A. (2000) 'Kön i teori och praktik.' In A. Meeuwisse, S. Sunesson and H. Swärd (eds) *Socialt arbete.* Falköping: Natur och Kultur.

Marks, D. (1995) 'Gendered "care" and the structuring of group relations: child–professional–parent–researcher.' In E. Burman, P. Alldred, C. Bewley, B. Goldberg, C. Heenan, D. Marks, J. Marshall, K. Taylor, R. Ullah and S. Warner *Challenging Women: Psychology's Exclusions, Feminist Possibilities.* Milton Keynes: Open University Press.

McLeod, J. (1997) *Narrative and Psychotherapy.* London: Sage.

McNamee, S. and Gergen J. (eds) (1992) *Therapy as Social Construction.* London: Sage.

Metteri, A. (1999) 'Researching difficult situations in social work: Morality and politics of expert work.' In S. Karvinen, T. Pösö, T. and M. Satka (eds) *Reconstructing Social Work: Finnish Methodological Adaptations.* Jyväskylä: SoPhi.

Middleton, D. and Edwards, D. (1990) 'Conversational remembering: A social psychological approach.' In D. Middleton and D. Edwards (eds) *Collective Remembering.* London: Sage.

Miller, G. (1997) *Enforcing the Work Ethic: Rhetoric and Everyday Life in a Work Incentive Program.* Albany, NY: State University of New York Press.

Miller, S., Duncan, B.L. and Hubble, M.A. (1997) *Escape From Babel.* New York: Norton.

Morrison, J.R. (1995) *The First Interview*. New York: Guilford Press.

Moustakas, C. (1994) *Phenomenological Research Methods*. London: Sage.

Muncie, J. and Wetherell, M. (1995) 'Family policy and political discourse.' In J. Muncie, M. Wetherell, R. Dallos and A. Cochrane (eds) *Understanding the Family*. London: Sage.

Murphy, C.M. and Baxter, V.A. (1997) 'Motivating batterers to change in treatment context.' *Journal of Interpersonal Violence 12*, 4, 607–619.

Nätkin, R. (1997) *Kamppailu suomalaisesta äitiydestä*. Tampere: Gaudeamus.

Niiranen, V. (2002) 'Asiakkaan osallistuminen tukee kansalaisuutta sosiaalityössäkin.' In K. Juhila, H. Forsberg and I. Roivainen (eds) *Marginaalit ja sosiaalityö*. Jyväskylä: SoPhi.

Niiranen, V. (2002) 'Asiakkaan osallistuminen tukee kansalaisuutta sosiaalityössäkin.' In K. Juhila, H. Forsberg and I. Roivainen (eds) *Marginaalit ja sosiaalityö*. Jyvästrylä: SoPhi.

Nijnatten, C. van (1995) *Het gezicht van gezag. Visies op gezagsrelaties*. Amsterdam/Meppel: Boom.

Nijnatten, C. van and Ackerveken, M. v.d. (1998) *De nieuwe ondertoezichstelling in de ogen van gezinsvoogden. Onderzoek naar meningen en observaties van gezinsvoogden onder de nieuwe wet op de ondertoezichtstelling*. Utrecht: AWSB/ISOR.

Nijnatten, C. van, Hoogsteder, M. and Suurmond, J. (2001) 'Communication in care and control: Institutional interactions between family supervisors and parents.' *British Journal of Social Work 31*, 5, 705–720.

Nikander, P. (1995) 'The turn to the text: The critical potential of discursive social psychology.' *Nordiske Udkast: Journal for Critical Social Science 2*, 3–15.

Nikander, P. (2000) "Old" versus "little girl": A discursive approach to age categorisation and morality.' *Journal of Aging Studies 14*, 4, 335–358.

Nikander, P. (2002) 'Moniammatillinen viestintä: Yhteistyö ja päätöksenteko sosiaali- ja terveydenhuollossa.' [Multi-professional communication: Cooperation and decision-making in the social and health sector]. In S. Torkkola (ed.) *Terveysviestintä [Health Communication]*. Helsinki: Tammi.

Nikander, P. (forthcoming 2002a) *Age in Action: Membership Work and Stage of Life Categories in Talk*. Helsinki: The Finnish Academy of Science and Letters.

Nikander, P. (forthcoming) 'Managing scarcity: Multi-professional decision-making in meetings.' In T. Heinonen and A. Metteri (eds) *Social Work in Health and Mental Health*. Toronto: Canadian Scholar's Press.

Norris, C. (1990) *What's Wrong with Postmodernism*. London: Harvester Wheatsheaf.

Nyqvist, L. (2001) *Väkivaltainen parisuhde, asiakkuus ja muutos.* Helsinki: Ensi-ja turvakotien liitto.

Offer, J. (1999) *Social Workers, the Community and Social Interaction: Intervention and the Sociology of Welfare.* London: Jessica Kingsley Publishers.

Olesen, S.P. (1999) *Handlingsplansamtaler: Intentioner og aktører. Arbejdstekst nr. 1.* Aalborg: CARMA, Aalborg Universitet.

Olesen, S.P. (2001a) 'Discourses of Activation at Danish Employment Offices.' In M. Seltzer, C. Kullberg, S.P. Olesen, and I. Rostila (eds) *Listening to the Welfare State.* Aldershot: Ashgate.

Olesen, S.P. (2001b) 'Handlingsplansamtaler – en hån mod de arbejdsløse eller konstruktivt samspil med systemet.' *Tidsskrift for Arbejdsliv 3*, 3, 7–28.

O'Neill, J. (1995) *The Poverty of Postmodernism.* London: Routledge.

Othmer, E. and Othmer, S.C. (1994a) *The Clinical Interviewing Using DSM-IV (Volume 1: Fundamentals).* Washington, DC: American Psychiatric Press.

Othmer, E. and Othmer, S.C. (1994b) *The Clinical Interviewing Using DSM-IV (Volume 2: The Difficult Patient).* Washington, DC: American Psychiatric Press.

Øvretveit, J. (1993) *Coordinating Community Care: Multidisciplinary Teams and Care Management.* Milton Keynes: Open University Press.

Packman, J. and Hall, C. (1998) *From Care to Accommodation: Support, Protection and Control in Child Care Services.* London: Stationery Office.

Packwood, A. (2002) 'Evidence-based policy: Rhetoric and reality.' *Social Policy and Society 1*, 3, 267–272.

Parsons, T. (1951) *The Social System.* Glencoe, IL: The Free Press.

Parton, N. (1985) *The Politics of Child Abuse.* London: Macmillan.

Parton, N. (1991) *Governing the Family: Child Care, Child Protection and the State.* London: Macmillan.

Parton, N. (1996) 'Child protection, family support and social work: A critical appraisal of the Department of Health research studies in Child Protection.' *Child and Family Social Work 1*, 1, 3–11.

Parton, N. (ed.) (1997) *Child Protection and Family Support: Tensions, Contradictions and Possibilities.* London: Routledge.

Parton, N. (1998a) 'Risk, advanced liberalism and child welfare: The need to rediscover uncertainty and ambiguity.' *British Journal of Social Work 28*, 1, 5–27.

Parton, N. (1998b) 'Advanced liberalism, (post) modernity and social work: Some emerging social configurations.' *Social Thought 18*, 3, 71–88.

Parton, N. (1999) 'Reconfiguring child welfare practices: Risk, advanced liberalism and the government of freedom.' In A.S. Chambon, A. Irving and L. Epstein (eds) *Reading Foucault for Social Work*. New York: Columbia University Press.

Parton, N. (2000) 'Some thoughts on the relationship between theory and practice in and for social work.' *British Journal of Social Work 30*, 449–463.

Parton, N. and Marshall, W. (1998) 'Postmodern and discourse approaches to social work.' In R. Adams, L. Dominelli and M. Payne (eds) *Social Work*. London: Macmillan.

Parton, N. and O'Byrne, P. (2000) *Constructive Social Work Towards a New Practice*. London: Macmillan.

Parton, N., Thorpe, D. and Wattam, C. (1997) *Child Protection: Risk and the Moral Order*. London: Macmillan.

Payne, M. (1980) 'Strategies for the management of stigma through social work.' *British Journal of Social Work 10*, 4, 443–456.

Payne, M. (1999) 'Social construction in social work and social action.' In A. Jokinen, K. Juhila and T. Pösö (eds) *Constructing Social Work Practices*. Aldershot: Ashgate.

Pease, B. and Fook, J. (eds) (1999) *Transforming Social Work Practice. Postmodern Critical Perspectives*. London: Routledge.

Peck, J. (2000) 'Work first: Workfare and the regulation of contingent labour markets.' *Cambridge Journal of Economics 24*, 119–138.

Peräkylä, A. (1995) *AIDS Counselling: Institutional Interaction and Clinical Practice*. Cambridge: Cambridge University Press.

Petrelius, P. (2002) 'Sosiaalityöntekijänaiset – marginalisoituja toimijoita työelämässä?' In K. Juhila, H. Forsberg and I. Roivainen (eds) *Marginaalit ja sosiaalityö*. Jyväskylä: SoPhi.

Pierson, J. (1998) Book Review of 'Social Work as Narrative: Storytelling and Persuasion in Professional Text.' *Community Care*, October 22–28, 34.

Pithouse, A. (1987) 'Social Work: The Organization of an Invisible Trade.' Adershot: Gower.

Ploug, N., Reib, J., Sidenius, N.C. and Winter, S. (1992) *A-kasserne og de ledige*. København: Socialkommissionens sekretariat.

Pomerantz, A. (1978) 'Attributions of responsibility: blamings.' *Sociology 12*, 115–121.

Pomerantz, A. (1984) 'Agreeing and disagreeing with assessment. Some features of preferred/dispreferred turn shapes.' In J.M. Atkinson and J. Heritage (eds)

Structures of Social Action. Studies in Conversation Analysis. Cambridge: Cambridge University Press.

Pomerantz, A. (1986) 'Extreme case formulations: a way of legitimizing claims.' *Human Studies 9*, 219–229.

Porter, T. (1995) *Trust in Numbers: The Pursuit of Objectivity in Science and Public Life.* Princeton, NJ: Princeton University Press.

Potter, J. (1996a) 'Discourse analysis and constructionist approaches: Theoretical background.' In J.E Richardson (ed.) *Handbook of Qualitative Research Methods.* Leicester: British Psychological Society.

Potter, J. (1996b) *Representing Reality: Discourse, Rhetoric and Social Construction.* London: Sage.

Potter, J. and Wetherel, M. (1997) *Discourse and Social Psychology. Beyond Attitudes and Behaviour.* London: Sage.

Ptacek, J. (1988) 'Why do men batter their wives?' In K. Yllö and M. Bogard (eds) *Feminist Perspectives on Wife Abuse.* London: Sage.

Queen's University Belfast, The Research Team (1990) *Child Sexual Abuse in Northern Ireland: A Research Study of Incidence.* Belfast: Greystone.

Rapp, R. (1979) 'Household and family.' In R. Rapp, R. Ross and R. Bridenthal *Examining family history*, Feminist Studies 181, Spring.

Ronkainen, S. (1999) *Ajan ja paikan merkitsemät.* Helsinki: Gaudeamus.

Rose, N. (1989) *Governing the Soul: The Shaping of the Private Self.* London: Routledge.

Rose, N. (1993a) 'Government, authority and expertise in advanced liberalism.' *Economy and Society 22*, 3, 283–299.

Rose, N. (1993b) 'Disadvantage and power after the Welfare State,' Finnish Translation, *Janus* (journal of the Finnish Society for Social Policy) *1*, 1, 44–68.

Rose, N. (1996) 'The Death of the Social? Re-figuring the territory of government.' *Economy and Society 25*, 3, 327–356.

Rose, N. (1998) *Inventing Ourselves: Psychology, Power and Personhood.* Cambridge: Cambridge University Press.

Rossiter, A. (2000) 'The postmodern feminist condition. New conditions for social work.' In B. Fawcett, B. Featherstone, J. Fook and A. Rossiter (eds) *Practice and Research in Social Work.* London: Routledge.

Rossiter, A. (2001) 'Innocence Lost and Suspicion Found: Do we Educate for or against Social Work?' *Critical Social Work 2*,1. http://www.criticalsocialwork.com/01_1_innocence_rossiter.html

Sacks, H. (1972) 'On the analyzability of stories by children.' In J. Gumpertz and D. Hymes (eds) *Directions in Sociolinguistics: The Ethnography of Communication.* New York: Holt, Rinehart and Winston.

Sacks, H. (1992) *Lectures on Conversation. Vols 1 and 2.* Oxford: Blackwell.

Saleeby, D. (2001) *Human Behaviour and Social Environments: A Biopsycho-Social Approach.* New York: Columbia University Press.

Sarangi, S. (1998) 'Interprofessional case construction in social work: The evidential status of information and its reportability.' *Text 18,* 2, 241–270.

Sarangi, S. (2000) 'Activity types, discourse types and interactional hybridity: The case of genetic counselling.' In S. Sarangi and M. Coulthard (eds) *Discourse and Social Life.* Harlow: Pearson Education.

Sarangi, S. and Roberts, C. (eds) (1999) *Talk, Work and Institutional Order. Discourse in Medical, Mediation and Management Settings.* Berlin: Mouton de Gruyter.

Sarangi, S. and Slembrouck, S. (1996) *Language, Bureaucracy and Social Control.* London: Longman.

Savornin Lohman, J. de and Steketee, J. (1996) 'Kwaliteit als legitimatie van het gezinsvoogdijwerk.' *Sociale Interventie 5,* 2, 68–76.

Schegloff, E.A. and Sacks, H. (1973) 'Opening up closings.' *Semiotica 7,* 289–327.

Schwartzman, H.B. (1989) *The Meeting. Gatherings in Organizations and Communities.* New York: Plenum Press.

Scott, M. and Lyman, S. (1968) 'Accounts.' *American Sociological Review 33,* 46–62.

Scourfield, J. (2001) 'Interviewing interviewers and knowing about knowledge.' In I. Shaw and N. Gould (eds) *Qualitative Research in Social Work.* London: Sage.

Secretary of State (1974) *Report of the Inquiry into the Care and Supervision Provided in Relation to Maria Colwell.* London: HMSO.

Secretary of State for Social Services (1988) *Report of the Inquiry into Child Abuse in Cleveland.* Cmnd 412. London: HMSO.

Shaw, I. and Gold, N. (2001) 'Introduction.' In I. Shaw and N. Gould (eds) *Qualitative Research in Social Work.* London: Sage.

Shea, S.C. (1998) *Psychiatric Interviewing: The Art of Understanding (2nd edn).* Darien, IL: W.B. Saunders.

Sheldon, B. (2001) 'The validity of evidence-based practice in social work: A reply to Stephen Webb.' *British Journal of Social Work 31,* 5, 801–809.

Shulman, L. (1991) *Interactional Social Work Practice. Toward an Empirical Theory.* Itasca, IL: Peacock Publishers.

Silverman, D. (1985a) *Communication and Medical Practice: Social Relations in the Clinic.* London: Sage.

Silverman, D. (1985b) *Qualitative Methodology and Sociology.* Aldershot: Gower.

Silverman, D. (1987) *Communications and Medical Practice.* London: Sage.

Silverman, D. (1993) *Interpreting Qualitative Data: Methods for Analysing Talk, Text and Interaction.* London: Sage.

Silverman, D. (1997) *Discourses of Counselling. HIV Counselling as Social Interaction.* London: Sage.

Silverman, D. (1998) *Harvey Sacks. Social Science and Conversation Analysis.* Oxford: Oxford University Press.

Simons, J.W. and Billig, M. (eds) (1994) *After Postmodernism: Reconstructing Ideology Critique.* London: Sage.

Sipilä, P. (1998) *Sukupuolitettu ihminen – kokonainen etiikka. Onko sukupuoli oikein?* Helsinki: Gaudeamus.

Slembrouck, S. (2002) 'Narrative accounts of class and parenting in the area of child protection – a discursive ethnography under construction.' Paper read at Sociolinguistics Symposium 14, Gent, Belgium.

Slot, N., Theunissen, A., Esmeijer, F. and Duivenvoorden, Y. (2001) *909 Zorgen. Een onderzoek naar de doelmatigheid van de ondertoezichtstelling.* Amsterdam: Vrije Universiteit.

Smart, C. (1992) 'Introduction.' In C. Smart (ed.) *Regulating Womanhood: Historical Essays on Marriage and Sexuality.* London: Routledge.

Smith, B.H. (1997) *Belief and Resistance: Dynamics of Contemporary Intellectual Controversy.* Cambridge, MA: Harvard University Press.

Smith, D. (1990) *Texts, Facts and Femininity: Exploring the Relations of Ruling.* London: Routledge.

Sommers-Flanagan, R. and Sommers-Flanagan, J. (1999) *Clinical Interviewing (2nd edn).* New York: John Wiley & Sons, Inc.

Spencer, J.W. (2001) 'Self-presentation and organizational processing in a human service agency.' In J.F. Gubrium and J.A. Holstein (eds) *Institutional Selves. Troubled Identities in a Postmodern World.* Oxford: Oxford University Press.

Spencer, J.W. and McKinney J. (1997) 'We don't pay for bus tickets, but we can help you find work: The micropolitics of trouble in human service encounters.' *The Sociological Quarterly 38,* 1, 185–203.

Stainton Rogers, R. and Stainton Rogers, W. (1992) *Stories of Childhood: Shifting Agendas of Child Concern.* London: Harvester Wheatsheaf.

Stamp, G.H. and Sabourin, T.C. (1995) 'Accounting for violence: An analysis of male spousal abuse narratives.' *Journal of Applied Communication Research 23,* 284–307.

Stancombe, J. (forthcoming) *Family Therapy as Narrative: Managing Blame and Responsibility.* Unpublished PhD Thesis, University of London.

Stearns, P. (1995) 'Emotions.' In R. Harré and P. Stearns (eds) *Discursive Psychology in Practice.* London: Sage.

Strong, P. (1979) *The Ceremonial Order of the Clinic.* London: Routledge and Kegan Paul.

Suoninen, E. (1997) 'Selonteot ja oman toiminnan ymmärrettäväksi tekeminen.' *Sosiologia 34,* 1, 26–38.

Suoninen, E. (1999) 'Doing "delicacy" in institutions of helping. A case of probation office interaction.' In A. Jokinen, K. Juhila and T. Pösö (eds) *Constructing Social Work Practices.* Aldershot: Ashgate.

Suoninen, E. (2000) 'Tanssilajit ja -tyylit asiakkaan kohtaamisess.' In A. Jokinen and E. Suoninen (eds) *Auttamistyö keskusteluna.* Tampere: Vastapaino.

Szmukler, G. (1996) 'From family burden to caregiving.' *Psychiatric Bulletin 20,* 8, 449–451.

Taft, C.T. and Murphy, C.M. (2001) 'Attendance-enhancing procedures in group counseling for domestic abusers.' *Journal of Counselling Psychology 48,* 1, 51–60.

Tainio, L. (2001) *Puhuvan naisen paikka: sukupuoli kulttuurisena kategoriana kielenkäytössä.* Helsinki: SKS.

Taylor, C. and White, S. (2000) *Practising Reflexivity in Health and Welfare: Making Knowledge.* Milton Keynes: Open University Press.

Taylor, J.R. and van Every, E.J. (2000) *The Emergent Organization: Communication as its Site and Surface.* Mahwah, NJ: Erlbaum.

Torfing, J. (2000) *Towards a Schumpeterian Workfare Postnational Regime? – a framework for analysing the changing face of Danish labour-market policy.* Arbejdstekst nr. 4, Aalborg: CARMA, Aalborg Universitet.

Turnell, A. and Edwards, S. (1999) *Signs of Safety: A Solution and Safety Oriented Approach to Child Protection Casework.* New York: Norton.

Vatcher, C-A. and Bogo, M. (2001) 'The feminist/emotionally focused therapy practice model: An integrated approach for couple therapy.' *Journal of Marital and Family Therapy 27,* 1, 69–83.

Vehviläinen, S. (1999) *Structures of Counselling Interaction. A Conversation Analytic Study of Counselling Encounters in Career Guidance Training.* Helsinki: Helsinki University Press.

Vuori, J. (2001) *Äidit, isät ja ammattilaiset – sukupuoli, toisto ja muunnelmat asiantuntijoiden kirjoituksissa.* Tampere: Tampere University Press.

Wagner, P. (1992) 'Liberty and discipline: Making sense of postmodernity, or, once again, towards a sociohistorical understanding of modernity.' *Theory and Society 22,* 467–492.

Wagner, P. (1994) *A Sociology of Modernity: Liberty and Discipline.* London: Routledge.

Wattam, C. (1996) 'The social construction of child abuse for practical policy purposes – a review of Child Protection: Messages from Research.' *Child and Family Law Quarterly 8,* 3, 189–200.

Wattam, C. and Woodward, C. (1996) '… And do I abuse my children? No! Learning about prevention from people who have experienced child abuse.' *Childhood Matters: Report of the National Commission of Inquiry into the Prevention of Child Abuse, Vol 2.* London: HMSO.

Watzlawick, P., Beavin, J.H. and Jackson, D.D. (1967) *Pragmatics of Human Communication.* New York: Norton.

Watzlawick, P., Weakland, J.H. and Fisch, R. (1974) *Change.* New York: Norton.

Weiss, C.H. (1979) 'The many meanings of research utilization.' *Public Administration Review 39,* 426–431.

West, C. and Zimmerman, D.H. (1987) 'Doing gender.' *Gender & Society 1,* 2, 127–151.

Wetherell, M. (1995) 'Social structure, ideology and family dynamics: The case of parenting.' In J. Muncie, M. Wetherell, R. Dallos and A. Cochrane (eds) *Understanding the Family.* London: Sage.

White, S. (1997) *Performing Social Work: An Ethnographic Study of Talk and Text in a Metropolitan Social Services Department.* Unpublished PhD thesis, University of Salford.

White, S. (1998) 'Time, temporality and child welfare: Notes on the materiality and malleability of time(s).' *Time and Society 7,* 1, 55–74.

White, S. (1999) 'Examining the artfulness of "risk talk".' In A. Jokinen, and T. Pösö (eds) *Constructing Social Work Practices.* Aldershot: Ashgate.

White, S. (2002) 'Accomplishing "the case" in paediatrics and child health: Medicine and morality in inter-professional talk.' *Sociology of Health and Illness 24,* 4, 409–435.

White, S. and Stancombe, J. (forthcoming) *Being Realistic about Clinical Judgement: Science, Morality and Case Formulation.* Milton Keynes: Open University Press.

Widdicombe, S. (1998) 'But you don't class yourself: The interactional management of category membership and non-membership.' In C. Antaki and S. Widdicombe (eds) *Identities in Talk.* London: Sage.

Widdicombe, S. and Wooffitt, R. (1995) *The Language of Youth Subcultures. Social Identity in Action.* London: Harvester Wheatsheaf.

Williams, F. (1996) 'Postmodernism, feminism and the question of difference.' In N. Parton (ed.) *Social Theory, Social Change and Social Work.* London: Routledge.

Winter, S. (1994) *Implementering og effektivitet.* Herning: Systime.

Wittgenstein, L. (1953) *Philosophical Investigations.* Oxford: Blackwell.

Wolf-Smith, J.H. and LaRossa, R. (1992) 'After he hits her.' *Family Relations 41,* 3, 324–329.

Wooffitt, R. (1992) *Telling Tales of the Unexpected. The Organization of Factual Discourse.* London: Harvester Wheatsheaf.

Woolgar, S. and Pawluch (1985) 'Ontological gerrymandering: The anatomy of social problems explanations.' *Social Problems 32,* 2, 214–27.

Young, K., Ashby, D., Bozaz, A. and Grayson, L. (2002) 'Social science and the evidence-based policy movement.' *Social Policy and Society 1,* 3, 215–224.

Zimmerman D.H. (1998) 'Identity, Context and Interaction.' In C. Antaki and S. Widdicombe (eds) *Identities in Talk.* London: Sage.

The Contributors

Christopher Hall is Senior Research Fellow at the Centre for Applied Childhood Studies, University of Huddersfield. He was a social worker and team manager in social services before becoming a researcher in child welfare and special education. His publications include social policy research, narrative and discourse approaches to social work.

Dr Gerard Hofstede is a youth care policy officer in South-Holland, The Netherlands, having previously worked as a research assistant on the Family Supervision project at the University of Utrecht. He has published several papers in collaboration with Dr Carolus von Nijnatten.

Arja Jokinen is Professor in Social Work, University of Tampere, Finland. She has been researching client–professional interaction in different social work organizations. She is co-editor, with Kirsi Juhila and Tarja Pösö, of *Constructing Social Work Practices* (Ashgate 1999), which brings a social constructionist perspective to social work research. Her current research topics include issues of marginalization and gender.

Dr Kirsi Juhila is Professor in Social Work at the University of Tampere. Her research interests include institutional interaction in social work settings and the issues of social exclusion, marginality and homelessness. She is currently working on a project on client construction and client careers in last-resort social welfare organizations. She is co-editor of *Constructing Social Work Practices* (Ashgate 1999).

Katja Kurri is a clinical psychologist who is doing her doctoral thesis in the Department of Psychology, University of Jyväskylä, Finland. Her dissertation is on the subject of morality as interactional phenomena in therapy. Previous articles include: 'Dialogical management of morality in domestic violence counselling' (with J. Wahlström), *Feminism & Psychology 11*, 2, 187–208.

Jim Laffer is a social worker with 35 years' experience working in Western Australia's statutory child welfare agency. He manages to remain moderately sane by bicycling to and from work each day and being married to the lovely Lorraine.

Gale Miller is Professor and Chairperson of the Department of Social and Cultural Sciences, Marquette University, Milwaukee, WI, USA. Professor Miller has focused much of his research on how language is used in diverse human service settings, including in therapy and counselling sites. His books include *Becoming Miracle Workers: Language and Meaning in Brief Therapy*. Professor Miller's writings are informed by a variety of social constructionist perspectives as well as studies of conversation and discourse. Most recently Professor Miller has begun to explore the applied possibilities of social constructionism and discourse studies.

Dr Pirjo Nikander is Assistant Professor in the Department of Sociology and Social Psychology, University of Tampere, Finland. Her research interests include studies of talk and interaction in meetings and the workplace, membership work and identities in talk, and moral discourse. Her recent publications include *Age in Action: Membership Work and Stage of Life Categories in Talk* (The Finnish Academy of Science and Letters 2002).

Dr Carolus van Nijnatten is Associate Professor Social Studies of Law at the University of Utrecht. Some of his recent publications include: Nijnatten, C. van, Boesveldt, N., Schilperoord, A. and Mass, M. (2001) 'The construction of parental authority and cooperation in reports to the Dutch court', *International Journal of the Sociology of Law*; Hofstede, G.P., Nijnatten, C. van, and Suurmond, J. (2001) 'Communication strategies of family supervisors and clients in organizing participation', *European Journal of Social Work 4*, 2, 131–142; and Nijnatten, C. van, Hoogsteder, M. and Suurmond, J. (2001) 'Communciation in Care and Control: Institutional Interactions between Family Supervisors and Parents', *British Journal of Social Work 31*, 705–720.

Søren Peter Olesen, MA (social sciences and history) is a senior lecturer at The National Danish School of Social Work in Aarhus, and an associate professor at The National Centre for Labour Market Studies (University of Aalborg). His research is on street-level institutional interaction in workfare and activation settings. He is a co-editor of the anthology *Listening to the Welfare State* (2001).

Terhi Partanen, MA (psychology) is a doctoral student in psychology at the Department of Psychology, University of Jyväskylä, Finland. Her dissertation consists of discourse analytic studies on therapeutic treatment processes and identity constructions of male perpetrators of domestic violence. The research project is funded by the Academy of Finland.

Nigel Parton is a qualified social worker and Professor in Child Care and Director of the Centre for Applied Childhood Studies at the University of Huddersfield, England. He is also Visiting Professor to the Department of Social Policy and Social Work at the University of Tampere, Finland. His most recent book (with Patrick O'Byrne) is *Constructive Social Work: Towards a New Practice*, Basingstoke, Palgrave, 2000.

Tarja Pösö is Professor in Social Work at the University of Tampere, Department of Social Policy and Social Work. Her research interests focus on social problems studies, social work and child protection. Recently Professor Pösö has been involved with some other researchers in contributing to or editing books about social work research and social constructionism, evil, child abuse and constructing clienthood, mainly in Finnish but also in English. Her current research concentrates on residential care for youth.

Stef Slembrouck is Professor of English Linguistics and Discourse Analysis at the University of Gent (Belgium). His research focuses on the role of text and talk in the construction of institutional identities. Publications include (with Srikant Sarangi) *Language, Bureaucracy and Social Control* (1996), a special issue (with Michael Baynham) on 'speech report and institutional discourse' in *Text* (1999), and two special issues with colleagues from the FWO/FSR Language, Power and Identity Research Group (see http://bank.rug.ac.be/lpi/): one on 'discourse and critique' (*Critique of Anthropology*, 2000) and one on 'ethnographies of hegemony' (*Pragmatics*, 2003). With Christopher Hall and Srikant Sarangi, he has published widely on the narrative and discursive aspects of case construction in social work (child protection in particular).

Eero Suoninen is Assistant Professor in Social Psychology in the Department of Sociology and Social Psychology at the University of Tampere. He is the author of two textbooks and a number of articles on discourse analysis. He has also edited (with Arja Jokinen) a book on professional helping work, *Social Work and Therapy*. His current interests are in the research of interaction between parents and children.

Ah Hin Teoh is a father to six children and lives with his family in the hills outside Perth, Western Australia. Ah Hin recently remarried and he and his wife spend much of their time focused on building up their newly established catering business.

Andrew Turnell is an independent social worker and brief family therapist of 19 years' experience. Andrew and Steve Edwards, in conjunction with over a hundred West Australian front-line workers, co-created the 'Signs of Safety' approach to child protection practice. Andrew regularly teaches this approach in Australia, Europe and North America.

Jarl Wahlström, PhD, is Professor in Clinical Psychology at the Department of Psychology, University of Jyväskylä, Finland. He has advanced training in family and systems therapy. He has published on therapy research in various international journals and books, mainly from a constructionist systems point of view.

Dr Sue White, an experienced qualified social worker, is Professor in Health and Social Care at the University of Huddersfield. She is the co-author, with Carolyn Taylor, of *Practising Reflexivity in Health and Welfare: Making Knowledge*, Buckingham, Open University Press, 2000.

Subject Index

Author Index